MW00570512

Vignettes of a Small Town

A Year of the Arts 1997 Project Sponsored By:
Department of Canadian Heritage
Government of Newfoundland and Labrador
NewTel

Robert C. Parsons

About the Cover Photo (Middle)

Grand Bank in the transition stages with a blend of old and new vessels. Left foreground the schooner tied to the wharf is in its dying hours as the hook and line bank fishery and coasting trade closes out; behind that, a dragger to bring fresh fish to the plant (far right). Behind the dragger a Portuguese salt boat discharges salt into Grand Bank Fisheries' shed. Squeezing between the western wharf and the eastern lighthouse, is the steamer *Burgeo*, most likely backing out of the harbour since few trucks and spectators are on the head of the wharf.

The top and bottom cover photos are included in Chapters One and Five.

Vignettes of a Small Town

A Year of the Arts 1997 Project Sponsored By:
Department of Canadian Heritage
Government of Newfoundland and Labrador
NewTel

Robert C. Parsons

Creative Publishers
St. John's, Newfoundland
1997

The Canada Council | Le Conseil des Arts
for the Arts | du Canada
since 1957 | depuis 1957

We acknowledge the support of the Canada Council for for the Arts
for our publishing program.

∞ Printed on acid-free paper

Published by
CREATIVE BOOK PUBLISHING
a division of 10366 Newfoundland Limited
a Robinson-Blackmore Printing & Publishing
associated company
P.O. Box 8660, St. John's, Newfoundland A1B 3T7

Printed in Canada by:
ROBINSON-BLACKMORE PRINTING & PUBLISHING

Canadian Cataloguing in Publication Data

Parsons, Robert Charles, 1944–

    Vignettes of a small town

    Includes bibliographical references and index.

    ISBN 1-895387-82-5

1. Grand Bank (Nfld.) — History — Anecdotes.   I. Title.

FC2199.G72P37 1997   971.8   C97-95152-0
F1124.5.G72P37 1997

DEDICATION

*I dedicate this book to my wife Sadie
who, in 1993, inspired me to begin this work
and eventually saw its conclusion.*

Foreword

Robert Parsons continues to be the premier writer of the triumphs and tragedies of Newfoundland seamen, particularly those who, during the past one hundred years, sailed out of his native town of Grand Bank. I have read with pride his several books which set forth in graphic detail life as it was for the mariners and their families of the South Coast of Newfoundland — their deeds, courage, and seamanship which made Grand Bank the deep sea fishing capital of this province.

In this most recent publication, Robert adds to his earlier collections of the life and times of those who lived in Grand Bank. Once again he has vividly rekindled the interest and nostalgia of Grand Bankers as we read, with pride and satisfaction, of the tales of our forefathers and those who generated the strong community spirit that so much belongs to Grand Bank.

I congratulate Robert Parsons on his initiative and the painstaking research he has carried out in preparing this book which I am sure will be of great interest to his readers and in particular, Grand Bankers.

> The Honourable T. Alex Hickman
> Chief Justice, Trial Division
> Supreme Court of Newfoundland

Introduction

In my search for historical material related to Newfoundland's maritime events, I came upon many delightful (to me, at least) articles written about Grand Bank — stories and articles that, if you love this historic town, are too good to miss. Some were written by born and bred Grand Bankers; others by visitors. For the purpose of *Vignettes of a Small Town*, I chose several of these, cleared copyright with the author where necessary or possible and fitted the story into *Vignettes*. Introductions for many articles explain when, why, or by whom each was written. Later I compiled endnotes to explain local terms or events mentioned in the stories.

Over the course of the years since 1987, I had written several nonfiction articles for various newspapers and magazines. While most articles featured local maritime history, others were of Grand Bank people and places. These articles I wrote as a pastime, a diversion, and they gave me an innocent pleasure to do so and, for the purpose of this collection of Grand Bank vignettes, I thought it would be a good idea to include some of these pieces. These original articles were short-lived since they appeared for a day or so in a local newspaper or regional magazine and then were gone. Not only that, in the magazine or newspaper each is embedded in extraneous material. In *Vignettes of a Small Town* you get only information related to Grand Bank.

In the intervening time, I put together other information on unique aspects of Grand Bank: the Grandy dory, soccer, schools and selected biographical sketches.

In the assertions above, of course, I pre-suppose that my writings or stories deserve to be in book form and that the reader is interested. To try and make some sense out of the mixed bag of odds and ends, I attempted to arrange them in some order to lead you, the reader, from one subject or stage to another. This became a problem for me since *Vignettes* is not entirely arranged chronologically.

One difficulty I had was that of presenting material that you may have read before. Some of the stories, especially those of the sea, appearing here overlap articles in my earlier books. Hopefully the subject matter is dealt with in a new context or from a different perspective with new information added.

Another aim of mine was akin to a collection of lists: be it the worst fires in Grand Bank, a listing of who's buried in the Main Street Methodist Cemetery, or the registry of vessels built in local shipyards. Included also are data banks of names, places and sources to help residents (or visitors) find out more about the town.

I believe Garfield Fizzard's history of Grand Bank, *Unto the Sea*, is one of the finest books written about a small Newfoundland town (or any town for that matter). *Unto the Sea* is unmatched in meticulous research and scholarly work. Given the excellence of that publication, I found it somewhat intimidating to produce another book of historical content on Grand Bank.

How will *Vignettes of a Small Town* differ? Perhaps what I hoped for was a volume about people, places and things — done in short sections. It's a book that, well let's say you were standing in a long queue or waiting to see the dentist, you could read a short section of it and not lose the sense of the entire work. You might scan a bit in the front about the versatile Chester Harris; flip to the back and read Les Stoodley's wonderful reminiscences of his growing up in Grand Bank. I realize that many interesting people or well-known events may not be covered in *Vignettes*, and I also know maps and diagrams are deficient.

A vignette, according to a standard dictionary, is a short descriptive work or story that depicts a view; an intimate scene. *Vignettes of a Small Town*, not strictly a history of the town, presents a closer and more intimate look at Grand Bank and its people in an earlier time. Throughout the chapters each vignette is simply called a story.

Some of the photographs in this volume fall short of the clear and distinct quality I would have liked. Unfortunately, they represent the only ones I had at my disposal or which others graciously loaned me. These photos are survivors from a period when not many people owned cameras and, if they did, the owner usually took pictures of family members or relatives. Despite the inadequate quality of some pictures, I chose to preserve them through this medium.

Contents

Chapter One   Historical Overview

In Search of a Small Town, Archivally

Bert Riggs

In the spring of 1987 I went to a Heritage Coalition meeting in St. John's. One of the featured speakers was Bert Riggs, a Grand Bank son who is an archivist in Memorial University. His talk was not only captivating, but it laid the basic groundwork for present and future researchers of Grand Bank or for anyone searching archivally for his roots. Bert's presentation later appeared as a journal article.

For this and certain other selections endnotes add further information.

Grand Bank celebrated its three hundredth anniversary in 1987. It may quite possibly be older than three hundred, and there are records which indicate at least seasonal contact before 1687, but it is for that year that the earliest extant record of definitive settlement exists. The year of celebration was marked in Grand Bank with special activities and events planned to honour the past and herald the future. For this reason ANLA asked me as an expatriate Grand Banker to address their public meeting[1] on the history of Grand Bank, and in a state of fleeting madness I said yes. I am now recovering nicely.

I discovered that the history of Grand Bank subdivided itself into five distinct periods which I designated as the periods of the French, the Early English, the Coming of the

1

Methodists, the Banking Fishery, and the Post-War. It was with these in mind that I began my search for substantive information. I discovered that there was only one written, published text upon any aspect of the history of Grand Bank: Charles Lench's *History of Methodism on the Grand Bank and Fortune Circuit* (1916), which covered the third period very adequately[2]. Apart from a few student papers and cursory references in House of Assembly or in books on related topics there was a dearth of published materials available. Official Newfoundland census records exist from 1836, and Grand Bank is included in these census returns, but the information they provide is for ten year (or sometimes longer) intervals. While this offers a base for growth comparisons, it does not provide the necessary data to enable a researcher to reconstruct a history of a three-hundred-year-old town.

For these reasons I turned to archival sources for information to complete my task. **The French Period** from roughly 1687 to 1714 is well documented archivally. Unfortunately, the original documents are in Paris and only selected transcripts are available in Newfoundland. However, even these provide valuable information on the first settlers and their life on a lonely French fishing station, three thousand miles from home, in the volatile decades of the late seventeenth and early eighteenth centuries. In 1714, at the end of another long string of wars between France and England, the French were ordered to quit all settlements on the island of Newfoundland, and so that period of Grand Bank's history comes to an abrupt end.[3]

French settlers were quickly replaced by English and the first record is contained in the official British fishery report of 1763, which also makes reference to the previous year. These fishery reports contain a wealth of valuable information, but unfortunately the Burin Peninsula and South Coast were not considered as important as the Avalon Peninsula or East and Northeast Coasts. Grand Bank, when it does appear, is included with a number of other settlements from as close as Fortune to as far as Boxey on the other side of Fortune Bay. The researcher must make educated guesses based on future development patterns to produce any sort of profile for Grand Bank in the period between 1762 and 1816. There is one brief light for the year 1781; in his autobiography, the Reverend Andrew Sherburne, who had been an American privateer during the American Revolution, gives an account of being captured by Grand Bank residents in Fortune Bay while he was part of a raiding party, and of his subsequent vigilante trial and rescue from hanging by an "English lady" who insisted that he and his compatriots were prisoners of war and should be treated as such. This episode demonstrates the influence this unnamed "lady" had over the settlers and provides a fleeting glimpse of the life in **The Early English Period**[4].

The Coming of the Methodists, which I have designated as the third natural division in the history of Grand Bank, covers roughly the period from 1810 to 1880. It is a period that is well documented historically and archivally. In Colonial Office correspondence letters exist from the residents of Grand Bank pleading for clergy; once the first clergyman arrives in 1816, church records begin to be kept, which result in a social record of the town as well as religious and historical ones. Birth, death and marriage records, financial statements, and minutes of church meetings still exist and Charles Lench has done a good job of documenting the history of the first hundred years of Methodism in Grand Bank in his book on the subject. Census records for the period provide other valuable, if scattered, data.

Approaching the twentieth century, I discovered that 1881 was the natural starting point for the fourth period, as that was the year that Samuel Harris took the first banking schooner to the Grand Banks, inaugurating what would become known as the Bank fishery. **The Banking Fishery** lasted until World War II, when depressed world markets and fresh-freezing facilities brought about its end. It is a period when much more information is available yet harder to come by. Official statistics are often scattered, while the records of the merchant houses which outfitted ships for the Bank fishery and European trade have too often been mis-

placed or destroyed. Those which have survived are store-
houses of information, containing records of the residents'
purchases at the general stores and wages paid, demonstrating the barter and credit system in use, and defining the
town, its people and the reasons for their existence. The
Centre for Newfoundland Studies Archives holds a complete set of the books of a Grand Bank merchant house and
should value them among its prized acquisitions[5].

There is much more information available on **The Post
War Period** because with Confederation came the Dominion
Bureau of Statistics (now Statistics Canada), the Canadian
Census, and a host of federal and provincial statistical, re-
porting and data collecting agencies which compile, analyze
and make information available on almost every aspect of
life in Grand Bank and every other town and community in
Newfoundland. There has also been a greater emphasis on
preserving the past. With the establishment of the Southern
Newfoundland Seamen's Museum in Grand Bank in 1970
and the formation of the Grand Bank Heritage Society in
1985, I am confident that future researchers will have a much
easier time "in search of a small town, archivally" than was
my lot in January 1987.

Endnotes:

1. Riggs, true to his feelings as an expatriate Grand Banker, worked
   closely with the tri-centenary anniversary committee, formed to help
   Grand Bank celebrate its three hundred years of existence. Bert also
   provided insightful commentary for the pageant and historic parade on
   that sunny Tuesday afternoon of August 11, 1987, when hundreds of
   people watched the re-enactment of the landing of Grand Bank's first
   English settlers.
2. Both Lench's book and Sherburne's memoirs are listed in the sources in
   the back. Another valuable written account of Grand Bank in the
   mid-1800s is that of Tocque's writings, also sourced.
3. In 1713, on the signing of the Treaty of Utrecht, the French colonization
   of Newfoundland came to an end. Four years later Captain William
   Taverner, a resident of Trinity, Trinity Bay, presented his survey of
   Newfoundland's South Coast to Britain's Board of Trade. He wrote
   brief descriptions of places once inhabited by the French; for example,
   Burin, Lamaline, Fortune, Belleoram, the Penguin Islands off Cape La
   Hune and settlements in Fortune Bay such as Bay de Nord and Rencon-
   tre East. Of Grand Bank he wrote:

"Grand Bank at present hath no inhabitants, there are 6 stages a great many good houses, very good Beech accounted by the French A good place for fishg and the best for Drying fish on that Coast, because the foggs are not so common in that harbour as in other places, its a Tide harbour fitt for boats only."

4. For the story of the English lady see Chapter 2, Story 1.

5. These are the meticulously-kept ledgers, account and supply books of Forward & Tibbo, a business which closed its doors on December 15, 1984 after nearly seventy-five years of operation in Grand Bank. It was formed in 1910 when Charles Ambrose Forward and Felix George Tibbo joined forces.

The ledgers, mostly recorded by Sarah Forward, are presently stored in the Centre for Newfoundland Studies Archives in Memorial University, St. John's.

A portion of Water Street, 1940, taken from the top of the former Grand Bank Fisheries Building. Businesses on the east side of Water Street: (far left) John Riggs & Son, Billy Matthews' barbershop, William Forsey Ltd., and Forward & Tibbo. Stores and sheds in centre foreground include French's confectionary store and the building where Fred Coxworthy once had his small business.

Chapter One   Story Two

As It Was In 1877

Philip Tocque

Rev. Philip Tocque (1814-1899), born in Carbonear and ordained a Church of England priest in 1854, wrote descriptive essays and books on Newfoundland for most of his life. He wrote three books, three almanacs and corresponded with the press on science, politics, religious, and economic issues.

Tocque's description of Grand Bank may have been based on his visits here between 1845 and 1849.

The following excerpt on Grand Bank is taken from Tocque's second book, *Newfoundland As It Was And How It Is In 1877*, which in its time was considered a guidebook for visitors to Newfoundland.

The most populous place in Fortune Bay is Grand Bank, situated on the south side of the bay...It affords no security in shipping, the entrance being barred[1]; small vessels, however, drawing from six to eight feet of water, can pass over the bar at high tides. To the westward of Grand Bank is Ship Cove, where there is good anchorage in eight or ten fathoms of water, sheltered from the south, west and north-westerly winds. Men-o'-war and other large craft always anchor there[2].

Grand Bank derives its name from the circumstance of its having a beautiful green bank. It has been inhabited about 180 years[3]. Mr. Jonathan Hickman, the oldest inhabitant, died in 1848, at the advanced age of 100 years. He piloted the celebrated Captain Cook along this part of the coast during the time he surveyed the coast of Newfoundland about 100 years ago[4]. Formerly Wm. Evans, Esq. the late stipendiary magistrate, carried on mercantile business to a considerable extent here; but owing to the want of a harbour for shipping, he was obliged to send his vessels to load at St. Jacques, on the opposite side of the bay. A mercantile establishment is still carried on here by Edward Evans & Co., sons of Mr. Evans, one of whom is in the commission of the peace, and the other a member of the House of Assembly[5].

Agriculture is more extensively pursued at Grand Bank than in any other part of Fortune Bay. Some individuals keep from 20 to 30 head of cattle. There is a stipendiary magistrate, a constable, a lock-up house; a doctor also resides here, and a Wesleyan missionary[6]. There is only one place of worship, which is Wesleyan. There is one school under the direction of the Wesleyans, and a small annual grant is given by the Government in aid of its support[7].

According to the returns made to the Government in 1844, the population of Grand Bank was 392...

Endnotes:

1. In 1765, almost one hundred years before Tocque's visit, English explorer and cartographer Captain James Cook reported Grand Bank as the most populous settlement in Fortune Bay. Its harbour was formed, according to Cook, with a baymouth bar "over which Boats can go at a Qt. flood." This situation provided excellent facilities for fishing shallops, but for the ships, other conveniences were necessary. They could "anchor under the Shore, anywhere between Great Garnish & Grand Bank, but would be sheltered only from offshore (south and southeast) winds."

2. The only cove immediately to the west of Grand Bank is Admiral's Cove; thus, up to the 1870s at least, Admiral's Cove was called Ship Cove. How, when and why it changed to its present nomenclature is not known.

    I was told by good authority that, in the 1930s when problems with Grand Bank's shallow harbour again became a town issue, a clergyman at a town meeting thought that the Cove was a far better harbour than the present one. He suggested Admiral's Cove Beach and Pond be dredged which would make an excellent sheltered harbour. It was an "admiral" idea, but not feasible financially.

3. Tocque described Grand Bank as it appeared in 1840s. One hundred eighty years before this date is approximately 1660, a period of French occupation. Grand Bank has been settled for over 300 years.
4. Captain Cook's logbooks, maps and crew rosters exist in England. Garfield Fizzard, in his history of Grand Bank, *Unto the Sea,* examined Cook's records and found no reference to Jonathan Hickman.

    Aaron Buffett, in his history of the town, mentions Jonathan Hickman piloting Captain James Cook. Percival Hickman, who was a direct descendant of Jonathan Hickman, wrote a short version of the town's past and also claimed Hickman piloted Cook.

    The truth may lie somewhere in between. If Cook spent time in Grand Bank, it is conceivable Hickman spoke to Cook about place names or sailed with him briefly on his ship, HMS *Grenville,* although he may not have been hired or paid a fee by Cook.

    Incidentally, the name of a small brook east of Grand Bank may have come from the name of Cook's vessel: today pronounced Gumbo Brook and Gumbo Runs, which may be a derivation of Grenville.
5. At this time Edward Evans and Co.(or Sons), founded by the father William Evans (1769-1845), was the most influential business in Grand Bank, predating the Harris and Buffett merchant houses. It was managed by Edward Evans and his brother.

    In Hutchinson's Directory of 1865 for Grand Bank, Edward Evans (1819?-1898), is listed as Justice of the Peace. On May 2, 1861, he was elected by acclamation to the House of Assembly as a conservative and was successful in two subsequent elections until 1873 when he chose not to run. After he retired from politics, he was appointed the local magistrate.

    When the Salvation Army set up their first place of worship in Grand Bank in September of 1887, they used a vacant tin shop owned by the Evans' business. This shop was located on the eastern side of Water Street, opposite the present-day George C. Harris Heritage House. The land now occupied by the Harris Heritage House was once the Evans' homestead property.
6. A stipendiary magistrate was usually a local man who was paid for his services. At Tocque's writing the magistrate was probably George Simms. The town was policed and the lockup house, or jail, may have been located in the vicinity of present-day Warren's Store. According to the 1870 population directory, Edwin MacGregor was the doctor who in turn was followed by Allan MacDonald.

    Tocque refers to the Wesleyan minister who at the time of his visit was Rev. Solomon Matthews. In 1881 an Ecumenical World Conference coalesced Wesleyan and Methodist groups into one body, eventually dropping the former name in favour of the Methodist Church. On June 10, 1925, the Methodists joined other denominations to become the United Church of Canada. In *Vignettes of a Small Town,* Wesleyan and Methodist refer to present-day United Church.
7. The Methodist school in 1886, according to Lench's *Rise and Progress of Methodism,* had two teachers and two rooms (departments) in an improvised church building.

Chapter One   Story Three

᷑napshots at the Newfoundland Conference

R.E. Fairbairn

This article, written forty-five years after Tocque's description of Grand Bank, is by R.E. Fairbairn, who along with several other Methodist delegates, attended a church conference in Grand Bank in August 1922. He describes his trip in an article, "Snapshots at the Newfoundland Conference", which appeared in the *Christian Guardian*, August 16, 1922. There is no indication of Fairbairn's role, but most likely he was a Methodist minister.

Fairbairn left St. John's on a Thursday, June 22, 1922, by train, connected with the coastal boat at Argentia on Friday, but with fog and stormy weather was delayed there until Tuesday — the last week in June. The first section of Fairbairn's article describes his journey to Argentia and, to a lesser extent, the trip to Marystown, Burin, and St. Lawrence.

He also writes of Conference proceedings, but I have lifted from his story the descriptive paragraphs on Grand Bank.

At seven a.m. we actually reach Grand Bank, which appears to be a smallish settlement with one church steeple on a slight swelling of a low shore[1]. We land in boats and a deluge of rain. We are a wan, dilapidated bunch — all except the two lady delegates, of course. Our hosts sort us out and escort us to our homes. Here, though still not greedy about solid food, we offer a fervent grace for a real cup of tea...

The ministerial session opens at nine a.m., so we are soon at work. The Methodist church...is an old-fashioned building with capacity for about twelve hundred worshippers[2]. The seats are well adapted to keep a congregation awake for an hour's service, and to produce a distinct ache in the small of the back in the case of repeated and prolonged sessions.

We had known, by the hearing of the ear, of the hospitality of the people of Grand Bank, but face to face with the reality we can only declare that the half had not been told. They do not actually try to kill us with kindness; it only appears so. Three times a day they spread a banquet before us in the homes. At first we were in excellent order to do justice to the fare, but after a day or two we can but sigh and wish that our gastronomic capacity were equal to the culinary generosity of our hostesses. Not content with this programme of three feasts a day, the ladies get together in secret conclave and plot for our confusion with a public banquet...!

By the way, in any other part of the world, codfish, whether fried, boiled, or baked, is just codfish, but here is an epicure's delight. Perhaps that is because it is so fresh; more likely it is due to the loving care with which it is cooked...Salmon, herring, caplin, etc. are specified by name, but codfish is just "fish". There was a lawsuit against a man who had undertaken to deliver all his catch of fish to a United States merchant, but handed over the cod only, keeping the other varieties on the grounds that he had so fulfilled his bargain in the local understanding of the term, and the court sustained his case!

This is, or was, one of the most prosperous of the outports, but was hit badly by the famous (here they declare "infamous") Fish Regulations of a few years ago[3]. It is said that there are no poor people in the place. Many of the houses are large and handsome within and without[4]. Many of the men and women have had college privileges[5] and most of the fishermen have experience of Canada or the States, which has enlarged their outlook[6]. The crowds of young people offer a challenge and an opportunity to the Church...

Elsewhere the work of fish-curing is done on fish "flakes", which are wooden structures lifted on poles, with a floor of brushwood, allowing of a free circulation of air around the split fish[7]. Here all the drying is done on the fish beaches, large areas of big pebbles, partly natural and partly made, and kept scrupulously clear of grass and weeds[8]. The women do most of this work. It is a back-breaking job setting out and picking up the fish, which must be carefully watched, hurriedly stacked when a shower threatens, and prevented from "burning" in the hot sun. The women and girls wear shady sunbonnets that remind the old-country-men among us of the headgear of the women in English villages[9]. A considerable number wear black dresses and bonnets. They are those who have lost husbands in the fishery with its manifold perils...[10]

A concrete pier is being built to replace an old wooden one, destroyed in a recent storm[11]. Sections are moulded in forms set on a cradle and then launched like a ship into the

One of the larger merchant homes which stood in Fairbairn's time was Felix Tibbo's home on Water Street. The front peaks were heavily ornamented with fancy scrollwork. Many fences along the main streets stood on low concrete walls with concrete gate posts.

harbour, floated into position, and sunk there by filling up
the hollow interior with stones and cement. It is gruesomely
fascinating to watch the diver at work preparing the bed for
the next section[12].

...Fine weather brings our boat back a day before we are
ready for it. Telegrams begin to fly between the Conference
and the authorities at St. John's with the final result that the
steamer is held for a day. To miss that trip would mean to
wait another ten days or so at least[13]. On Thursday afternoon
we are all aboard again. The sea is calm and the sunshine
brilliant. Three motor boats filled with young people are
circling us, dodging one another. To salvos of cheering we
get under way, our escort racing alongside for awhile. It is a
pleasant contrast to the conditions of our arrival.

We are on our way home[14]...we find ourselves in the
harbour of St. Lawrence when we wake in the morning. Alas!
Another change of weather. It is blowing hard and foggy.

Endnotes:

1. Grand Bank's population at this time was around nineteen hundred
   people with approximately four hundred dwelling houses.
       Fairbairn's view of the 'slight swelling of low shore' must have
   been similar to that seen by the early French and English settlers which
   probably gave rise to the town's name: Grand (high or large) Bank
   (ridge or low shore); an embankment which extends from the west at
   Admiral's Cove extending to the harbour entrance near the present day
   Thorndyke Bed and Breakfast Home.
2. Wesleyanism (Methodism) was brought to Grand Bank in 1816 by Rev.
   Richard Knight, a missionary from Devonshire, England. The first
   church was called the "Little Chapel" and after thirty years it was
   considered inadequate. In 1846 a second building was erected during
   the ministry of Rev. Adam Nightingale.
       The third structure — the one which Fairbairn attended — was
   opened in 1876 during the tenure of Rev. Solomon Matthews and
   served the congregation until 1965. The fourth, today's building, was
   opened May 9, 1965, by Canada's moderator of the United Church, Rev.
   E.M. Howse, while Reverend Calvin Evans was the resident clergy.
3. William F. Coaker's Fishery Regulations, introduced in 1919, were
   attempts to control and to reform Newfoundland's salt fish trade.
   Coaker, as president of the Fishermen's Protective Union, and as
   Minister of Fisheries from 1919-23, established minimum export prices
   but these were disregarded in the winter of 1921 and were later
   repealed.
       The chief adversaries for Coaker's laws came from the South Coast

businesses, especially Grand Bank's G & A Buffett and Samuel Harris Ltd. Harris ignored government fish inspectors although he later claimed he was "stabbed in the back" when exporters in other South Coast communities, who initially agreed to disregard the Fishery Regulations, secretly went along with Coaker and exported fish under government regulations.

Two men with white shirts carry a draft bar across a long plank to a schooner. Since there is no lighthouse on the eastern pier, this photo dates pre-1921 when the lighthouse was built.

4. Grand Bank's older buildings and homes have been catalogued in the Newfoundland Historic Trust's book *Ten Historic Towns*. This book claims, "Architecturally, Grand Bank is interesting, since many of its earlier homes are built in variation of the Queen Anne style, popular in England and America from 1870 to 1890."

The larger homes which were standing in 1922, the time of Fairbairn's visit, were John Thornhill's Thorndyke built 1917-18; George C. Harris' home built in 1908; Buffett house on George Street built in 1905 and other three-storey dwelling houses. High impressive halls and stores were: Freemason's Hall built 1904 and Foote's Store built around 1910. Fairbairn would have also been impressed with the U.C. Parsonage — a three-story Queen Anne style home built in 1914 and taken down in 1975. Other highly visible buildings existing during the Methodist Conference have since disappeared — homes of Thomas Foote and Samuel Harris, the Frazer Hall, Temperance Hall and the Postal and Telegraph Office.

Despite Fairbairn's assessment, the majority of people at this time lived in smaller two-storey peaked roofed houses.

5. Mount Allison, in Sackville, New Brunswick, was founded in 1840 as a Wesleyan (later Methodist) College. Grand Bank's predominant religious denomination prior to, and for several years after, Fairbairn's visit was Methodist. Thus many students went to Mount Allison after graduation from the local Methodist school. A high ratio of girls, in proportion to the general population, attended Mount A obtaining degrees in fine arts, education or business (See Appendix G). Many Grand Bank men studied there including George Foote who, in his brief autobiography, says he followed family tradition and attended Mount Allison.

6. Many sailors employed on the town schooner fleet travelled to the great seaports of the world: Boston, Halifax, Gloucester, New York and the European cities, especially Oporto, Cadiz, Malaga, Gibraltar and ports of Greece. Schooners also travelled south to the West Indies and returned with cargoes of salt, rum, molasses and supplies. Educated by experience in world travel, these men brought home bits of culture, knowledge and expertise in a wide variety of areas.

7. This would include neighbouring towns like Burin which, although it had a large banking fleet, dried its fish on wooden flakes similar to those described by Fairbairn. As well, in old photos of Fortune the raised flakes can be seen in the vicinity of today's Lake and Lake Building, the Irving station, and Mavin's Variety.

8. The Trimm, Patten and Buffett beaches were three of the main curing areas. A little codfish was dried at Admiral's Cove Beach by the Piercy business. Stones or beachrocks, were taken from Admiral's Cove and the western end of Trimm's Beach (near today's Irving Oil tanks) to create beaches near Marine Drive. One such built-up beach which can be seen today lies, partially grassed-over, near the parking lot of the Seamen's Museum.

Another small beach, commonly called "John Thornhill's Beach", existed near where the Town Hall is presently located. Thornhill, a banking captain who owned or had part ownership in several schooners in the 1930-40s, entered into the fish-drying business relatively late. All the best beaches had been long claimed by established merchants; thus, he created a beach on the flats of the brook, Riverside West. His beach was used for three or four years.

9. This is one of the few written accounts where beach bonnets are compared to those in the old country — England. The headgear for shading the neck and face from the sun existed in other countries. Examination of photos of French women curing fish at St. Pierre show similar beach bonnets and dresses as those of Newfoundland.

10. In the years leading up to 1922, when this article was written, there had been several major shipping disasters in which all crew had been lost. Many drowned seamen were married men of Grand Bank. The widows of these men, as Fairbairn says, wore black and had no choice but to raise their family and try to earn a living on the beaches making fish. Contrary to Fairbairn's belief most of the losses at sea came not from the banking or fishing voyages, but from the coasting trade in winter.

The Grand Bank schooners lost with full crew in a fifteen year period prior to Fairbairn's arrival were: *Nellie Harris* - November 1906; *Tubal Cain* -January 1907; *Orion* - October 1907; *Elfreda May* -December 1910; *Arkansas* -November/December 1911; *Dorothy Louise* -January 1912; *Jennie Duff* -January 1917; *John McRea* - December 1917; *General Horne* - February 1921 and *Jean and Mary* in December 1921. All of these except the banking schooner *Orion* were in the coastal or foreign-going trade.

In addition to shipwreck, there would have been other losses at sea resulting from missing or overloaded dories, men washed overboard, and wrecks where some of the crew had been rescued.

11. This destruction may be the results of ice carried down by Grand Bank Brook. The *Evening Herald* carried the following piece on April 1, 1911. The wharf was temporarily repaired; later, a more permanent structure was built and finished in September 1922, a month after Fairbairn's visit.

Headlines from Herald

"River ice broke up last night; harbour packed full of vessels preparing for fishery; force of ice irresistible, snapped moorings and carried out a number of vessels; many badly wrecked. Damages estimated in thousands. One side of beacon carried away, will require rebuilding or extensive repairs. Lantern intact and light can be kept going by temporary stopping opening. Permanent repairs impossible at present. Every available man engaged in repairing vessels."

A similar occurrence happened in March 1948 when the Brook rafted or "riftered", as it was termed locally. The schooner *Isabel Corkum* was totally wrecked and several other vessels received damage including bankers *Freda M, Pauline C. Winters, Jean and Mona,* M.V. *Ariel* and *Doris V. Douglas,* a coal carrier commanded by Captain Tom Snook.

12. Who this diver was is not stated. He probably came from St. Pierre. Grand Bank later had a professional diver, George R. Diamond (1895-

March 1948. Harbour filled with brook ice.

1967), born at New Melbourne, Trinity Bay. Diamond moved to Grand Bank at an early age, attending Diving School at Halifax and worked at Burin, St. John's and at St. Pierre for six years. Most of his diving experience came while he worked in Nova Scotia just prior to and during World War II. After the War, he returned to Grand Bank where he found employment diving for the company that dredged the harbour and repaired the wharf. He was married to Lucy Patten of Grand Bank.

13. Two coastal steamships, *Glencoe* and *Portia*, serviced the South Coast at this time. Beginning around 1910 Reid's S.S. *Glencoe* plied the South Coast route from St. John's to Port aux Basques. In 1940 she was replaced by S.S. *Burgeo* and S.S. *Baccalieu*, both of which operated alternatively on the South Coast run. In 1943 the S.S. *Bar Haven* replaced the *Burgeo*.

In 1904, Bowering Brothers entered into a contract with the govern-

A picture taken from the masthead of a schooner in Grand Bank harbour probably around 1935 as evidenced by Model T vehicles on pier. S.S. *Portia* discharges from head of the wharf while the S.S. *Glencoe* waits on the bar.

The United Church choir in 1925, three years after Fairbairn's visit: Back row (l-r) Gerald "Ged" Patten, Sam Patten, Sam Stoodley, unidentified teacher (below the X), Charles Patten, Elic Stoodley, George Harding.
The women of the choir in the front row (l-r) with their marriage names bracketed: Sally Foote, Almeda (Eveleigh) Matthews, Meta Forsey, Ethel Foote, Grace (Forsey) Francis, Essie (Forsey) Stoodley, Nellie (Penwell) Rose, Hannah Mullins.
In the left background is Simeon Tibbo's house which stood on the corner of Ralph and Church Street. It is said that Tibbo had an old-fashioned English garden on the premises with a variety of unique plants and flowers. Photo courtesy of C.O. Eveleigh

ment to operate two steamers, one from St. John's to Battle Harbour, Labrador, and the other (*Portia*) from St. John's to Bonne Bay via South Coast ports. The contract expired in 1919 and the two ships, *Portia* and *Prospero*, were taken over by the government. *Portia* continued on the South Coast run until it was sold in 1940.

Fairbairn's misgivings of delays and untimely connections for the *Glencoe* and the *Portia* are well noted. South Coast residents and visitors were frequently upset with the "steamers" interrupted schedules.

Rev. Lench, writing in *The Newfoundland Quarterly* (1912), noted the coastal steamer's irregular departures and arrivals:

Our one drawback in Grand Bank is our isolated position and the infrequency of the mail service. The *Glencoe* calls on Thursday and on her return from Port aux Basques. The *Portia* calls on her fortnightly trip, going and returning. If the *Glencoe* fails to connect with the train at Placentia, which is quite frequently, the "hang up" may mean for eighteen or twenty hours. This is great inconvenience to the travelling public of the Western Coast...

14. Fairbairn's visit as part of a church delegation was one of many such conferences. According to the *Encyclopedia of Newfoundland and Labrador*, in 1892 the Methodist Newfoundland Conference gathered at Grand Bank — the first time it had been held off the Avalon Peninsula. After that the Methodists, which later became the United Church of Canada, met here seven times: in 1907, 1916, 1922, 1935, 1949, 1959 and 1971.

Chapter One   Story Four

The Old Home Town

Philip Forsey

The following article written by Philip Forsey appeared in the *Atlantic Guardian* in April 1945. The Honourable Philip Samuel Forsey (1912-1965) was born in Grand Bank, the son of Aaron and Maude Forsey. He received his university training at Memorial College and Mount Allison, taught school for seventeen years and actively campaigned for Confederation in 1949. In April of that year Premier Smallwood appointed him acting Minister of Provincial Affairs and Forsey subsequently won the provincial riding of Burin in May 1949. He resigned from cabinet in 1954 and left politics in 1956 to resume teaching.

Writing twenty-three years after Fairbairn's description, Forsey expresses his feelings on the changes sweeping, not only Grand Bank, but all Newfoundland: improved educational facilities, the credit system, and the establishment of local town councils.

I have no doubt that the shades of my forbears will visit me in a nightmare for writing a Grand Bank march of time in a vein of levity. However, grandfather and I[1] would both be surprised if we were to visit the old town today and see what changes had occurred. And yet perhaps grandfather would feel at home even more than I because fundamentally it has not changed at all.

Politics, the price of fish, the prospects for good crops of hay and potatoes are the age-old topics still hotly debated on the stageheads on bright Sunday mornings. The local wise-acres still congregate in the several barber shops that the town boasts.[2] Here in the winter evenings you are regaled with tall tales concerning the feats of strength of some local Hercules of a past generation, or perhaps an argument as to when the capelin struck in last year.[3] Again, two people allergic to one another may each be claiming the best load of firewood hauled that winter.

The sailing of the deep-sea fishing fleet still abounds with the same old hopes and fears; hope that the season's catch will be a good one,[4] fear that some homecoming vessel will show her flag at half-mast, to herald the untimely and tragic death of a bread-winner.[5]

Such tragedies still happen and the bereaved widows still assume the arduous responsibilities of raising a family by working on the beaches making fish. With their picturesque sunbonnets they can still be seen before the sun is up going to their work on the half trot and returning in the late afternoon still hurrying, still chattering. They work hard, these women,[6] but they stick with it and with thrifty cunning they keep homes together and educate their children.

Housewives still trudge miles to pick a bucket of berries which they proceed to jam for the winter.[7] And woe betide the precocious laddie who braves the wrath of an irate mother and dares to remove a handful of berries from the pail before she gets a chance to go jamming.

Boys still catch tom-cods on the stage-heads. They still gorge themselves on lobster bodies after the local lobster-canning factory[8] has had a "boil". They still burn tar-barrels on bonfire night, and braver spirits are still willing to risk running foul of the local constable by indulging in minor escapades ranging all the way from gate-removing to carrot-stealing.

A modern academy now replaces the old schoolhouse which, though not red in colour, is still red and redolent in many memories. The old outhouses liberally inscribed with doggerel verse have disappeared,[9] and there are now no half holidays because the stove pipes intervened and suffered a K.O. in a fracas between teacher and a refractory scholar.

The church, tribute to foresight of its planners, still meets the needs of the community and the "change and decay" of the old hymn, still so heartily sung by large Sunday evening congregations,[10] is mostly wishful thinking. The annual spring revival meeting, though perhaps not as demonstrative as in grandfather's day, are still largely attended.

Philip S. Forsey (above), one of Newfoundland's first Cabinet ministers, was appointed Minister of Provincial Affairs by Premier Smallwood a few weeks after Confederation with Canada in 1949.

After Forsey left politics, he taught in the Roman Catholic faith in a boys' school in Montreal where he was regarded with such high esteem that his picture hangs in the foyer today.

Right now there is a social pain in the old home town attendant upon the birth of the idea of local government.[11] But the church and school have been progressing towards the idea of personal civic responsibility all down through the years and local government is the cards for the future.

Grandfather, no doubt, symbolic of the diehards who still worship the feudal squire idea,[12] is looking down with the morbid fascination of a gladiatorial spectator awaiting the killing of another new-fangled notion. I, egoistic self-styled prophet of the future that I am, look towards the death of the prejudices of the past and hope to see the old home town arise from the dead ashes of its past to the heights of vibrant citizenship, which is so old in well meaning intentions and so sadly young in action, in Newfoundland's old home towns.

Grand Bank fish being washed out in pounds in the 1940s as Philip Forsey would have viewed it. From the brook on Riverside East fish was taken by horse and cart to the Marine Drive (Long Shore) beaches. The four homes (l-r) in the background are those of Capt. Charlie Rose and his son Abner; Arch Rose; Sam Rose and the home, far right, was John Pardy's and later occupied by Edith Grandy.

By the mid-fifties, a crisis (similar to the fish moratorium legislated in 1992) affected Grand Bank. As the markets for salt dry cod disappeared, banking dories were beached, turned bottom up and abandoned. Fish washing pounds of a decade ago are heaped in useless stacks. The crane and trucks prepare the land for the fish plant. Insert shows the plant walls going up.

Endnotes:

1. Philip Forsey's father was Aaron "Kit" Forsey. Philip had two sisters: Meta Forsey and Mary (Meeb) Forsey; the latter resides in Dashwood, Ontario.

   Philip Forsey's grandfather was Robert Forsey.

2. At least four barbershops existed in 1945: those of Levi Bungay, Billy Matthews, Morgan Handrigan, and Jim Welsh. Bungay's once stood at the bottom of Patten's Hill near J.B. Patten's store; Billy Matthews' shop still exists a little north of Forward & Tibbo's store on Water Street; Handrigan had a barber shop on Church Street on the site of the present day public building, and Welsh, who was also a cobbler, had a barbershop which stood a little west of the bridge.

   In her book *A Small Town Nurse*, Alfreda (Smith) Marsh, the daughter of Grand Bank sea captain Alex Smith, writes about her home town in the 1940s. Of barbers she says:

   Our barber Mr. Billy Matthews was the main hairdresser. He would cut a man's hair and shave him with a straight razor for fifty cents. He was most particular about the sanitation of his shaving brushes and mugs. Each male customer had a personalized pigeon hole in a cupboard for his mug.

   He would have a contract with my mother to cut all the girls' hair year round for a small fee. Otherwise a boy's bob or a "shingle" cut for the girls would cost her fifteen cents each.

3. Capelin "struck in" in Grand Bank around mid-June to late June/early July. Young and old spent many memorable hours at L'Anse au Paul, Trimm's Beach, Admiral's Cove or Kelly's Cove dip netting or catching capelin in buckets or by cast net. Sadly, today capelin scull in such prolific numbers is no more. (See Chapter 6 Story 3)

4. Usually the schooner bank fishing fleet left in early March. Most insurance companies began coverage on the first of that month.

5. A flag flying at half mast on the schooner would have been seen as she rounded Grand Bank Cape meant a crewman was missing, usually because of dories that gone astray in the fog-shrouded Atlantic.

   In a few instances these weary men, after several exhausting days of rowing, were picked up by another schooner or made land. All too often the flag meant a dory, which carried two men, had overturned, had been swamped from overloading or was missing. To set trawl lines, the men rowed out into the fog often up to a half mile or a mile from the schooner and at times were unable to find their way back to the mother ship.

   For example, on December 3, 1934, Clifford Smith, age twenty-eight, and Albert Elms, twenty-six, of Grand Bank fishing from the schooner *Christie and Eleanor* drowned when their dory overturned. It is estimated that scores (and the exact number may never be known) of men who lived in Grand Bank were lost while dory fishing from schooners.

   Not all missing dories and their two-man crews ended in tragedy; some were fortunate enough to make land; others were picked up by other schooners or passing ships. Marie Forsey in the booklet *United*

Church School Record (1941) relates this story of her grandfather, Edward Riggs.

Lost and Found Some years ago one of the fishing vessels of the Grand Bank fleet left here with twenty-two men on board for the Grand Banks. They arrived there all right and fished for a few days with great success. One day while the dories were away from the vessel it became very foggy and one dory, in which there were two men, failed to return.

A search was made but no trace could be found of the missing dory and when the vessel came in she reported one dory missing. The two men were given up for dead and their relatives mourned their loss. One day, a long time afterwards, a message was received from Belfast, Ireland, saying that two men who had been picked up by a steamer on the Grand Banks had been landed there.

Everyone was overjoyed to hear such good news, though it was a long time before the men reached home to tell of the hardships they had endured before their rescue.

On another occasion in the summer of 1920, Thomas Forsey and Grandy Matthews strayed away in the dense fog from their fishing schooner *Admiral Dewey*. They drifted for seven days and six nights until a jackboat fishing off Cape St. Mary's spotted the dory and towed the two men to safety. By then, they were near the end of their endurance, not so much from cold or exhaustion, but from hunger. To reach home, they connected with the westbound *Glencoe*.

When the *Admiral Dewey* came into Fortune Bay with flag at half mast, the two men were on the *Glencoe*, also steaming into Grand Bank from Placentia Bay to South Coast ports. *Glencoe*'s captain asked both

Dredge *Sydney M* removing sediment deposited by Grand Bank Brook.

men if they would know their schooner from a distance and they did, recognizing the schooner and realizing the black flag at half mast was for them. Both the schooner and the two missing men reached Grand Bank about the same time.

6. Sunbonnets may have been, as Forsey describes it, picturesque; but in reality, they were highly functional and protected the neck and eyes from the burning glare of the sun. In addition to working on the beaches, most women, if they had no older daughter to help out, had to do house and garden work — bake bread, prepare meals, make hay, care for the livestock, wash clothes, keep the house clean, and raise large families.

   Widows of the men lost at sea faced insecurity on many fronts; not only for a few meagre dollars for basic food and supplies, but also to raise a family. One man of Grand Bank related the story of his mother, recently widowed by a tragedy at sea, who had left her eldest son at home to care for younger brothers. As she spread or piled fish on the beaches, the young mother kept glancing back over her shoulder to the road. The other women working beside her asked why she kept looking up every few minutes. She replied, "I expect any minute someone will run down to the beach to tell me my house is on fire." Extended family members were working and she had left her very young son home to care for his two even younger brothers.

7. Blueberries, partridgeberries, bakeapples, and marshberries (mishberries) were common berries picked and to a lesser extent raspberries, squashberries, blackberries, and English blackberries. Some of the more frequented berry-picking grounds within walking distance: Lewis Hill, Maloney's Hill, L'Anse au Loup, foot of Bennett's Hill, Gumbo Runs, Bragg's Path, Martha's Mish (Marsh), and the Old Road from Sally's Rock down to the L'Anse au Loup Tee.

8. In the 1890s, lobster canning factories were big businesses. Foote's carried on extensive collecting, canning and shipping. George Foote (1901-1990), in an *Evening Telegram* article, claimed, "There were four or five canning factories around Fortune Bay. Lobsters teemed the waters and were sold for thirty-five cents a hundred during the 1870s and 1880s. Fishermen caught them unwisely, bringing in small as well as large and the fishery was ruined."

   By the time of Forsey's writing the industry was but a shadow of these former times. Simms' lobster plant still operated in the 1940s near the western end of L'Anse au Loup Tee, about a mile east of Grand Bank.

9. The Academy, built in 1922, was painted grey. Before the town water system was installed, only a few establishments had their own sewage systems. Forsey refers to outhouses located near the school. *Memoirs*, a Salvation Army School reunion booklet collated/edited by T. Maxwell Snook and produced in 1991, has this to say about outdoor toilets: When the water and sewerage system was put through Grand Bank in 1953-54, it ended the epic of the "out house" and the memories associated therewith. One student recalled, "I will never forget the aroma and having to hold my nose when entering...We never did envy the janitor's

task in disposing the night soil during his nightly promenade to the land wash."

10. Forsey refers to the hymn *Abide with Me* and the second verse, "Change and decay in all around I see Oh Thou, who changeth not, abide with me."

11. The Town Council disturbance of 1944. (See Chapter 6, Story 1)

12. Feudal squire system and the credit/merchant system existed in Grand Bank up to 1949, when Confederation with Canada put real cash in families' hands through the baby bonus and old age pensions. Up to that time fishermen and beach women saw little cash or dollars although it is generally agreed no one suffered for lack of food, supplies or shelter.

The credit system, according to Hollett, Jackman, Rose, and Taylor in *A Changing Fishing Technology in the Community of Grand Bank*, existed in Newfoundland and this book claims that "when the fishing season was over, the fishermen did not receive cash in payment for the total value of his catch. The value was used to balance the cost of the supplies given to him by the merchant. If the payment for the fish exceeded the cost of supplies, then the fishermen received the difference in either 'cash' or a 'credit note'. If the opposite were true, then the fishermen became indebted to the merchant until the next fishing season."

The domineering master-servant system was more pronounced in communities along the South Coast that had only one merchant. In Grand Bank, this was not the case because, as former mayor and businessman Curt Forsey says, in *A Changing Fishing Technology...*, "There were a number of merchants, and competition was strong. To attract good workers, the merchants treated them with respect and justice; otherwise, they might lose them to some other merchant in the community."

Alfreda (Smith) Marsh writes of Grand Bank in the 1940s and makes this point:

As I remember my town I recall class distinction among the people. Those classed as the rich, included the merchant, the minister, the doctor and the teachers. The middle class were the labourers, fishermen, and the servants. The poor were less fortunate and some lived on the "Dole" similar to our welfare today.

Around 1938-40, near the outbreak of World War II, Greece ordered a large quantity of salt-bulk fish from Grand Bank and sent their ships over to collect it. The mounds covered with white sail are piles of "wet" fish stored near Plant Road.

The white fence around a single gravestone at far right — George Aaron Forsey (1799-1888), the author's great, great grandfather — is a single remaining marker in an area where many are buried. Insert shows the workers moving and culling fish for the Greek freighter

Chapter Two Prominent Grand Bankers
from our Recent Past

The Lady With An "Excellent" Education

Accounts which feature Grand Bank women is one aspect of this work which is deficient. Had I been able to locate stories by or about women, the information certainly would have made a welcome addition. Yet the person in this story and her intervention is not only one of the earliest recorded "acts" by a local personality, but is also one of the most intriguing.

One of the many problems that plagued early Newfoundland settlers was the presence of pirates and privateers. A privateer differs from a pirate in that the former have permission from the head of a government to raid settlements and other ships; pirates were outside the law. Any sea raiders unlucky enough to fall into the hands of Newfoundlanders could expect death. Grand Bank, nearer the American mainland than most parts of Newfoundland and also close to St. Pierre, a well-known and frequented international port of call, most likely saw more than its share of sea raiders.

In 1781, one group of Yankee privateers, which included a "boy privateersman" named Andrew Sherburne, was captured by a group of irate Grand Bankers. The Americans were saved from death, most likely by hanging, by an unidentified woman — a respected town leader, educated, and knowledgable in certain English and American laws regarding privateers.

Captain Willis, with his crew of American privateers on his ship *Greyhound*, had been striking quick raids in Fortune Bay. They looked for a small British warship known to be in the bay, but had only found, looted, and captured some fishing shallops, large open boats which were often decked at both ends and about thirty to fifty feet long. One captured shallop was owned by Charles Grandy of Garnish.

Captain Willis had ordered five of his crew, including seventeen-year-old Andrew Sherburne, to take one of the captured shallops back to the United States. The *Greyhound* sailed away leaving the overloaded shallop off St. Pierre. Bad weather had forced them into the mouth of Fortune Bay, perhaps off Fortune or Green Island. The privateers were in this general area when another vessel was sighted on the horizon heading toward them.

Sherburne, who later wrote a book of his life (*Memoirs of Andrew Sherburne*, 1970 reprint), described what happened next:

> Shortly, however, most of us were rather inclined to think it was the enemy. The shallop continued to gain on us and we discovered that her crew were rowing...
>
> They soon began to fire upon us with long buccaneer pieces, into which they put eight or ten common musketballs for a charge. The first time they fired they did not strike us, but we heard their bullets whistle over our heads.

The unknown crew soon lowered their aim. Subsequent shots went through the head of the mainsail. The third rounds were lower still and hit the middle of the sail. Apparently the privateers were not armed and were outnumbered. At any rate, they stopped, knowing well their lives were in danger. As Sherburne relates:

> In a few minutes they were alongside of us and 20 men sprang aboard with these long guns in their

hands, loaded, cocked, and primed, and presented
two or three at each of our breasts without ceremony, cursing us bitterly and threatening our
lives...They seemed determined to take our lives,
after they had sufficiently gratified themselves
with the most bitter imprecations that language
could afford.

There were one or two who interceded for us.
One of these was their commander, but their en-
treaties seemed to increase the rage of some of the
others. We stood trembling and awaiting their de-
cisions, not presuming to remonstrate, for some of
them seemed to be perfect furies. At length their
captain and several others, who seemed more ra-
tional, prevailed on those heady fellows to forbear
the rashness.

The privateers were taken to port which they eventually
learned was Grand Bank. It was about two or three o'clock in
the evening. On the way into port, the privateers were ques-
tioned closely about what had happened since they had left
Fortune Bay. One captured man had a written copy of the
Greyhound's commission from the United States government,
but this piece of information meant nothing to the Grand
Bank men. The wind was fair into Fortune Bay and before
nightfall captors and captured arrived in Grand Bank. Sherburne wrote:

...Almost the whole village were collected to see
the Yankee prisoners. We were taken on shore and
soon surrounded, perhaps by a hundred people.
Among them was an old English lady of distinction who appeared to have an excellent education,
and to whose opinion and instructions they all
seemed to pay an especial deference. She was the
only person among them who inquired after papers. I presented the commissions.

This lady took them and commenced reading

them audibly and without interruption until she came to the clause in the privateer's letter of marque and reprisal which authorized to "burn, sink or destroy," etc.

As the old lady with "excellent education" read aloud the people listened quietly. Perhaps the words "burn, sink or destroy" incited the Grand Bankers to anger again for they again wanted to lynch the privateers. The lady called for order and quieted the murmurings for violence. What Sherburne produced was a letter of marque —defined as "naval commissions or authorizations to distinguish the holder from a pirate" — they now had to be treated as prisoners of war and not as common criminals.

According to Sherburne the townspeople were mostly West Countrymen of England or from Ireland. He continued:

They were rough and quite uncultivated, and were in a state of complete anarchy. There was neither magistrate nor minister among them. They appeared very loyal to his majesty. The old lady interposed, and soon called them to order. She informed them that we were prisoners of war and ought to be treated with humanity and conveyed to a British armed station. She then went on with her reading, and closed without further interruption.

Again the woman gave directions, ordering the townspeople to prepare food for the Yankee prisoners. Sherburne, in his description of his first and only meal in Grand Bank, wrote:

When it was boiled sufficiently, they took the pot out of doors, where there was a square piece of board which had a cleat on each edge. They then turned the pot upside down upon the board, and when the water had sufficiently drained away the board was set upon a table, or rather a bench, something higher than a common table. The company stood around this table without plates or forks. They had fish knives to cut their pork, but generally picked up the fish with their fingers, and had hard baked biscuit for bread. Having taken our refreshment, we were conducted into a cooper shop and locked up, the windows secured, and a guard placed outside.

This ended Sherburne's stay in Grand Bank. No more is said of the lady who intervened to save their lives. Sherburne and the four other Yankee privateers were put aboard a shallop and locked in a dark and filthy fishroom located in the front of the boat. Everything was taken from them except clothes, but their shoes were confiscated. Taken to Garnish, they were again locked up, but treated well by a man named Charles Grandy (this may have been the Charles Grandy whose shallop had been captured) who offered them a loaf of bread and a plate of butter.

The next morning the prisoners were transported six miles up the Garnish River, landed so as to set a course across the Burin Peninsula and marched barefooted, with seven men still guarding them with muskets, the twenty miles to Mortier.

A celebration of guns firing greeted the party of guards and their privateer prisoners when they arrived in Placentia Bay. From there they were taken to Placentia, the largest fishing station in that part of Newfoundland. It was then May, 1781[1].

Endnote:

1. It is interesting to create a description of Grand Bank, 1781, from what Sherburne writes about the town he was forced to visit.

    He doesn't, however, describe the layout of the town or the waterfront. At the time the population numbered over one hundred. As Sherburne describes it, the men were uneducated, lawless and well-armed with long buccaneer pieces loaded with several musket balls. No civil authority nor clergyman was present, British law being apparently located in Placentia Bay.

Sherburne states the South Coast ships were shallops, capable of sailing some distance from land and were fairly large since twenty men boarded one to apprehend the five Yankee crewmen. When the men rowed to catch Sherburne's group, most likely the wind was against them or sails would have been used.

Food, as described by Sherburne, was corned (salted) fish, pork, hard biscuit for bread and, in Garnish, a loaf of bread and butter. In that one and only meal in Grand Bank, the Yankees and their captors ate outdoors using their fingers from a large board-like table. Although the men who served them were rough fishermen, planters, i.e., the more prosperous landowners and permanent population, may have had better homes, eating utensils, etc.

Sherburne's cooper shop prison indicates some trades: barrel making, which in turn implies importing and exporting products, timber cutting, fishing, perhaps shipbuilding.

Some Grand Bank people in that era had immigrated from West Country England and Ireland. The lady who saved Sherburne was English and quite possibly was Jonathan Hickman's (see Chapter 1, Story 2) mother who, according to local histories and tradition, migrated from England to St. Pierre. In 1763-64 she moved to Grand Bank, eighteen years prior to the incident with the privateers.

Chapter Two Story Two

George Robert Forsey: Several Walks of Life

> Stories of George Robert Forsey appear in several sources, notably *Life on the Fringe* and the *United Church Record Book*. In March 1994, using some of these references, I gave this account of his life to a gathering of members of Fidelity Lodge, an organization Forsey helped bring into Grand Bank over one hundred twenty years ago.

According to the late Senator Eugene Forsey, his grandfather George Robert Forsey (1842-1916), was a quiet man. He was born in Grand Bank, and because of limited educational opportunities had little formal education. In his book *Life on the Fringe,* Senator Forsey claims that in the 1850s all the town could do for education was to hire one teacher. Each child of well-to-do families was able to get some semblance of education for six months. Fortunately, this early teacher was dedicated and George R. Forsey became an excellent reader, in English and in French.

He entered into Grand Bank's commercial business early in life putting his French to good use. Forsey did a great deal of business with St. Pierre and subscribed to the Montreal newspaper *La Presse.* He built most of the equipment and machinery he used on his little farm and tile-drained his land. In addition to table vegetables, he also planted a number of apple, cherry, pear, and plum trees.

In middle-age this merchant, shipbuilder and shipowner was appointed resident magistrate and for a number of years served in Burin. Transferred back to his home town he held the positions of magistrate, port warden, custom's officer for Fortune and Grand Bank, and later operated the town's Postal Telegraph Service. He had a monopoly on practically every government job in his community.

Between 1876 and 1878 the telephone was invented and improved. Five years later, before it had gotten widespread use in cities like New York, Toronto, Montreal, Forsey bought a telephone apparatus in St. Pierre, wrote Alexander Graham Bell for instructions and installed a system of three instruments, connecting his home, shop and farm. The *United Church Record Book* (1941) details the purchase and installation of Forsey's telephone:

> In 1883, the first telephone in Grand Bank was installed by Mr. G.R. Forsey, connecting his place of business with his home. With the exception of the one at the General Post Office, St. John's, there was no telephone in any other settlement in the island. There was a telephone in St. Pierre, in the office of a merchant, Mr. Cordon. Forsey who had long been a subscriber to *The Scientific American* and had read with interest articles about the new invention, saw this telephone and asked Cordon if he had a telephone to sell him. The gentleman replied that he had one, constructed by himself but it had proved a failure, but that Mr. Forsey could have it to experiment with if he wished.
>
> Forsey brought it back to Grand Bank with him, installed it successfully and used it for many years. In 1886 the first telegraph office was opened in Grand Bank and the telegraph company requested Mr. Forsey to pay a tax for his telephone.

The Honourable James S. Winter, who later became the Prime Minister of Newfoundland, came to Grand Bank speak the first words over the system. Born in Lamaline, Winter studied law after he finished his schooling and was first elected to Newfoundland's House of Assembly in 1873; eventually became the leader of the Conservative Party and then Prime Minister in 1897. During Winter's terms as member for Burin district, he and Forsey developed a close friendship, although they were rivals politically.

Today the fad of "time capsules" is fashionable. Organizations and individuals seal pictures and documents in airtight canisters and bury them. George Robert Forsey, with the idea of preserving documents for the future, had a similar concept. He had been the first master of Fidelity Lodge when the organization was formed in Grand Bank in 1877. Because of his stature in the town and his importance in the lodge, Forsey gave the speech at the dedication of the newly-erected Masonic Lodge in 1905. The text of the speech he had sealed in the cornerstone to be placed on the northeast corner of the lodge. The stone, with the text, is still there today. (See Chapter 5 Story 2)

George R. Forsey ran for the Newfoundland legislature in 1882 and was narrowly defeated by James S. Winter and John E. Peters (up to 1924 many districts in Newfoundland were represented by more than one person).

Forsey married Jane Forsey and they had ten children, the eldest of which was Eugene, a clergyman. Due to failing health, Rev. Eugene Forsey and his wife lived in Mexico. Forsey wanted his child to be born in Grand Bank and sent his wife back home to give birth. This son was christened Eugene, after his father and eventually became Senator Forsey as noted above.

George Forsey's grandson, Senator Eugene Forsey (1904-1992), academic scholar and journalist, was a Rhodes Scholar for Quebec, lecturer in political science at McGill University, and was appointed to the Senate in 1970. For Senator Forsey's long service to federal and provincial politics, he was awarded twelve honourary degrees from various Canadian universities.

When George R. Forsey died in 1916, John Edgar Peters,

the man who had defeated Forsey when both ran for the district of Burin, had this to say about him:

> In the early eighteen sixties and onward a number of the smartest looking sailing schooners that entered the narrows were from Grand Bank and Fortune. One of these vessels (*Nellie Gray*) was owned and commanded by Mr. Forsey, then quite a young man...After a time he gave up going to sea and opened up a business in a thriving town and Mr. Forsey's visits to the city were less frequent, but our friendship did not suffer...I knew him in several walks of life.

Chapter Two   Story Three

𝕾amuel 𝕳arris: 𝕾elf-𝕸ade 𝕸an

For the past several years *The Newfoundland Quarterly* has had a section, "Prominent Figures from our Recent Past", which are short biographical sketches edited by Melvin Baker of St. John's. Many prominent figures hailed from St. John's or the Avalon since that's where the bulk of Newfoundland's population lived. But I felt, however, that Grand Bank's Samuel Harris was of such stature to warrant equal billing with many other renowned Newfoundlanders, past or present.

In the winter of 1992, I submitted his biographical sketch to the *Quarterly*; in December 1994, it appeared in print.

𝕭orn in Grand Bank on August 2, 1850, Samuel Harris was the sixth of eight children of Thomas Harris, a schooner master, and Eleanor (Hickman) Harris. At a very early age, Samuel became a breadwinner for his family when his parents separated and his father left Grand Bank. Living in a seafaring town, Samuel Harris gave up any chance at formal education at the age of ten, and went to sea on a local coasting schooner. But as Reverend Charles Lench wrote in the *Newfoundland Quarterly* (Dec. 1912), "...he can well claim the title of a self-made man."

By the time he was twenty-three, Harris was captain of his first vessel, and while being a master at this young age is not unusual, the fact that he stayed afloat when other vessels were lost, is proof of his skill and good judgement. In his personal memoirs, dated August 24, 1923, Harris wrote of one death defying experience: "Today is the 50th anniversary of the great gale of August 24th, 1873 which swept the Nova Scotia coast and carried scores to a watery grave. I was off Canso on my way to Sheet Harbour in the schr. *'Jennie S. Foote'* my first year master."

By the late 1870s Samuel Harris owned his first vessel. In 1881, according to Aaron F. Buffett's local history, he sailed the seventy ton *George C. Harris* to the offshore banks for cod becoming the pioneer of the South Coast schooner fishery. Presumably he learned of the lucrative bank fishery and the method of catching cod by baited hook and line on his earlier voyages to Lunenburg or Gloucester. He already knew the climate and geography of Grand Bank was well suited, in terms of its total hours of sunshine and its proximity to the fishing grounds, to curing and shipping the finished product.

Following Harris' initiative, other businessmen in Grand Bank and along the South Coast began their own enterprises and exported their fish directly to Europe bypassing Newman's Company at Harbour Breton and the St. John's merchants. Harris helped break the well-established salt fish exporting monopoly cornered by St. John's firms.

By the turn of the century, Harris owned a fleet of banking schooners — the total number of schooners owned by Harris' interests throughout the years was well over sixty. One of his vessels, the *Castle Carey*, abandoned at sea in 1922, was named for the town in Somerset, England, his grandmother's birthplace. Samuel Harris established businesses at Grand Bank, Lamaline, Marystown and Garnish and also had a branch business at Change Islands on the Northeast Coast. To export his products, he bought or had built nearly a score of tern schooners, fourteen of which he christened 'Generals' after British or Canadian World War I commanders — *General Allenby, General Byng, General Gough, General Smuts*, etc. By 1918, Samuel Harris Limited had an annual turnover of a quarter million dollars.

According to Lench, Samuel Harris "used every means to

inform himself of how to become a successful businessman and encouraged his six children to get higher education." All except one entered Wesleyan College (Mount Allison) at Sackville or at other colleges.

Harris was an active and liberal supporter of community institutions: he helped found Grand Bank's Freemasons, actively supported the Methodist Church, Foreign Missions and the Grenfell Labrador Mission. One of his local contributions was the large clock built into the church bell tower.

Harris became a member of the Harbour Board which brought a dredge and wharf improvements to the harbour. The first dredging of the harbour was begun in 1898. The first dredge was wrecked in 1903 and the Harbour Board arranged for Lemoines of Montreal, a company dredging at St. Pierre, to come to Grand Bank. As a result the harbour was deepened from the entrance to near the bridge. The cost was covered by a tax on each barrel of flour, ton of coal, etc. entering Grand Bank harbour.

After the Great War, Harris' fortunes began to decline: shipping losses decimated his fleet, several schooners disappeared with crew while on transatlantic voyages. Fishery regulations, introduced by Coaker and legislated by the

Samuel Harris in his later years with his grandchild in his arms. Behind him are two homes on Blackburn Road; left the house once occupied by Eugene West (now owned by Hubert Vallis) and the home with the mansard-type roof was Richard Rose's (now owned by Edward Rogers).

Squires' government, dictated the prices and quality of exported fish.

Harris, in a letter to the *Daily News*, criticized the actions of government appointed fish inspectors, claiming that in October 1920, his agent had no say in the kind of fish exported nor the price Harris' business could ask for it in Oporto. He claimed that, "the *General Currie* loaded at Lamaline a cargo of five thousand seventy-four quintals..." and when the account came back to Grand Bank, "the voyage had lost $42,372.00 beside freight on the same."

In 1923, as world markets declined, his business went into receivership and re-emerged under new management as Samuel Harris Export Limited. Subsequently it became Grand Bank Fisheries, managed by his son-in-law, Percy L. Carr.

Samuel Harris married twice: first to Mary in 1875, the

This is how the *Evening Telegram* of May 8, 1923, depicted Harris heading the polls.

Mr. George Harris Heads Poll

BURIN RETURNS ONE OPPOSITION AND ONE GOVERNMENT.

Burin District has returned the Opposition Candidate, 'Mr. George Harris, at the head of the poll with a majority of 106 votes over Hon. S. J. Foote, the Government candidate. Capt. Eric Chafe, colleague of Mr. Harris, polled a splendid vote, considering that he was a new man in the field and was also handicapped in his canvass of the district by being held on the Kyle for 14 days. The final count was:—

BURIN.

Harris (Opp.)	1288
Foote (Govt.)	1182
Cheeseman (Govt.)	1150
Capt. Chafe (Opp.)	1148

St. George's Count.

BIG VOTE POLLED.

The count for St. George's District

(Founded in 1879 by W. J. Herder.)

Evening Telegram

The Evening Telegram, Ltd., Proprietors.

All communications should be addressed to the Evening Telegram, Ltd., and not to individuals.

Tuesday, May 8, 1923.

daughter of Aaron Forsey, thus becoming a brother-in-law to his business contemporary, George A. Buffett. In 1915 he married Marion Harding. He died in his Grand Bank home on April 29, 1926.

His children: George received at least one university degree in commerce, managed the Harris' business and married E.J. Pratt's sister, Charlotte (Lottie). George also had a successful but short run in politics when he was elected in Burin District in 1923 as a Liberal-Progressive candidate; the next year he was defeated by H.B. Clyde Lake of Fortune, the Liberal-Conservative candidate.

Chester was a doctor and the first mayor of Marystown. (see Chapter 2, Story 6) and Garfield was employed in his father's business until the 1920s when he moved to Western Canada. Samuel Harris had three daughters: Mary, Emily, and Eleanor (Nellie). Eleanor married the above-noted Percy Carr.[1]

Endnote:

1. General William Carr (1923 -), the son of Percy and Eleanor and grandson of Samuel Harris, was born and educated in Grand Bank. He joined the Canadian Air Force in 1941 rising through the ranks as pilot and commander. He piloted the plane that, at various times, carried Queen Elizabeth, Prince Philip, Princess Margaret, General De Gaulle and Prime Minister John Diefenbaker. In 1975 Carr became the first Commander for the new Canadian Armed Forces for Air Defense.

A.E. Hickman: Prime Minister of Newfoundland

Where in Grand Bank did he live? That became a focus of
my interest for Prime Minister Albert E. Hickman, a man who
was born in Grand Bank and spent his boyhood playing
around and exploring the waterfront. He later served in the
highest political office Newfoundland had to offer.

In time, the site of his ancestral home will be appropri-
ately recognized with signage by local or provincial authorities.

A man with many diversified interests, Albert E. Hickman
has the distinction of having served the shortest term of any
Prime Minister of Newfoundland, one month, but that dubious distinction belies the many facets of his colourful life.

Born in Grand Bank on August second, 1875, the son of
Henry and Ann (Hillier) Hickman, Albert was educated at
Grand Bank graduating from the Methodist Academy
around 1892-93. He attended Mount Allison University in
Sackville, New Brunswick. After graduation he joined Smith
and Company Ltd at Halifax, but returned to Newfoundland
entering into the fish buying and exporting business at St.
John's in partnership with Smith & Company.

Not long after, he bought out his partners and established
his own business under the name of A. E. Hickman Company
Limited which dealt in general supplies, marine equipment,

hardware, and insurance. His foreign-going sailing fleet was once one of the largest in Newfoundland carrying Hickman's products to the Mediterranean, Brazil, and the West Indies. By the end of World War I there were fifteen sailing vessels operating under his flag. Some of his schooners included *Helen Stewart, Henry L. Montegue, Florence Swyers* and included a fleet of tern schooners which, interestingly enough, carried one-word descriptive names such as *Armistice, Kinsman, Workman* and *Vogue*. At least nine of his vessels were built in Newfoundland.

Even at the height of his business successes, he diversified into buying and distributing coal throughout Newfoundland. In 1919, he foresaw the impact the automobile would have on the island and imported a small quantity of motor cars. Four years later, he obtained the franchise for selling Ford automobiles; then changed to General Motors products. From those modest beginnings with a few cars, the A. E. Hickman Company was for decades one of the largest car dealerships in Eastern Canada. In 1933 he contracted to build a brewery for a client. When problems arose he finished the brewery himself and guided its management. As a result, this became the leading brewery in Newfoundland until it was sold, years later, to a national company.

Hickman's organizational skills and personal qualities overflowed into politics. In 1913, he was elected in Bay de Verde as a Liberal supporter of Sir Robert Bond. In 1919 Sir Michael Cashin formed an administration for Newfoundland and Hickman was invited to become the Minister of Militia. After a by-election defeat Hickman remained out of politics for a few years until he ran in the Harbour Grace district in 1923. The Newfoundland political scene between May 1923 and May 1924 under the W.R. Warren leadership was a confusing one with resignations, defections, and dissolutions. While this was happening, the opposition — Liberal-Progressive —elected Hickman as its leader.

On May 10, 1924, after he had been asked by the governor to form the government, A.E. Hickman became the seventeenth Prime Minister of Newfoundland. He remained in

A.E. Hickman, a former Prime Minister of New-foundland when Newfoundland was an inde-pendant country, was born in Grand Bank in 1875.

office until the June 1924 election. Hickman's term of office was one month and the House of Assembly did not met while he served. In the subsequent election Hick-man's party was defeated and he officially resigned on June 11. He lead the Opposi-tion until his retirement from politics in 1928. At the end of his political career, Hickman continued to expand his al-ready successful business operations. He passed away on February 9, 1943.

According to the late Joshua Forsey and Grace Sparkes who both remem-bered the house, Albert Hickman's Grand Bank residence was situated on the present-day site of the Thorndyke Bed and Breakfast Home on Water Street. Although it was a large and grand house, it looked lower than the surrounding structures and had a large verandah around the front or side. The house, which was painted a bluish grey, was torn down around 1915-1917. Around that time Captain John Thornhill bought the land and built his house, the Thorndyke. By then Hickman had already left Grand Bank. However, he occa-sionally returned; in 1899, aged twenty-four, he joined Fidel-ity Masonic Lodge in Grand Bank.

Hickman's father, Henry, had always been well-to-do, but he had had a serious financial loss in the Newfoundland bank crash of 1894 when Newfoundland's two banks, the Union Bank and the Commercial Bank, closed permanently. After the father died, A.E.'s mother went away to live with a daughter in Dartmouth, Nova Scotia, and the ancestral home lay unoccupied for some time.

Through the oral traditions passed on locally, it is known

A.E. Hickman would spend some of his summer days in Lamaline, the home of his maternal grandparents. There he went out in boat with his grandfather to help him catch, clean and salt away fish.

When he lived in Grand Bank as a young boy, A. E. Hickman did what many ten to fifteen-year olds do today: climbed the cliffs and jumped the chasms of Point Bouilli, explored the beaches and fishstores a stone's throw from his home, and fished for connors and tom-cods on the head of the wharf. He saw the banking schooners bringing the raw products and the foreign-going vessels taking the finished product from the Burin Peninsula to European markets. Growing up in a typical fishing community, Hickman witnessed the great salt fish enterprise which became so much a part of his future.

Church Street in 1940. Much of the land on the right (or north side of Church Street where the public building now stands) was residential: A meat market at bottom right; King's restaurant is just out of view and Dr. Burke also had a clinic in this area. Much of the land along the north side (right) was once owned by the Hickman family.

Chapter Two   Story Five

Marystown's Mayor Poet, Dr. Chester Harris

As I read about poet E.J. Pratt's connection with the Burin Peninsula, I became fascinated with the idea that Pratt occasionally visited Marystown to see Chester Harris. Harris, I discovered, was a prominent Newfoundlander in his own right and had a varied and interesting career.

I brought this piece to the *Southern Gazette* and editor George Macvicar published it in the November 30, 1993 issue. Coincidentally, the same issue carried the announcement of the winner of Marystown's Chester Harris Scholarships. That article is appended to this biography.

Doctor, decorated soldier in the Great War, artist, award-winning poet, friend of E.J. Pratt: this, and more, was Marystown's first mayor.

Born in Grand Bank in 1887, Chester Harris attended the Methodist School in his home town. Upon graduation he enroled in the Methodist College in St. John's and later attended Mount Allison University in Sackville, New Brunswick. In one university photo of him, he is identified as the captain of Mount Allison's ice hockey team.

Shortly after completing his undergraduate studies, he entered the Faculty of Medicine at Edinburgh University, Scotland, and received his medical degrees in 1916. He had intended to be a medical missionary to the Far East, but

This was the home of Chester's parents, Samuel and Mary Harris. The house was located on Blackburn Road. Its extensive garden, barns and outbuildings were separated from the street by a high board fence. The front door step, like many homes of a by-gone era, was practically on the street. The William Baker and Allister Buffett homes today occupy the site where the Harris' house once stood.

around this period changed his career becoming a medical doctor.

That same year Harris enlisted in the Royal Army Medical Corps. During his service in this branch, Dr. Harris was mentioned by General Douglas Haig, the Commander of the British Expeditionary Force, in his "Dispatches" several times. Cited for bravery and effort, Harris was awarded the Military Cross, receiving the decoration from King George V at Buckingham Palace, February 1919.

After the army disbanded, he served for a short time on the Balkan Peninsula fighting a war of a different nature — the great influenza epidemic that spread world-wide. For his efforts, Harris received an award from the Bulgarian government. Shortly after, he was Medical Officer on the passenger ship *S.S. Tieresias* travelling between England and China. Following this, Dr. Harris established a practice in Toronto where he remained for three years. In 1924, Chester Harris decided to return to Newfoundland and settled in Marystown as a community doctor. He married Eleanor Forsey of Grand Bank.

Harris was devoted to his medical practice. In earlier years Marystown, like most Burin Peninsula towns, had inadequate roads and no cars which necessitated travel by horse-drawn buggy or sleigh. Often the doctor travelled by open motor boat across the harbour to Marystown South, down the coast to smaller communities like Jean de Baie or Spanish Room or out to the Placentia Bay islands.

His was the era before cottage hospitals and he sometimes performed surgery and dentistry in lamp-lit homes, often on kitchen tables. It is said that the first baby delivered by him in Marystown was Effie Murley (Legrow). In 1961, Dr. Harris was honoured by the Canadian Medical Society with Senior Membership, a distinction given to few Newfoundland doctors.

In addition to his heavy medical practice, Harris found time to participate actively in community affairs. In the early fifties, his interest and enthusiasm in civic matters resulted in his election as mayor of Marystown. Marystown was incorporated as a town in 1951, and in the first municipal election held the following year, Dr. Harris led the polls becoming the town's first mayor and held that position for eight years.

During his term, he worked tirelessly to improve local roads, fire protection and garbage removal. Marystown was one of the last large towns on the Peninsula to receive electricity and Harris was instrumental in bringing electric lights as well as street lighting, and a telephone service to the town. He foresaw the need to bridge Mortier Bay to connect Marystown North and South, and he worked to put a bridge in place.

Harris had varied artistic interests. He, like most of his brothers and sisters, was enthusiastic about art, painting, drama, poetry and literature. At least one of Dr. Harris' water paintings exists in Marystown today. As well, he had been writing poetry all his life, although most poems were circulated among family and friends.

Marystown's first mayor, Dr. Chester Harris, was highly respected by his patients and friends in the Marystown area. Described as soft-spoken and sincere, Harris was known to have paced the floor for hours in silent prayer while attending a particularly difficult childbirth. His wife, Eleanor Forsey of Grand Bank, who had a degree in nursing, often worked with him. They had one son, Chester.

Occasionally Harris submitted a poem to magazines. His creations earned him distinction in Newfoundland; a relationship which no doubt strengthened the ties of friendship between him and E.J.(Edwin John) Pratt. Pratt's sister, Lottie, was married to Dr. Harris' brother, George; thus E.J. Pratt and Chester Harris had common bonds and a close friendship. E.J. Pratt, Canada's well-known and loved poet, sometimes visited the Burin Peninsula spending as much time in Marystown as he did in Grand Bank, where Lottie lived.

In June of 1925, E.J. Pratt came to Newfoundland from Toronto and visited Marystown, or Mortier Bay as it was then called, to see his friend Chester Harris. According to David Pitt (1984) who has made an extensive study of the poet's life and has written two books about him, Pratt travelled from St. John's to Placentia by train, and then crossed Placentia Bay to Marystown by coastal boat. When the weather turned foul, he was forced to stay there a week longer than originally planned.

The time was well spent. Chester Harris showed him around — out to Merasheen Island and to the whaling stations at Rose-au-rue, cod jigging on the rich grounds just offshore, and salmon fishing in the rivers near Marystown. Pratt also accompanied the doctor on his medical rounds by motorboat to the smaller communities.

Most likely Pratt and Harris talked of poetry and writings, successes and failures, for both had a common interest. But this is not to say that Harris' ability to create poetry was in any way aided, influenced or guided by Pratt for the doctor was a fine poet in his own right. Several years later Chester Harris had a sparkling poem which gained island accolades. In early 1947, this report appeared in the *Newfoundland Quarterly*:

> On Christmas Eve it was announced that Dr. Chester Harris, practising at Marystown, was the 1946 winner of the F. M. O'Leary Newfoundland Poetry Award with the first prize of fifty dollars.
>
> Dr. Harris' winning poem is entitled *Metamorphosis* in which the poet deals with nature's change of a grub to a dragon fly in comparison with man's change from Life to Immortality. In it the author goes deep into the mystery of Life in a poem that is definitely a prize winner.
>
> Congratulations to Dr. Harris on his success in the realms of poetry with this fine creation. Mr. Roy Evans, now at Mount Allison University, was also a prize winner in a similar contest when he was a student at the U.C. Academy. (Roy Evans, son of William Evans of Grand Bank, attended school in Grand Bank. He now teaches music in Milan, Italy.)

Metamorphosis

Bound in her sombre caul,
Patient to suffer all
The ills that may betide;
Couched in the dark inside
Her clayey dwelling;
By steady toil and slow,
She trusts in time to grow
From grub to dragon fly,
Urged to perfection by

Instinct's propelling.

When comes the warmth of June,
Bursts from the dark cocoon,
Enters the light of day,
While the dull house of clay
Back falls to the ground,
Splendour, accomplished now,
Sits on the topmost bough
Fluttering her pinions new,
Forth soars she in the blue
In glory, unbound.

Now, when my time comes due,
Shall I go soaring too
Forth from my chrysalis,
Bursting my carapace
Quickly asunder?
Shall I through azure ways
Flit in celestial rays,
With bright wings silver-lined,
Leaving my shell behind?
Greatly I wonder!

In 1964, Chester Harris retired from the medical profession and moved to St. John's where he died in 1971. Today Harris Drive, a street in Marystown, honours the mayor-poet.

(*Southern Gazette* article November 30, 1993) Peter Rogers of Marystown is the winner of the Dr. Chester Harris Memorial Scholarship. He was selected the winner after 1993 graduates were nominated by both Marystown Central High School and Pearce Regional High in Burin.

A first-year student of Memorial University's program at Eastern College in Burin, Mr. Rogers is hoping to pursue a career in the medical profession. Peter is the son of Peter and Rose Rogers of Marystown.

Dr. Harris was the first Mayor of Marystown, and the scholarship is awarded annually by the town council through the scholarship committee.

Chapter Two   Story Six

Coxworthy's Car

In 1993 I attended a Royal Canadian Legion Conference and met Edward Coxworthy. He asked if I knew of his grandfather, Fred, who once lived in Grand Bank, and gave me a picture of Fred Coxworthy. So many people in Grand Bank remembered Coxworthy and his car that I felt this short piece would be appropriate.

Fred Coxworthy was born in 1872 in Ontario, lived in St. Pierre as a young man, and later came to Grand Bank to set up a ships' chandler business — rope being his most common item. His store, which doubled as a general repair and junk shop, was located directly across the road from Forward & Tibbo's premises, a little east of J.B. French's confectionary store.

Coxworthy would buy, sell, and repair any item and made a living with his mechanical ability. It is said that a Grand Bank woman brought him a small sewing machine to be repaired, and he charged her $1.50. When asked about the high charge, Coxworthy replied: "Fifty cents for doing the repairs and a dollar for knowing how to do it."

For a few cents, fishermen would sell their old fishing boots at his store. "Throw them out back in the junk pile," Coxworthy would tell them. Later he repaired the leaky boots and sold them back to another unsuspecting fisherman for a quarter. Young boys were not adverse to snitching odd items from the junk pile and then selling them back to

Coxworthy. Someone claimed the same rubbers were sold and resold several times.

Coxworthy's Model T became an attraction, of a dubious nature, in Grand Bank. It is said he set a record for going off the road and down over High Bank — a steep embankment west of Grand Bank. Once he ended up in the landwash without any damage to his vehicle or injury to himself. He also liked cards and was not adverse to high-stake gambling.

He was married to Margaret Hennebury and had two sons, Pierre and Frank. Coxworthy died in 1932 at age sixty.

Frederick Coxworthy at the wheel on his Model T Ford, said to be the first car owned in Grand Bank. Sitting behind him is the bank manager. His tin-lizzy had to be cranked from the front and had a squeeze horn near the steering wheel.

Many people liked to catch a ride in his car and Coxworthy was obliging. Many a penny given to children for Sunday School or the church collection ended up in Coxworthy's pocket when he charged them for a Sunday's ride to Fortune. Courtesy Edward Coxworthy

Chapter Two   Story Seven

Grand Bank's First Mayor

As a boy I can remember this distinguished gentleman walking along Water Street; although I had a nodding acquaintance, I scarcely knew Curtis Forsey. Thirty years later, while searching for information on the marine history of Grand Bank, I visited him often at his nursing-home room in St. John's. He was a remarkable, reliable and enthusiastic source; he had so much historical knowledge of the town it is our loss the information was not all recorded. With help from his children, coupled with several talks I had with Curtis, I put together this short (considering the many facets of his long life) biography.

Curtis Forsey was born November 3, 1895, at Grand Bank. In a conversation with him in 1989 he told me his earliest memories were of his father, William Forsey, coming home to say Queen Victoria, England's longest reigning monarch, had passed away and the town was preparing for mourning. Queen Victoria died on January 22, 1901, which means Curtis was five years old when he formed clear impressions of events in Grand Bank. That year he began his formal education at the Methodist Academy in Grand Bank. Christened in an era when many males received standard names like George, William, John and Aaron, Forsey's first name is linked to Rev. Levi Curtis, the Methodist clergy stationed in Grand Bank from 1891-1894.

In 1912, Forsey attended Mount Allison University in

New Brunswick. One of his many friends was Roger Lench whose father, Charles, had once been the Methodist minister in Grand Bank. To find temporary employment, both young men went to New York where Forsey worked with a newspaper company. But the Great War curtailed his university education and career. When England called for volunteers, the two friends returned home to enlist.

After initial drill instruction in St. John's, Forsey and his regiment went to Salisbury, England, and then to France for further training. While in Salisbury, he met and talked briefly with Winston Churchill who, at this period of his long military and political career, was secretary of state and minister of munitions. Churchill said the Forsey name originated in Normandy and that the first Forsey, albeit with a different spelling, had come to England from France in 1066 with William the Conqueror.

Curtis Forsey saw military action in France and was wounded in Ypres on September 27, 1918. The first wound was in the ankle and he later received another more serious injury in the groin. The latter injury healed and the ankle injury seemed not to bother him at first, but it later caused trouble all his life. Taken from Calais, France, to England on a hospital ship, he was transferred to a London hospital and spent over a month there. Forsey was released from hospital, on crutches, on November 11, 1918, Armistice Day.

Before demobilization, Forsey was sent to Ayr, Edinburgh and Glasgow, Scotland, to recuperate and then to receive further military training. While in Ayr, in a chance encounter, he met a friend and business acquaintance of his father.

H.B. Clyde Lake (1887-1965), who was later to become the Liberal MHA in the Newfoundland government, of the Lake business interests of Fortune was the young skipper of the schooner *Margaret Lake*. While sailing to Oporto, Portugal, with fish the *Margaret Lake* had rammed another schooner, *Lottie B. Silver*, owned by Forward & Tibbo of Grand Bank and captained by Parmineas "Min" Banfield of Bay

L'Argent. The *Silver* sank but Banfield and his crew were rescued and taken aboard the *Margaret Lake*.

Lake journeyed from Oporto to London, England, to talk to Lloyd's of London insurance company concerning the accident. Lake heard of schooners for sale in Troon, Scotland, and went up to look at them. A day or so later Lake travelled to Ayr to meet the boys from Fortune who, like Forsey and several other Newfoundlanders, were in Scotland for training.

Forsey was at the end of a long queue in the crowded Ayr train depot when he recognized and went up to greet H.B. Clyde Lake who was farther up the line. His fondest experience of the war years was not the damage inflicted on the enemy nor his views of France or Belgium, but this coincidence when among hundreds of strangers in a foreign country, he met a friend from Fortune. Roger Lench also survived the war and returned to live in St. John's. Both Curtis and Lench remained in contact over the years.

After troops disbanded, Forsey probably came to Grand Bank for a while; then went to Epworth, near Burin, to manage a branch of the family business. His father, in partnership with J.B. Patten, had an extensive fish procuring and exporting firm in Grand Bank. Patten and Forsey's business had been established around 1900, but in 1922 William Forsey and Patten mutually agreed to break off the partnership and each established his own store in Grand Bank —Forseys becoming William Forsey Ltd.

In 1922 he married Hazel Tibbo of Grand Bank. For some time he and his wife resided in Epworth while he managed Forsey's business there. They had four children: Jane, Helen, Amelia and William.

But by the 1920s world prices for fish had dropped and, like most fish exporting companies in the pre-Depression years, Forsey's business was in financial trouble. In 1925 the Burin branch closed and he moved back home.

On March 1, 1930, a fire destroyed several stores, sheds and businesses on Water Street, including the stores of Patten, Buffett and Forsey. Curt's father hired Saunders and

Howell of Carbonear to rebuilt his store which was relocated further north on Water Street (Sharon's Nook is presently located there). William Forsey's new store opened on July 30, 1930. When William Forsey, the founder of the business, died six years later, Curtis ran the store until it ceased operation in the 1950s.

A line drawing by Jean Ball of the former residence of Curtis Forsey (left) with the Thorndyke home on the right. Forsey's house, built in 1891, was owned by Jane (Hickman) Tibbo and Wilson Tibbo, a captain and owner of Grand Bank schooners like the *Mary E; Annie C. Hall; Beothuck* and *Coronation*[1].

William Forsey acquired this house, today termed a salt-box, and a number of others in Grand Bank in the 1920s giving the residence above to his son in 1930. Many homes built around the turn of the century were salt-box; that is, a one or sometimes two-storey house with a steep pitched roof with either an attic or bedrooms in the upper storey and the structure built around a massive stone chimney. Many had an extension added to the rear.

Forsey played an active role in local politics. In 1943, when Grand Bank applied for the formation of a town council, he was secretary of the committee appointed to draft the act for incorporation. From 1944 to 1948, council members were appointed and Merrill Tibbo became the chairman (or mayor). In 1948, when the town held its first elections, Curtis Forsey became the chairman of the new council — Grand Bank's first elected leader. In 1952, he was appointed to assist Magistrate Sparkes on a storm damage report for Placentia Bay. He was the co-founder and first president of Grand Bank's Royal Canadian Legion and the town's Justice of the Peace for many years.

Forsey was keenly interested in local and island history; many a school student went to him for interviews and information on the town's history. Appendix I is an interview with Forsey done by a Grand Bank school student.

He had extensive knowledge of the Bible; while a soldier in the Great War, Curtis kept a small Testament in his uniform. He disliked war intensely, rarely talked of it and became distressed when he knew of the young men, especially those of his home town, who had been killed in World War Two.

In later life he resided in the Agnes Pratt Home in St. John's and on October 20, 1993, this soldier of the Great War, mayor, businessman, and amateur historian died.

Endnote:

1. The loss of the *Coronation*, owned by Captain Wilson H. Tibbo (1855-1917), has been recorded.

   Built in 1902 in Shelburne, Nova Scotia, the ninety-eight ton *Coronation*'s registry was sold to Wilson Tibbo of Grand Bank two years later. Tibbo sold sixteen shares to Harvey and Company in St. John's. According to the February 18, 1912, edition of the *Morning Chronicle* of Halifax, Nova Scotia, the *Coronation* was abandoned while en route from Oporto to Newfoundland. The crew was taken off safely and carried to Halifax.

The Fabric of Her Life: Louise Belbin

> Most people growing up in Grand Bank in the 1950s and 60s recall Louise Belbin's two confectionary stores, one on Riverside East; the other, directly across from it on the other side of the brook, on Riverside West. It was later in her life this unassuming woman received the praise she deserves.

A travelling exhibition of the 1970s included Louise Belbin's work; it was displayed in six galleries in England, one of which was the Canada House Gallery in London, plus others in galleries across Canada, including the Museum of Man in Ottawa. The curator travelling with the exhibition claimed her work was "beautiful and she deserved the honour." Lynn Verge, then Newfoundland's Minister of Education, praised each piece in the exhibition for the beauty of the work. On April 9th, 1980, Memorial University's Art Gallery opened *The Fabric of Their Lives*, an exhibit in which Louise played a significant role.

When Louise's traditional Newfoundland craft went on public view in the Arts and Culture Centre, she was there, at age eighty-one, demonstrating her craft and answering questions. The previous year, 1979, the Media Unit of MUN Extension produced a film on the process of her hooked mat craftsmanship.

Born in Jacques Fontaine in 1898, Louise (Johnson) Belbin lived there until she was twenty-three when her husband and his work took her to Grand Bank. In 1922 she married

Thomas Belbin: "My husband was from Grand Bank. He was a foreign-going captain of a three master in his younger days."

Louise Belbin's husband was at sea much of the time. "I only saw him for a month and a half the year we were married," she says, adding that she took up mat-making to pass time. As she recalls:

> I can't stand the wind. My father and husband were sea captains and every time the wind came up, I used to worry and I suppose that's why I can't stand the wind. My father went to sea on a banking schooner and my husband sailed to places like Brazil and Gibraltar with dried fish and returned with salt, rum and molasses.
>
> The first five years he was always going down south to Brazil, Portugal, Spain, Gibraltar, Turk's Island and Barbados. The first thing I asked my husband when I was married was to make a mat frame as I had to do something in the long winter evenings.

In 1944, she opened a small confectionary store in her front yard in Grand Bank. After her husband died Louise found she had more time to make her hooked mats and to practise her unique designs while waiting on friends and customers. "Sunday was my only day to have a spell," she says. In her youth mat making was something she had to do. The houses were cold and drafty, and the mats helped keep a house warm and cheery during the long windy winters. There were always several mats in the kitchen, mats along the threshold of a door to keep out the drafts, and mats by the bedside.

Most mat designs and colours are Louise Belbin's creations, but she gave credit to artist Don Wright who gave her ideas on mat designs. It was Wright who originally brought Louise's work to the attention of the MUN Art Gallery. The gallery immediately bought a number of mats. Other mats

Water Street facing north in 1958. The bike is situated in front of Forward & Tibbo's store. The next two stores — William Forsey's, and Billy Matthews' barbershop — have flagpoles on the building extending over the street.

were bought by private collectors, some of whom specified the designs they wanted.

While Wright was in Grand Bank, he operated a small studio in the Temperance Hall and started craft classes in the Seamen's Museum. Louise taught mat-hooking. "I used to teach two nights a week for two hours a night," she recalled. "I had twelve in my class — all the doctors' and technicians' wives from the hospital."

When I spoke to Louise Belbin in her daughter's home in Grand Bank on December 18, 1994, she was still artistically active and mentally bright. Louise showed me her handicraft — knitted mitts, caps and chair coverings. Hands which had produced hundreds of hooked mats could no longer handle the heavy material: "But I still feel the need to knit. It's what keeps me going, you know."

Chapter Two   Story Nine

𝔅iographical 𝔖ketches

George Abraham Buffett was born in Grand Bank in 1847.
While he was a fisherman, he educated himself and regularly read current books, works of literature, magazines
and leading periodicals. After marriage, he collected books
for his well-selected home library. Like Samuel Harris, his
brother-in-law, George A. Buffett helped introduce the
bank fishery into Grand Bank, took his own vessels to the
bank fishery as early as 1883, and set up a business partnership with Harris.

According to the *Newfoundland Quarterly* (December
1912), Buffett purchased a small fleet of banking schooners
around 1883 and split from Harris setting up his own enterprise, G. & A. Buffett, Limited. Around 1908, with his fleet
increasing and his enterprise expanding, Buffett added a fish
collecting and trading store in Marystown.

Five schooners owned by George A. Buffett and his son
in the early 1900s were the sixty ton *Julia Forsey*; forty ton
Sunbeam; *Quero*, a seventy-four ton banker built in 1887;
Pointer II, constructed in Grand Bank by shipwright
"Pointer" John Forsey, and the fifty-six ton *Kitty Clyde*, built
in Grand Bank in 1871 and jointly owned with Benjamin
Buffett. *Kitty Clyde* was eventually sold to the Northeast
Coast and her last registered owner was Peter Blackwood of
Brookfield, Bonavista Bay. Up to a few years ago, her kelp-
covered keel and rotten bottom timbers were visible at low

tide near Brookfield where she had been beached in the late
1940s.

   George A. Buffett became an extensive traveller journeying to Paris, London, Vancouver, the United States, and
Hawaii. Heavily involved in Methodist Church work, he
taught Sunday school for
sixteen years and in 1904
travelled to the World's Sunday School Convention in Je-
rusalem. In his later years he
became Justice of the Peace
for his home town and was
one of the founding mem-

A 1940 ad for G. & A. Buffett shows the extent
and types of enterprise of the business. Bottom picture shows the original Buffett store in
Grand Bank.

bers of the Masonic Lodge.

George A. Buffett married Julia Forsey, the daughter of Aaron Forsey who had drowned in the attempt to save his son who had fallen overboard. Knowing the value of university education, George A. Buffett's four children attended college: Claude became a medical doctor who practised in Honolulu; Maria acquired a Bachelor of Arts; Georgina attended Wesleyan College (Mount A) at Sackville and Toronto's Conservatory of Music. His other son Aaron, also attended Mount A and subsequently obtained a B.A. degree from McGill, but choose to stay in Grand Bank to work in the family business.

After George A.'s death in 1929, Aaron managed the firm, which by then had been renamed G.& A. Buffett, Limited. G.& A. Buffett became one of the leading businesses on the South Coast and managed its salt-fish and general retail enterprise out of Grand Bank for approximately one hundred dred years.

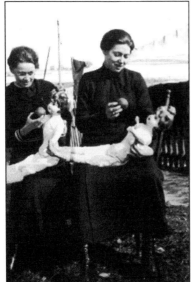

Woodland (right) in 1920 at Grand Bank when she was a captain in the Salvation Army. She and Olive (Batten) Evans reminisce with toys from their youth. Note: hanging on the fence (r), is a hoop used for bringing buckets of water. Courtesy Ruth Gosse

Major Sarah (Shute) Woodland (1897-1994) spent more than sixty years of her life as a Salvation Army officer. She became well-known for her dynamic speaking ability as she travelled extensively in the province preaching the Word of God. Daughter of Dinah Matthews and Ebenezer (John) Shute, a fisherman, she moved to St. John's to work, returned home and then began her career as a Salvation Army officer and evangelist.

She assisted her husband Major Charles Woodland as

he served in several Newfoundland communities, including her home town (a rarity for Army officers). She spearheaded the development of the Salvation Army's police court and welfare programs in St. John's.

After retirement, she remained active in the Army and received her Silver Jubilee Medal in 1977. She was awarded an honourary doctor of laws degree by Memorial University in 1981, the first Grand Banker to receive the honour. Dr. Otto Tucker, in making the award, said her life "... has been spent helping others to find hope and joy, and to experience meaning in life."

Chapter Three   Ships and the Men Who Sailed Them

Our Foreign-Going Captains

By the mid-1940s, the foreign-going voyages made by schooners out of Grand Bank and other Newfoundland ports were practically at an end. Very few Newfoundland captains went overseas in wooden vessels for several reasons: German subs had sunk several schooners during the war years and the voyages through enemy waters were considered dangerous; the salt-dried fish production and the demand for salt declined; and by the late 1930s and early 1940s, the Portuguese were sending their own large steamers to Grand Bank, Fortune and St. John's to deliver salt and to load dry fish.

Not all schooner masters were foreign-going; many had no formal training in navigation. In the early years skippers used the log, compass and their judgement. In later years, they used a sextant for a twelve o'clock sighting, called the 89-48 and four lines of calculation to find latitude only. Writing for *Trade News*, Bruce Woodland in his article "Newfoundland Schooners Made History" claims:

> Grand Bank alone exported 126,000 quintals of salted fish in one good season. Quite often the men who shipped the foreign-going vessels had but the bare rudiments of navigation. The story is told of one skipper who took a load of fish to Italy before World War I. He could neither read nor write and

knew little of the significance of charts. However,
he succeeded in making the run back and forth
across the Atlantic in excellent time. When asked
how he did this, he replied, "I stopped everything
I saw on the ocean and asked the way."

It is not recorded which Grand Bank master was the first
to take a vessel overseas nor is it known which Grand Bank
schooner was the first to make a transatlantic voyage. Most
likely navigational skills of the pioneer schooner captains
were studied or picked up by experience through the
barques, brigs and schooners sailing out of Trinity Bay,
Carbonear, and St. John's before the turn of the century.

In that era for example, Captain Sam Piercy (1867-1948)
moved to Grand Bank from Scilly Cove (now Winterton) in
Trinity Bay; many of the Piercys there were noted vessel
owners and captains. By 1898, he was captain of Samuel
Harris' banker *Mary Harris*, and he eventually made foreign-
going voyages to Europe.

The first Grand Bank schooner to disappear while en
route to Europe was the *Arkansas*, a two-masted vessel. In
1903, the *Arkansas* was launched at Lunenburg, Nova Scotia,
and some years after was brought to Grand Bank under the
registry of George C. Harris, the business manager of Samuel
Harris' firm.

On November 6, 1911, this one hundred eleven ton
schooner left Grand Bank with a cargo of fish for Gibraltar,
both ship and cargo insured against loss. After sixty-seven
days out, the *Arkansas* still had not been heard from. Shortly
afterwards, the schooner, seaworthy in all respects, was
officially declared lost with crew. Only her captain's name is
known: Charles Deveaux, of French origin probably from
Neil's Harbour, Nova Scotia. Although local oral history has
not left us any names of crew, it is likely they were young
men from smaller towns in Fortune Bay.

One of the last captains to lose a Grand Bank ship on a
foreign-going voyage, through no fault of his own but by the
whim of a German submarine commander, was Captain

John Ralph. His schooner the *Helen Forsey* was intercepted by a U-Boat and sent to the bottom on September 6, 1942. Ralph, Jacob Penwell, Thomas Bolt, and William Keating survived; Leslie Rogers of Grand Bank and Arthur Bond of Frenchman's Cove were killed by the German attack on an unarmed merchant schooner.

The following list of foreign-going captains is incomplete; some captains I may have missed, others may have made one or two voyages, then moved away. It not only contains men born in Grand Bank, but those who came to Grand Bank as young sailors, learned the skills of navigation and eventually became masters of local schooners. Many stayed; others left for larger ports and greater opportunities in places like Boston, Gloucester, Halifax, Sydney and St. John's. Generally, the list contains those masters who went to sea after 1910. Before this general era, records are obscure, and it wasn't until the first decade of the 1900s that most Grand Bank businesses shipped their fish overseas in their own vessels bypassing the St. John's merchants.

On the return voyage, the ships carried salt from Portugal or Spain. Deeply laden, the little ships laboured in violent Atlantic storms — sails were often blown away, seams opened, and over-worked pumps became clogged with brine.

Other schooners not otherwise engaged in foreign trade sailed to Nova Scotia and Prince Edward Island for supplies and produce and were forced to face the treacherous Gulf of St. Lawrence in harsh winter conditions. Many ships and men, especially in the years between 1900 and 1940, disappeared without a trace while plying the coastal trade.

The following captains sailed to Europe, the West Indies or South America:

Grand Bank's Foreign-Going Captains

*Charles Anstey
Parmineas "Min" Banfield
Thomas Belbin
Absolum Bellman
James Bellman
Samuel Bradley
Wesley Breon
William Courage
*Robert Courtney(Daisy Dean)
*Robert Courtney(Lucy Howse)
William Courtney
*Charles Deveaux
George Douglas
**Thomas Evans
George Follett
Steve Will Forsey
Lawson Fox
Hughie Grandy
Thomas Grandy
George Handrigan
*John Thomas (J.T.) Handrigan
Robert Haskell
*Lionel Hickman
Thomas Hickman
*Thomas A. Hickman
*Samson Hiscock
Heber Keeping
Walter Keeping

Harry Lee
Morgan Matthews
Fred Parsons
John Benjamin (J.B.) Patten
Sam Patten
*Walter Patten
Sam Piercy
*John Ralph
*Berkley Rogers
Charles Rose
George Rose
Alex Smith
John Smith
Benjamin Snook
Thomas Snook
Cyril Squires
*Frank Stoodley
Harry Thomasen
Arch Thornhill
Frank Thornhill
**Harry Thornhill
Reuben Thornhill
Will Thornhill
George 'Pluck' Tibbo
Wilson Tibbo
Edwin Vallis
*Amiel Welsh
Clarence Williams
Gordon Williams

*Those marked with an asterisk indicate schooner captains who were lost at sea.

**Thornhill was lost on a Portuguese vessel during World War II; Evans died of natural causes on a British ship during World War II.

The sextant and the homemade wooden case (above) was owned by Captain Thomas Snook (1898-1987), a foreign-going schooner master. Snook was born on Sagona Island in Fortune Bay and moved to Grand Bank at an early age to find work. In his thirty-five years as a mariner, Thomas Snook made thirty-seven trips to Europe on sailing vessels. His ports of call were many including Oporto, Portugal; Malaga, Spain; and Genoa, Italy; his early ships were *General Gough*, *General Plumer*, and later the coasting vessels *Bermuda Clipper* and *Arichat*.

Despite a minimum of formal or school education, Captain Snook learned navigation picking up experience while sailing with other foreign-going captains. After schooners acquired engines, Captain Snook plied the coastal trade for Batten Brothers based in Corner Brook and for Dixon's *Arichat* in Fortune until he retired from the sea in 1973 at age seventy-five.

Another well-known captain who moved to Grand Bank from Fortune Bay was Alex Smith. Born in Harbour Mille, the son of Margaret and Joseph Smith, Alex went to sea at an early age while shipped with his father. As a young man, Alex Smith moved to Grand Bank where steady employment or work on the sea was more readily available.

Although seamen like Smith had little formal education, it was not for the lack of ability that such men were forced to leave school at an early age to help provide a livelihood for the family. Smith soon proved his capabilities by learning to use a sextant, to read charts and maps, and to "box the compass". Young men aspiring to become more than simple labourers and dory fishermen had to learn navigation, weather lore, laws of the sea, and how to manage a schooner in all types of weather and circumstances.

At age twenty-four, Alex Smith took command of his first schooner, the sixty-five ton *Portia*, built in 1905 and owned by Patten and Forsey. While this first vessel was small, Smith's next command, the *Thorndyke*, which netted over two hundred ton, was the largest banking vessel owned in Grand Bank. Her previous captain, John Thornhill, had made many successful fishing voyages in her. But as Thornhill was in the habit of changing schooners practically every year, the *Thorndyke* was offered to Captain Smith.

In the *Carrie and Nellie,* Patten and Forsey's eighty-five ton banker, Captain Smith sailed to Portugal with a cargo of salt dried fish. Foreign-going voyages were usually made in the fall or early winter when the cured fish had been prepared for market. But these winter voyages across three thousand miles of winter-lashed seas were very treacherous. Smith survived the storms and eventually took charge of other Grand Bank schooners like the *Christie and Eleanor, Helen Forsey,* and Buffett's schooners *Nina W. Corkum* and *L.A. Dunton.*

Many of Grand Bank's well-known skippers took their schooners to the offshore grounds to the best fishing areas. Many were not qualified navigators, but were expert seamen. John Thornhill made several voyages overseas in schooners of which he was part owner —*Thorndyke, Vera P. Thornhill, Dorothy Melita, Theresa Maud, Robert Max, D.J. Thornhill* — all named for his children, his wife, or his home. Since Thornhill was not a certified navigator, he usually hired a qualified navigator to go with him. When he fished Banquereuo, George's Bank, the Grand Banks, and St. Pierre Bank, he sailed there himself by paying careful attention to his log, sounding line, and ship's speed. He became one of the top procurers of cod, a highliner or "fish killer".

There were many other Grand Bank captains — Joshua Matthews, Joseph Grandy, George Follett, Harvey Banfield, Les Dodman, Morgan Riggs, Morgan Matthews, Will and Jake Thornhill — all of whom were recognized as the best in their business.

Chapter Three   Story Two

Aftermath: The Great St. John's Fire and a Shipping Disaster

August 1992 marked the one hundredth anniversary of one of the worst shipping disasters in the history of Grand Bank when two vessels went down in a late August gale in 1892. I thought it too important an event not to recognize it in some small way.

My account of the August gales and the circumstances surrounding the loss of twenty-three lives was sent to St. John's *Evening Telegram* and to the Burin Peninsula's *Southern Gazette*. The *Telegram* chose not to publish. However, editor George Macvicar of *Southern Gazette*, always helpful and kind toward my offerings, ran the story in its September 8, 1992 edition.

> "He (Clarence Foote) hearing of the conflagration (St. John's Fire) came to see the destruction done."
> *Evening Telegram* September 7, 1892

Taken from the newspaper of the day, this quote typifies the attraction manmade and natural calamities have for sightseers. No doubt people from many outports around St. John's came to view the ruins of a fire which on July 8, 1892, razed the city. As with most disasters, people gravitate toward it, lured by the spectacle of devastation.

So it was for the "he" in the above quote, which refers to

Clarence Foote, a young man of Grand Bank, who sailed to St. John's on his father's schooner, the *Maggie Foote*. However to "see the destruction" was not his prime intention — distance from St. John's and his work in a small fishing settlement wouldn't allow for idle time and pleasure trips.

A round trip between Grand Bank and St. John's, a sailing disance of over five hundred miles, was to be made on the *Maggie Foote*. This was not a large schooner, but a coaster or trader, designed to carry fish and supplies along Newfoundland's rugged coastal seaways. Built in Grand Bank in 1891, the twenty-two ton vessel had an overall length of forty-nine feet and was registered to Thomas Foote's Grand Bank business.

Maggie Foote transported dried fish or canned lobster collected at the canning factories at Grand Bank and Garnish to St. John's. From there she would bring building materials, supplies, food —barrelled flour, sugar, pork, apples and other living necessities to the South Coast.

To finish a summer's work in his father's business, Clarence, age seventeen, made the trip. His older brother George would be going too for he was a crewman on the *Maggie Foote*. George had recently married, and he had to buy furniture at St. John's for his new home. (Today the former home of Marjorie and Ray French, 29 Water Street)

Clarence had other reasons to travel: not only would he see the destruction of St. John's laid in waste from a fire of a month before, but a sea voyage would be a fine way to end the summer before going back to school. Moreover, he intended to buy the clothes and suits necessary to continue his studies at Wesleyan College in Sackville, New Brunswick. The trip would be timely. He would arrive back home around late August, spend a week or so in Grand Bank and then leave for mainland Canada.

On this voyage, *Maggie Foote*'s crew was Captain Morgan Riggs, George and Clarence Foote, George Buffett, and Sylvester Shea. Riggs, of Grand Bank, was married with two children; Buffett, age twenty, hailed from Jersey Harbour and Shea, about the same age, was from English Harbour. The latter two were not married.

The schooner arrived in St. John's in good time and, no doubt, her crew spent some time walking around and viewing the heaps of smoke-blackened bricks and rubble of once impressive buildings.

Port records and documentation indicate the little schooner was laden with one hundred thirty barrels of flour and other shop goods. *Maggie Foote* left St. John's at noon, Saturday, August 20, 1892.

She sailed for home but never arrived at her destination. A twist of nature originating much further south near the Tropic of Cancer saw to that. In this area, late summer hurricanes are born and they howl their way northward devastating parts of the southern United States. Winds often exceed one hundred miles an hour.

By the time the violent tropical storms reach the Maritimes much of their fury is spent, but the final flick of the hurricane's dying tail often lashes the waters off Newfoundland. These wind storms, while lacking the intensity of a full-blown hurricane, were still powerful and dangerous to shipping. Around the island they were termed the 'August (or September) Gales'.

Such storms were weather phenomenons well-respected by schooner captains and crews. Early coasting or banking vessels, ranging in size from twenty to sixty tons, were no match for the heavy winds and high seas which seemingly sprang from nowhere without warning. In those years of limited communication and inaccurate long range weather forecasting, boats caught miles from shelter met with devastating results.

One week after leaving St. John's the *Maggie Foote* was again sighted; this time bottom up, a lifeless derelict.

Beacon Light with Captain Tibbo, a schooner owned in Burin by James Viguers, spotted the wreck about twenty miles off Cape Race. Tibbo sailed near the overturned hulk and had his men row a dory over to it. After noting her position and name, the men from the *Beacon Light*, seeing

Going To St. Pierre ?

FOR RESERVATIONS WIRE :

STOODLEY'S SERVICE STATION GRAND BANK

PHONE 14—2 or 26—2

IN ST. PIERRE CONTACT MARC MORAZE

M. V. RODCO

Of Good Speed — Radar Equipped

LEAVES GRAND BANK :

MONDAY — WEDNESDAY — SATURDAY — 10 A.M.

LEAVES ST. PIERRE :

MONDAY — WEDNESDAY — SATURDAY — 5 P.M.

By the time of this photo, the 1960s, vessels equipped with radar and ship-to-shore radio made transportation by sea much safer.

An advertisement from the early 1960s when a St. Pierre Ferry operated out of Grand Bank harbour. Robert Stoodley of Grand Bank owned and managed a ferry service to and from St. Pierre under Captain Edwin Vallis and crew John Douglas, Tom Evans and Bob Thornhill.

nothing could be done to tow the hapless vessel to shore, cut a hole in her bottom salvaging fifty barrels of flour. No sign of *Maggie*'s five crew was ever seen.

News of the lost schooner was relayed to the schooner *Pointer*, owned and captained by Charles Pardy of Grand Bank, who, in turn, gave some details of her crew and destination to the newspaper *Evening Telegram*. It could only be speculated that the *Maggie Foote* sailed into the wind on Monday, August 22, but the storm was too heavy and she capsized.

Ironically, as if the loss of one schooner and five young men was not tragic enough, the 'August Gale of 1892' claimed another schooner from Foote's business: this one with even greater loss of life. News of that disaster came later after the banking fleet returned home in early September.

Foote's seventeen-man banker, the *George Foote*, collided with the Nova Scotian schooner *Corsair* while riding out the gale on the offshore fishing grounds. Both sank on the night of August 22, as witnessed by a third vessel which somehow escaped the ravages of wind and water. But that's another disaster, another story following the aftermath of the Great Fire of St. John's and the August Gale over one hundred years ago.

Chapter Three   Story Three

ꬵast ꙏoꙗage of the ꬁarꙗ ꙳. Ꙗhalen

Mary A. Whalen's fast voyage from Newfoundland to Oporto, Portugal, was first mentioned to me by Curtis Forsey, a former Grand Bank mayor and businessman. I had talked to him in July of 1990 and, although he was unsure of the exact year the *Whalen* sailed, he recalled the stories of the event this way.

"*Mary A. Whalen* went across in a few days with Captain J.B. (John Benjamin) Patten in command and his young brother Samuel, navigator. Patten and Forsey (Grand Bank salt fish exporting business of which Forsey's father William was part owner) brought her down from the States and on the first voyage from Grand Bank to Europe the captain took Sam Patten with him. When father received the cable from Oporto that the *Mary Whalen* had arrived, no one could believe it. It was a record never beaten," recalled Forsey.

And a record for Grand Bank sailing ships that endured, although other Newfoundland sailing ships later made the trip in less time.

Three years after Forsey told me of *Mary A. Whalen's* initial voyage, I received a written account of it which substantiated the story. It was a typewritten memoir of *Mary A. Whalen's* mate and navigator, Sam Patten. At the time of the voyage in 1910, he was a teenager although the article was written when Patten was much older. It is likely he studied navigation from his older brother, John B., who knew navigation and taught it in his office at night to interested seamen.

Mary A. Whalen, one hundred thirty-four ton gross, was originally owned by Captain (Bat) Whalen of Boston, Massachusetts, and used as a fresh fishing schooner out of Boston until she was purchased and commanded by John B. Patten of Grand Bank. *Mary A. Whalen* was built to sail fast. Her masts were one hundred feet high, the main boom seventy-five feet long and she carried a mainsail of approximately a thousand yards of heavy canvas. In the competitive American fresh fish market at the turn of the century, the first ship to market commanded the best prices. Therefore, Captain Whalen could fish for a longer time and still make port early.

But by 1910, fishing ports on the Eastern American seaboard were switching from sail to engine; steam-driven trawlers were replacing sailing ships. Schooners like *Mary A. Whalen* were for sale at good prices.

Patten purchased *Mary* early in the summer of 1909 when she was a two-masted craft. Her first trip under new ownership was from Boston to Burgeo under full sail since the weather was moderate. Most likely Patten took her to Halifax first to load supplies and food for Newfoundland. When she arrived in Grand Bank, the schooner underwent alterations. As Sam Patten writes:

> After arriving Grand Bank the big mainmast was taken out and cut shorter and a third mast erected giving the *Mary* three masts and a smaller mainsail.
>
> After the three masts were erected and everything in readiness there was time to make a trip to Sydney for a load of coal which was taken to Bonavista. She then returned in rock ballast to Grand Bank where a cargo of dry fish was ready for the schooner to take to market.
>
> She knew it; she actually shined before she sailed when the cargo was loaded as all hands were busy

with the paint brushes to give her a good lick and look.

Mary A. Whalen sailed from Grand Bank on a Thursday evening at four p.m. The weather was moderate and it took the schooner until Saturday evening to reach Cape Race. At six p.m. on Saturday evening Cape Race was abeam with a light wind, overcast skies and a fair barometer showing. Patten, the young navigator, says of that fast overseas trip to Oporto:

> During the night the wind freshened gradually with drizzle and light seas; all sails set — balloon, main jibs, jumbo, foresail, mizzen, three gaff topsails and two staysails, all drawing well and the *Mary* was set on her course (SE by E) for the objective. Because of the limited number of crew, the barometer was watched practically every minute.
>
> Sunday and Monday the *Mary* was averaging at least thirteen miles per hour, the log showing fourteen miles per hour at intervals which wasn't bad going. Tuesday and Wednesday she couldn't do so well because the wind was slackening and she averaged about 11 in those two days. Thursday the wind slackened again and lessened the speed to about 10 miles per hour and on Friday morning land was sighted but this was not too surprising.
>
> Meantime the question with the *Mary* was, was I north or south of my objective. As the day went on the schooner kept getting closer to land when about three p.m. something like a huge crane was sighted. Then smoke appeared on the horizon ahead; later some small fishing boats were sighted.

Captain Patten wanted to luff up alongside one of the fishing boats to find out the schooner's exact position. Then a boat came alongside asking and the captain asked if he could take *Mary A. Whalen* in tow. This was an old time paddle boat with paddles on each side. Patten agreed.

As *Mary A. Whalen* neared land another boat hove to with pilots aboard. The pilots were employed to guide ships over the Duoro River bar, outside Oporto. All sails were lowered and tied up for the first time since *Mary A. Whalen* left Grand Bank. Sam Patten's impressions of the quick trip were:

> On Friday evening at 5 p.m. and on the sixth day practically to the hour after passing Cape Race, Newfoundland, the *Mary* was tied up to the quay in the River Douro in Oporto, Portugal, a few gunshots from the bridge which links Oporto to Villa Nova da Gia across the river.
>
> *Mary*'s small cargo consisted of about 3500 quintals of dry fish which was discharged alongside of the quay, weighed on her deck and taken ashore in baskets, each Portuguese man carrying about 50 kilos on his head.

After discharge, which took about six days, *Mary A. Whalen* was taken to anchor in the stream and sufficient salt loaded for ballast for the return tip to Grand Bank which took about twenty-five days. The total number of days for the round trip from Grand Bank and return was thirty-four days.

In those years many small craft, both local and foreign owned, battled the Atlantic taking salt fish to Europe and returned with salt. Small Danish and Norwegian craft often manned with as few as four crew would visit Grand Bank and wait months for a cargo of fish. Their sails were small and easy to man; none of the ships would have any power other than a man's muscles.

The years between 1904 and 1913, when small Newfoundland schooners began to ply the European fish trade, were not without tragedy. An article appeared in the Newfoundland newspaper *Herald*, dated May 14, 1913, which documented the disappearance of several ships including *Pearl Eveline*.

The vessel posted missing was the *Pearl Eveline* reported to have put to sea from St. John's on January 6 last, and she is understood to have left Grand Bank on or about January 14, bound for Oporto. Under normal circumstances the little craft ought to have completed her voyage in a month or so. Towards the end of February, she came on the overdue market...hope for her safety was abandoned a considerable time back.

There is nothing definite to indicate how the *Pearl Eveline* met her fate, but having regard to the furious gales which swept the Western Ocean during the early weeks of the year, it is but natural to assume that she fell a victim to the terrific weather she undoubtedly encountered.

The missing vessel, which sailed under command of a shipmaster named Pinel, was built at Shelburne, Nova Scotia in 1909 and was of 99 net tons. She is registered at Lunenburg and owned by N and M Smith of Halifax, Nova Scotia.

We give the names and other details of all ketches, schooners and other small sailors which since January 1, 1904, have been posted as missing:

Vessel	Net Tons	Bound	Date Posted
Forget Me Not	—	W.	July 1, 1904
Nelly	79	E.	March 8, 1905
Conquer	59	E.	March 8, 1905
Norseman	96	W.	August 30, 1905
Energy	129	W.	February 28, 1906
Girl of Devon	130	E.	March 28, 1906
Scintila	100	W.	July 4, 1906
Challenger	57	E.	May 19, 1909
T.W. Aston	85	E.	February 2, 1910
Ruth	116	E.	April 15, 1911
Skudesnaes	85	E.	January 3, 1912
Arkansas	98	E.	February 14, 1912
Dorothy Louise	125	W.	May 22, 1912

Reliance	96	W.	May 22, 1912
Beatrice	89	W.	May 22, 1912
Grace	129	W.	May 22, 1912
Pearl Eveline	99	E.	April 30, 1912

* See Chapter Five, Story Three

Courtesy of Trevor Bebb

Dorothy Louise on her launching at Lockeport, Nova Scotia. Registered to George C. Harris, she was commanded by Samson Hiscock, age twenty-nine, who, with his mate Jacob Hickman vanished in 1911. Newspapers of the day reported her overdue, but gave no mention of her crew.

Chapter Three   Story Four

Letter to Grand Bank, 1919

𝕯espite the horrendous losses at sea after the turn of the

This photo of my father Charles Parsons was on an Oporto postcard with a message/address space on the back. The note to his sister Fanny and his step-mother, Jennie, was dated Oporto, November 18, 1919. It reads:

"Just a line to let you know I am well and hope all of you are too. This is some class "eh". No strange news to tell you. I don't know where we are going from this but I expect to Lamaline. I don't know if I will be coming home or not. Remember me to all my friends. Sorry I can't send one apiece. I had a dozen taken and haven't one left. Now I hope father got the ox by this time. Tell Fanny and the rest they will get theirs next time.

Had a rough passage coming over was 34 days, expect to be about 80 going back.
This is all
From Charlie to Jennie."

century, schooners continued to ply the trade between Newfoundland and Europe. Grand Bank depended on foreign markets and as long as fish were caught, cured and barrelled, willing sailors manned the terns headed for Oporto, Portugal.

While in Oporto, many Grand Bank seamen saw the enterprising Portuguese photographers on the Oporto quays and had their photos taken for a few pennies. These were poses with the man dressed in his best "going ashore" clothes in front of a painted backdrop usually of the sea and a ship.

It is not known which schooner this was. Parsons had been shipwrecked in St. Pierre harbour on Samuel Harris' tern *Mary D. Young* in

November of the previous year and, with the reference to Lamaline where Harris had a branch business, it is likely his ship was another of Harris' fleet.

Parsons mentions the long and treacherous westward voyage which, for Newfoundland salt-laden schooners, often lasted from eighty to one hundred days. He also refers to the ox which his father was buying. Up to the 1920s, many Grand Bank families kept oxen as beasts of burden.

Jennie is his step-mother. His mother, Emmaline, had died when Charles was twelve, and before his father remarried, he stayed home from school to cook for his three younger sisters — Fanny, Dianne and Rose. This gave them the opportunity to go to school; a sacrificial deed which the sisters never forgot.

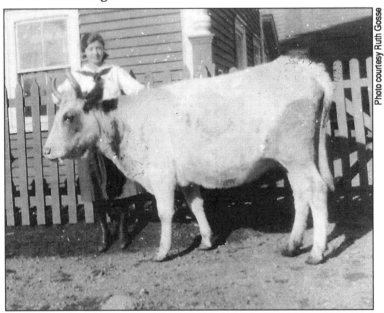

Photo courtesy Ruth Gosse

As shown in this photo dated 1921, not all oxen had disappeared from Grand Bank by the 1920s; here Vida (Camp) Evans stands by a picket fence and a rather docile ox. This picture was taken in front of Capt. William Evans house which once stood on Main Street (Fortune Road), but was taken down to make more room on the United Church School property.

Rev. Lench, writing about Grand Bank in 1912, had this to say about oxen: "One of the unique and interesting features of Grand Bank has been the yoking of oxen for the purpose of hauling wood from the forest. A short time ago there were upwards to one hundred and fifty of these fine animals weighing eight hundred pounds or more." Eventually oxen were replaced by horses.

Chapter Three   Story Five

Finding the Nina Lee's Painting

Several years ago, I wrote to the Shelburne County Museum looking for information about the Shelburne-built schooners (*Wilfred Marcus, General Horne, General Maud, Emily H. Patten, Robert Max* and several others) purchased by Grand Bank businesses. Curator Betty Stoddard referred me to Trevor Bebb, a resident of Lockeport, who had a collection of pictures, information and statistics of many of the vessels I was searching for. Over the next several years Bebb and I exchanged much information.

I learned that Bebb was searching for paintings of schooners done by artist Edwin Locke of Lockeport, and he sent a list of pictures of schooners Locke had painted. Several schooners built in Lockeport or Allendale were eventually sold to Grand Bank merchants — William Forsey (*Edith Pardy, Theresa Maud, Mary F. Hyde*); Samuel Harris (*Dorothy Louise*); Forward & Tibbo (*Ella M. Rudolph*); J.B. Patten (*Nordica*); John B. Foote (*Nina Lee*) — and Bebb thought the pictures might have come with the schooners. In the 1970s Bebb had written to Buffett, Tibbo, Foote, and others, including the Pennys of Ramea and Petites of English Harbour West, but no one had any knowledge of the large, beautiful paintings of Lockeport-built schooners.

Three or four years ago, I had a casual conversation with Jack Foote who said he had a painting of the *Nina Lee* hanging in his living room. I went to look at it and upon close examination the name 'E Locke' was written in the lower left

Picture courtesy Jack Foote

Nina Lee sailing south out of Lockeport, Nova Scotia. *Nina Lee*, launched April 1913, registered at seventy-nine ton, was built for John B. Foote. This schooner was slated to be named Dinah Lee, after the wife of Captain Harry Lee, a veteran skipper for Foote's business. Lee would assume command of the new schooner. However, through mis-communication combined with the fact that Dinah is not a familiar name in Lockeport, the vessel was christened and registered *Nina Lee*.

hand corner. Foote kindly consented for me to take a picture of the painting. I engaged local photographer Rosalind Downey to do the work.

When I sent the evidence to Trevor Bebb that a Locke painting still existed, he was delighted and sent the following information about the artist: Edwin Locke, known around Lockeport as "Trap", seemed to do little else but paint — one of his most popular and frequently reproduced work is that of a trout with a fly-hook in its mouth, a rod close by, all lying on the bank of a stream.

Locke painted at least two pictures (from imagination) of American privateers coming into Lockeport and being frightened away by women's red petticoats. Artist Locke also did pictures of yachts especially with taut sails. Of the picture of *Nina Lee*, Trevor Bebb says:

> I recognize the faint background to the *Nina Lee* as being, at the left, a portion of South Street and on

the right the Lockeport Cold Storage and maybe
the spire of the Baptist Church. There is now a large
breakwater where the two rocks are shown, so the
vessel is heading south out of the harbour with
what is called (hereabouts) a "smoky sou'wester"
on her starboard beam or quarter. She doesn't
seem to have much in the way of rails or trunk and
the bowsprit doesn't seem too well fitted — but
overall a very pretty picture.

Chapter Three   Story Six

Letter from Grand Bank, 1914

In his book *Quest of the Phantom Fleet*, historian Trevor Bebb (in the previous story) tells of Lockeport's shipbuilders and their ships. In the section related to Newfoundland schooner-building agreements, Bebb writes that he has in his possession a number of letters written between 1910-1915 by various Grand Bank businessmen to the Lockeport Ship-building Company.

When I wrote Bebb to ask if he would send me a copy of correspondence pertaining to the ordering of a schooner, he graciously complied and sent a fairly typical letter, a mixture of business and social items. Yellowed by time, hence the darkened reproduction, this is William Forsey's correspondence to William McMillan, the last of the Lockeport ship-builders and a friend of Forsey.

Grand Bank, around the turn of the century, had a fine fleet of schooners; this piece of correspondence gives insight into deals, bargains, and the inquiries for vessels.

1913
Dear Wm McMillan

Kindly accept my many best thanks for the beautiful presents received by Capt. Petite.[1]. I will never be guilty of thinking after now, that you forget me.

Your letter came to hand last week. I was delighted to hear from you again and to hear that your business is all that you can handle was still more pleasing. I hope you will

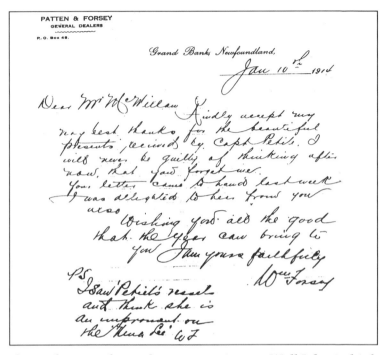

always have such good news to write me. Well I don't think
we need complain either, our vessels did well. "Theresa
Maud" led with 3212 quintals, the best voyage ever landed
here in the history of the fishery, "Hyde" 2300 qtls, "Pardy[2]"
2000, the others 1500 to 1760 qtls, so you see that we have
fared fairly well for the unlucky year of 1913.

Our shipments have all paid us a little profit. We have
one cargo at Oporto now and one to go about Feb. 1st. The
last cargo will be all shore fish of prime quality.

Jack wants a new vessel built for him next summer and
would like Mr. Payzant[3] to make the model of a knockabout
type say 115 tons of five lines and a little narrower than the
"Pardy" say 24 ft. He is greatly taken up with some lines Mr.
Payzant sent down last year and would like one on the same
lines, a clipper he wants next time.

Yes, I do expect you to come down next summer and we
will have a good time fishing and we will go to St. Pierre in
my yacht which I will have in readiness for you. I moved in

my house on the 15th of last month and find it more conven-
ient.[4] I have it heated with hot water. I must fit up a room for
you by the time you come to visit us.

John Thornhill had his leg broken last month. He will be
laid in all winter. Poor Jack is very much put out. It will keep
him home from his winter trip.

The weather is very fine all the last month and it looks as
if we are in for a mild winter.

We are a little busy now fixing up the year's work.

Give my best wishes to all the friends. Wishing you all the
good that the year can bring to you. I am yours faithfully,

Wm Forsey

PS I saw Petite's vessel and think she is an improvement on
the "Nina Lee".[5] WF

Endnotes:
1. Capt. Jerry Petite, born in Mose Ambrose, was the son of Jeremiah Petite
   who had moved to English Harbour West just after the turn of the
   century and established a salt-fish exporting business there. The reference to Petite indicates the extent to which South Coast shipowners and
   business people from Placentia Bay to Port aux Basques intermingled
   and socialized.
2. The three vessels mentioned are: Forsey's *Theresa Maud*, captained by
   John Thornhill and named for Thornhill's oldest daughter (who married Sam Stoodley, Grand Bank's second mayor). *Mary F. Hyde*, a
   banker owned by Forsey and captained by George Hyde; and Forsey's
   Edith Pardy, commanded for many years by John Hickman Matthews.
   All three were built in Lockeport by Howard Allen.
3. "Jack" most likely refers to Captain John Thornhill.
   Freeman Payzant was a Lockeport vessel designer, but not a
   builder. He later became the first mayor of Lockeport, owned some
   vessels and was somewhat of an inventor —reportedly having the
   patent to a solderless method of sealing tin cans.
4. William Forsey's home was located at today's #32 Church Street — his
   son Chesley later lived there. It was subsequently owned by Randolph
   Emberley, then became the Grand Bank Group Home and today is a
   boarding home managed by Guy LaFosse.
   As indicated by Post Office Box 48 in the letterhead, in 1913 the
   Grand Bank Postal and Telegraph Building contained mailboxes.
   Larger local businesses, which received more mail and often corre-

sponded with the foreign markets in North America and Europe, had
the convenience of this service.

5. Jeremiah Petite's new vessel was the eighty-three ton *Effie May Petite*,
launched at Lockeport in the fall of 1913. *Nina Lee* was launched in April
of 1913 for John B. Foote of Grand Bank.

R.C.A.F. Plane Makes Forced Landing

Crew Picked Up By Local Schooner

A message from the Telegram's special correspondent at Renews reports that a Royal Canadian Air Force plane made an emergency landing in the sea off Newfoundland yesterday morning about 9.30 and the crew were picked up by a schooner in command of Capt. Keeping, and landed.

Our correspondent, who inter-

Photo courtesy Jerry and Otto Kelland

On June 22, 1941, a Douglas "Digby" Bomber #752 based in Newfoundland, was returning from a submarine patrol mission and ran short of fuel. The pilot had to make a forced landing in the ocean off Cape Race.

Forward and Tibbo's tern schooner *Chesley R*, above tied on at the business premises on Point of Beach, with Captain Heber Keeping (inset), mate Walter Keeping was in the area between Clam Cove and Cape Race. The bomber's five-man crew spotted the schooner, landed near it and Keeping manoeuvred *Chesley R* nearby. Keeping landed the airmen at Renews. A naval tug was sent to tow in the plane which remained afloat for some time, but the ditched bomber sank a short distance from Cape Race. Except for a wetting and a few minor injuries, the bomber's crew were none the worse for the experience.

Captain Heber Keeping is the father of Max Keeping, one time sports editor of the *Evening Telegram* and noted broadcaster with CTV radio and television in Toronto. Max is now a news director of CJOH-TV, Ottawa.

Chapter Three   Story Seven

𝕿𝖍𝖊 𝕾𝖙𝖔𝖗𝖞 𝕭𝖊𝖍𝖎𝖓𝖉 𝖆 𝕾𝖙𝖔𝖓𝖊

This article originally appeared in *The Newfoundland Ancestor*, a publication of the Newfoundland and Labrador Genealogical Association. Between the years 1991-1994 the NLGA provided the funds to hire students to document inscriptions on Grand Bank headstones. To focus on the many unique gravestones in Grand Bank, I submitted an article to the *Ancestor*. There are many headstones in Grand Bank cemeteries engraved "Lost At Sea"; Frank Stoodley's was one.

The line drawing of the stone in the original story was not suitable for reproduction, but since that time I acquired a picture of the wreck of the ill-fated schooner.

Towns that send a fleet of ships to the sea have always had shipping losses; the litany of vessels lost with crew or missing without a trace are often reflected in the local gravestones and monuments. So it is with a granite marker in the Grand Bank United Church Cemetery erected for a drowned seaman. The inscription reads "Frank Stoodley who was lost at Burgeo in the *Russell Lake* on March 17, 1929, age 39 years".

On March 15, 1929, the *Russell Lake* left her home port, Fortune, to load fish destined for Oporto. Her cargo was to laden at Burgeo Lapoile Export Company at Burgeo, but on the way the vessel stopped at St. Pierre for supplies. A tern schooner built at Fortune a few years before, the *Russell Lake* was owned by Lake's fish exporting business at Fortune. On

The earliest stone in Grand Bank related to a loss at sea. It reads: "Robert Forward, father of Sarah Jane Forsey, born Nov. 1829. Lost at Sea 1862". According to lists of Grand Bank vessels this was the schooner *Watchword*, owned by Forward. She disappeared with crew while on a voyage to the mainland. (Note: building in centre background is the former Hickman Motors Garage, now Metal Manuworks, a metal fabrication shop.)

this voyage she was under the command of Frank Stoodley of Grand Bank and his bosun George Day, a resident of Fortune.

By the time the schooner left the French Islands on the evening of Saturday, March sixteenth, the wind had freshened from the southeast which quickly increased to gale force accompanied by driving snow. Visibility dropped to zero, forcing Captain Stoodley to navigate by instinct. He was a veteran skipper with good knowledge of the rugged shoreline — experience that came with years of sailing the South Coast.

The sea off Burgeo has many small islands; many are dangerous hazards to shipping. Folklore says there are three hundred sixty-five, one island for every day of the year, but in actual fact there are just over one hundred. As the *Russell Lake* approached these rocky environs, one of the crags, Boar Island, could barely be seen through the driving blizzard. It was almost twelve o'clock on Saturday night.

Stoodley tried to manoeuvre between them as the wind and waves pushed him off course. Between midnight and one a.m., the vessel hit the rocks with a terrifying grind. The *Russell Lake* struck Small's Island, located about a quarter of a mile northwest from Boar Island and almost inside Burgeo harbour.

Breaking up almost immediately, the shattered remains of the schooner seemed to hold no refuge for the doomed men. Most of the crew came to a general agreement that, to save their lives, it would be best to lash themselves to heavy boxes or boards. This would enable them to reach the rocks of one of the small islands in case they were washed off the shattered schooner.

One by one bosun George Day saw four crewmates disappear in the boiling surf. But the cook, Billy Spencer, clung on; he and Day, long time friends who had grown up together in Fortune, were near each other on the wreck. In the long hours that followed, both men, suffering from exposure as the lashing sea drenched them constantly, lapsed into a state of shock and hypothermia. Spencer slowly lost the strength to hold on. Day encouraged his friend not to give up, but due to his weakened state he could not help as *Russell Lake*'s cook slipped into the water a short time before rescuers arrived.

Day, however, managed to lock his arms onto a portion of the wreck until daylight came. By then, not much remained of the ninety-six foot vessel except for the lone piece the fortunate man stubbornly held. Some residents of Burgeo, who were out and around early in the morning, saw the

Picture courtesy Walter Simms

Burgeo men sift the debris that was once the tern schooner *Russell Lake*. "Dry rot," they claimed, "She fell to pieces and there was no wind to speak of". The schooner broke up within minutes after hitting Boar Island, almost within Burgeo harbour. Gordon Noseworthy of Fortune once told me *Russell Lake* was built with no iron nails, but with wooden tree nails or trenails.
   The large section on the right was the part George Day held to save his life.

wreckage on the shore and knew the storm had driven a vessel onto the island. Braving the blizzard and heavy swell that Sunday morning, they rescued George Day, who by this time had reached the limits of his endurance. Of the six crew, he alone survived.

Rescue completed, Burgeo residents then gave their undivided attention to recovering victims. The three bodies — mate Ron Martin and George Witherall, both of Fortune and Leo Foote, Lamaline — that were found by Sunday night indicated that the battered sailors had been dashed against the rocks before they could save themselves. Spencer was found later that day. By Monday, Captain Frank Stoodley's body was located and, with the others, brought to Grand Bank by the coastal steamer *Daisy*. From there each victim was carried to his home town for burial.

Today the only visible reminder of this sea disaster is a single marker with the story and its attendant grief summarized in a dozen engraved words. Around our island stand many such stones and stories; it is our duty to preserve them.

Chapter Three   Story Eight

Three Short Sentences

As a high school student in the early 1960s, I tried to get down to studying geometry theorems and geography in the kitchen, a place often frequented by my father's friends who came to visit him 'after supper'. One elderly man in particular told fascinating sea stories; in fact often he repeated many particularly gruelling and spellbinding sea stories. It was hard for me to keep attention focused on school books.

In June 1987, when I began to search out Grand Bank's numerous sea stories and oral retellings of tragedy and heroism, the same veteran seaman who had been to my father's home was still alive. I went to him to ask if he would retell some of the yarns. Sadly his mind was not as keen, but he recalled, sketchily, stories of his true experiences.

In February 1990 I sent his version (with the section on the chocolate box embellished) of the sinking of the *Jean McKay* to the magazine *Newfoundland Quarterly*. It was one of my first sea stories submitted for publication, and I heard nothing from the editor for months. Then out of the blue, almost two years later, a large brown envelope came in the mail; inside, a copy of 1991 fall edition of the *Quarterly* and there was the story. The *Newfoundland Quarterly* pays contributors a small honorarium, but the satisfaction of seeing George's story in print far outweighed any monetary gain.

George was well over eighty years of age and straight as a whip when I talked to him in his Grand Bank home. On his faded photo showing the town's soccer team of long ago, he stands tall in the second row, his height suggesting a defender, or as he said a full back. George had a ready smile and was delighted to recount his seafaring days as he sat in his high backed chair, talked, showed me his diary and asked only anonymity in return.

In his early years he fished from a dory on one of the dozens of banking schooners operating out of his home town. After some time at that he handled sail on tern schooners. When the era of sail passed, he worked on steamers and Canadian freighters until he retired from the sea.

I knew from previous conversations George had been a crew member on a schooner, *Jean McKay*, where disaster had struck, and wanting to learn how that ship sank and the details of the loss at sea, I asked him about his experiences.

George kept a diary — a journal about his life at sea. It was just a cheap notebook stored in a chocolate box along with other papers, documents, and photos. It was yellowed foolscap containing entries written long ago in blunt heavy pencil. It was not a daily account, but contained snippets of information about significant personal happenings experienced in a long sea career; entries pencilled months, and sometimes years after the event.

It was amazing really that such a notebook had survived at all considering the number of life-threatening situations George had endured: ship fires, severe ocean storms, crewmates washed overboard or lost while dory fishing, the inevitable wreck, sinking vessels and rescue. Three times he had abandoned ship in various areas of the North Atlantic when his battered schooners, seams opened during violent throes of mid-ocean gales, slowly sank beneath him.

To George's way of thinking, surviving storms on gale wracked hulks was just another job hazard — something to be faced and when over, it was back to the sea on another ship if work was readily available. Many young men, family men he knew had disappeared over the years, all victims of the treacherous Atlantic. Patras, Oporto, Cadiz, Pernambuco, Turk's Island were exotic ports of call, but the journeys there or back claimed Newfoundland ships and men by the score.

The diary — there it was, none the worse for wear, considering. It was not secret; George proudly showed his words to anyone interested in reading it and listening to his stories. No doubt family members had seen it often, friends occasionally and strangers, like me, rarely. His entry on the *Jean McKay* was pencilled in as three short sentences, so I asked him if he could tell me more about that misadventure. Here is George's story, slightly edited for clarity. He wrote:

(Diary entry) *That fall I signed on the Jean McKay for a trip across.*

Built in 1918 at Shelburne, Nova Scotia, the one hundred ninety-four ton *Jean McKay* was owned in Grand Bank by Patten's, a local business that cured and exported salt cod. For twelve years this tern or three-master in local terms, had plied the waters between Europe, the West Indies and Newfoundland. In September 1930, the *Jean McKay*, with a fish cargo loaded at Harbour Buffett, Placentia Bay, headed for Oporto. On the return journey, deeply laden with salt, a typical mid-Atlantic storm opened her seams. For four days the schooner wallowed deeper and deeper as water poured into her bilges faster than the pumps could keep it out.

Picture courtesy George Squires

The tern schooner *Jean McKay* anchored in an European port, probably loading salt.

Captain Cyril Squires ordered his crew of five men to work the pumps and to keep a sharp lookout for a passing ship in the hope of rescue. Then, on October 16 (as verified by the October 21, 1930 edition of the *Daily News*) that ship appeared. But George's memories are not of the trauma of getting plucked off a sinking ship just before it went under; rather, the unforgettable conditions aboard the rescue ship.

The Jean McKay had to be abandoned at sea.

George voiced it this way: "The Captain had ordered lookouts and signs, so we went up in the rigging to the masthead and put up distress signals. Several steamers sighted us and saw our signal fires, but turned away. By this time our schooner was down quite a bit in the sea. Although we had lots of drinking water, most food was gone. Rationed bread, a slice or two a day; biscuits; several sacks of Spanish onions and that was about it. By the time we were rescued, everyone was ravenous hungry and dog tired from manning the pumps continuously for four days.

We were picked up by a passing ship...

"This night a freighter came along that saw our signal fire and took us off the sinking *Jean McKay*. I can't remember her name, but it was a British steamer about five thousand ton coming west from out of the Far East, China, perhaps and had passed through the Suez Canal and Gibraltar. Let me tell you she had a strange cargo and that knowledge came as a surprise to all of us Newfoundlanders.

"That night her cook put food on the table for us. Although we were starving — without a solid meal for over a week — we wouldn't touch it. It seemed to be a pudding, about the size of an ordinary water bucket, and it was red, blood red in colour. That was all was on the table beside our tea. We wouldn't eat it; afraid of what it was and waited till the next day to eat.

...and taken to...

"Anyway our rescue ship had three hundred Oriental passengers, all men, going to the United States as labourers. For the most part, they stayed below in the hot, overcrowded steerage but we sometimes saw them on deck in good weather, standing and lying around, passing time.

"Not long after we were called up to the bridge by the captain of the steamer.

"Pointing at me, the captain said, 'You broke path for the coolies.'

"I was kind of thunderstruck at first. 'What do you mean broke path?'

"'In the companionway you stepped aside to allow coolies to pass,' he said. He waited a few minutes to allow that to sink in. 'I guess you noticed that all the officers on this ship wear side arms.'

"I had. Each had a small holstered gun attached to his belt.

"The captain stared the crew of the *Jean McKay* in the eyes. 'There are only a few of us Englishmen controlling this ship and three hundred of them cooped up in a hold where there's only room for fifty and they're not fed well. If they see any sign of weakness, it would be a simple matter for the coolies to take this ship, throw all of us overboard, and no one would know what became of us. We're outnumbered about a hundred to one.'

"The meaning of the captain's words came clear to me then. Of course we treated all people with courtesy and dignity; it's something that's born and bred in us, but that time respect got us in trouble.

"Not long after, we struck another Atlantic storm which sent mountainous waves across the decks of the freighter. On deck there had been several cages of wild animals captured in Africa —birds, monkeys, other small creatures destined for American zoos. A cage containing six or seven monkeys broke open in the gale scattering monkeys everywhere. Two or three were washed overboard and the rest managed to escape to the ship's steel stays and riggings, wireless cables and so on in the masts.

"The caretaker, a Frenchman whose job was to ensure the safety of creatures, paid us to climb the masts to try and get them back. The prospect of a few dollars made us risk the danger, but the terrified animals were too wild in that storm to let anyone get near them. They bit, clawed and clambered out of reach, so we had to come down and wait for better weather.

"By the next day, there were no monkeys left in the riggings. During the night in the cold wind and heavy seas, they must have perished for we never saw them again.

...Curacao where arrangements were made for our transportation home.

"After that incident the weather changed for the better. The captain had no further problems with his various passengers; it was smooth sailing until we reached the island of Curacao in the West Indies. From there arrangements were made for our passage to New York and then home."

Words pencilled in a modest diary. What would happen to them? What would happen to the stories between the lines? Like the passing of the tall ships, the ranks of schoonermen grow thinner each day and many of their heroic tales of wreck and rescue have gone from our knowledge. As George finished his story and put his diary away, I could only marvel at and admire this unassuming seaman. He had been snatched from a watery grave and carried to safety by a strange and unforgettable rescue ship and had recorded the event in three short sentences — brief entries that left more unsaid than said.

Chapter Three　　Story Nine

Battle of the Banks

by S.E.A. Young

This article appeared in the March 1945 issue of *Atlantic Guardian*, nine years after the loss of the Grand Bank schooner *Partanna* with her crew of twenty-five. In the original version, the vessel's name appears as *Southern Coaster*; I believe the story is that of the *Partanna* and so closely parallels her loss that if one takes the liberty to change the vessel's name to *Partanna*, the similarities are striking.

S.E.A. Young is Ewart Young, editor of the *Atlantic Guardian* in the 1940s.

To hundreds of fishermen on the South Coast of Newfoundland, the Bank fishery represents the Pot of Gold at the end of the rainbow. Year after year they go forth to match their strength and their wooden ships against the forces of the sea, to conquer more often than not and return with the Pot of Gold.

But sometimes King Neptune triumphs and a ship does not return at all and then, instead of the Pot of Gold, the wives and families must share a Cup of Sorrow.

Take the case of the banking schooner *Southern Coaster*, lost with her entire crew. Ten of them belonged to one community, and there was scarcely a home that was not directly touched by the tragedy.

When the previous banking season closed, the people

were buoyant as all their men had returned safely. There was much work at home for the men to do during their short stay. Everyone was happy. Houses were repaired, wood was hauled, barns improved and towards spring fertilizer was carried to the fields and everything done to make the work for the womenfolk light when planting time arrived.

I watched my next-door neighbour with his ox draw load after load of firewood, which he and his wife sawed into usable lengths till the shed was overflowing. I watched him build a new barn to house the sheep and oxen, haul loads of manure to his fields, and perform what seemed an unending round of duties.

Meanwhile the womenfolk spent their evenings knitting woollen comforts for their men. No thought of the coming separation was allowed to interfere with these precious weeks together. But time moved on. The season for departure drew near and the men became busy with preparations for the voyage.

Community Banquet The clergyman of the village, wishing to give the men and their womenfolk a good time before they separated, suggested a free-for-all banquet. The whole community agreed and for days the wives and mothers were extra busy in their kitchens.

Finally the night came. Cold and stormy it was, but that proved no deterrent. A table groaning with good things was spread in the Community Hall. Old men and their wives, young men and their sweethearts, mothers with babies, school children of all ages, sat at the festive board.

After the inner man had been satisfied, all settled back for the entertainment. Some sang, some gave speeches, others made up an orchestra composing violins, accordions, and the organ. The old salts told stories of their experiences and concluded with warnings to the 'freshmen' bankers, "Don't overload your dories!" "Don't stay out when ye see the fog gatherin'!" "Don't go too far from the ship!"

The event was such a success that it was agreed to have another when the men returned in the fall. No shadow of tragedy loomed over the gathering.

The time to embark came all too quickly. Wives, mothers, sweethearts and friends, gathered at the quay on that cold March morning to bid their men "Bon voyage".

The Banker usually stays out three weeks on each baiting. Several such periods went by and the men paid an over-night visit to their homes while the ship was in port. Toward the end of April the usual three weeks had gone by and there was no sign of the ship.

One week passed, and another. Women could be seen leaning over fences, lingering at the gate, gathering on the road corners. Faces became grave with anxiety. Old seamen shook their heads and spoke in worried tones. More days with apprehension mounting and no news of the vessel.

Bad News Comes Then the fateful day arrived. Looking through my window I saw the telegraph operator making his way up the hill carrying a small box under his arm. "It's come!" he said, as I opened the door.

"What?" I asked.

"The awful news", was the reply. "The *Southern Coaster* has been given up. I have the message here for the minister. I had to bring this box under my arm to throw off suspicion. They're watching me through the window."

The minister took the yellow paper with shaking hands and slowly read its contents:

'Regret to inform you that as the *Southern Coaster* is long overdue we are now obliged to announce her as lost with all on board. Only clue a battered dory with pair of mitts on thwart initial M.K. Please break news to relatives of men.'

Realizing acutely that he was to be the bearer of this tragic news, the clergyman shrank from the task but knew that it must be faced as a part of his duty.

It was an exceptionally gloomy day. The skies seemed in sympathy. Storm clouds gathered, a coppery hue spread over the landscape, and the heavens wept copiously. The minister wended his way on leaden feet from home to home.

A son here, a husband there, a brother in the next. In one home a young wife soon to become a mother learns that she has lost both her husband and her father.

Form T 6—"DN"—200M—23-11-36

Department Posts and Telegraphs
NEWFOUNDLAND

Operating in Connection with

COMMERCIAL CABLES TO ALL PARTS OF THE WORLD

```
16K 2PD STJOHNS 1128AM JULY 11TH 1936

J.F. HYDE GRANDBANK

      DISPENSATION GRANTED.

          BARKER.

              1258PM
```

Typical "message" or telegram dated July 1936.

In another a mother sat around the table with her seven children. It needed great courage to tell her that the bread-winner would come home no more.

An aged mother said of her son, with tears streaming down her wrinkled cheeks, "Thank God! — He's safe at last. — These long years I've prayed for him. — Now he's safe in port. — Thank God!"

There were few loud demonstrations of grief. The bereaved amongst the fisherfolk are stoical in their acceptance of sorrow. One women only became hysterical.

Through my window I watched my next-door neighbour's wife tidying her yard. I prayed that she might go in before the messenger came. But she raked on. Soon I saw several women approaching. One was her mother. She was weeping. They all went into the house.

"Poor Tom is gone, my dear," the mother said, weeping.

"Yes!" the reply came with a sob. "He knew he was goin'. He said to me, 'Maid, if anything happens to me you'll hear me scream'. And I heard him the other night".

Still a Mystery There is no further tidings of the ship. The wrecked dory was the only clue. It still remains a mystery as no survivor was spared to tell the tale. Conjectures were many, but the consensus was that she had been cut down by another vessel in the fog. Fog and sudden storms are the two worst enemies on the Banks of Newfoundland.

The fisherman builds his house gradually, year by year adding a little till the final touches are put on, windows fitted, paint on the exterior. Then the wedding if all things go well. But when tragedy comes the house remains untenanted. Many of them stand as sad reminders — their vacant windows like staring eyes looking out to sea for the ship that never returns, for the lovers for whom they were so hopefully planned.

The wives of the fishermen live in constant anxiety. They suffer through the storm, thinking of their men away on the Banks. Meanwhile they keep the home fires burning and carry on even when the worst comes.

Some battles with the elements are lost, but not because of fear or cowardice. The Newfoundland fishermen are as courageous in danger, ingenious in emergencies, and as calm even in the face of death, as any that sail the seven seas.

And maybe in the not-to-distant future, the Newfoundland Banker enveloped in his dreaded enemy, fog, will ride on the radio beam in safely to the haven where he would be.

(Appendix J is Ches Burt's song "Mystery of the *Partanna*")

Chapter Three   Story Ten

The Last Schooner Built In Grand Bank

This story was previously published in another of my books, but since then other information and photos have come to light. At the time of the writing of these events, two of the principal workers gratefully shared their stories of logging in the Garnish woods and of schooner building in Grand Bank.

During Newfoundland's Commission Government (1934-1949) ship builders were paid a subsidy per ton for vessels built. Although the ship building incentive was short-lived, it was an attempt to stimulate local economy. During 1935-36, as many as four schooners were built in Garnish at the same time, which then had a population of fewer than five hundred.

In Grand Bank one enterprising and ambitious captain and schooner owner, John Thornhill, took advantage of the government's bounty and made plans to construct a ten-dory banker, the last schooner built in Grand Bank. An *Evening Telegram* article dated March 16, 1935, announced the news with this lead:

Banking Captains See Bright Future

Building Vessels for 1936 Fishery
    Captain John Thornhill, famous fish killer of Grand Bank, has a crew of men in the woods

getting timber for a banker of 120 tons to be built
this summer at Grand Bank for the 1936 fishery.

Captain Thomas Grandy of Garnish is having a
50-ton schooner (*Jean and Mona*) built at Garnish
this summer for next year's fishery. A crew went in
the woods last week to cut the timbers for the
vessel. Capt. Thornhill for years has been a high
liner amongst Newfoundland fish killers. He is
now on the Banks in command of the schooner
Helen Forsey.

Four Grand Bank men at Boston in posed photo; the painted background is a country scene, the model
T car is staged. From left to right, John Green, a carpenter and also a coasting schooner skipper who
had *Freda M* for at least two winters; Captain Harry Thornhill; Captain John Thornhill, in the front seat
next to the driver, and Joshua Matthews (not to be confused with the Joshua Matthews lost in the
schooner *Carranza* in 1930).

Thornhill knew many skilled shipbuilders in Garnish,
and he employed one of the best schooner builders, Bill
Henry Grandy, from there to construct his schooner. Grandy
also headed up the team of Grand Bank men sent up the
Garnish River to cut timber: Bob Riggs, brothers Elic and
Robert Stoodley, Philip Riggs, Philip Stoodley, Thomas
Forsey, Henry (Harry) Hickman, cook Tom Keating and
Chas Stone who liked to use a double-bladed axe. Stone's
work experience stood him well in later years when he was
employed on many town and government jobs. He generally
was foreman on local wharf repairs and road construction.
Chas Stone became skilled at drilling rock and using dyna-

mite. Many people remember that he would order everyone hundreds of feet away before a blast while he stood nearby amidst the falling rock with his hands over his ears.

Bill Henry Grandy's son, Fred, worked there, as well as a young man, Jacob Grandy of Garnish, who helped the cook and brought water to the men in the woods. Robert Stoodley kept an informal set of books tallying wages, amount, and cost of food.

Logging lasted for one month beginning in the first week of March and ending in early April. After supplies were hauled by horse and sleigh to a site five miles up the Garnish River, the men built a camp bunkhouse. The crude bunkhouse had a small barrel stove for heat at night. A cook shack was already on site, but was so small Keating prepared most food outdoors, baking his bread every day in large covered pots. Crusty on the outside, the bread was not baked in the middle. One of the woodsmen would pull apart the stringy dough in the middle of the loaf and say: "Cook, what a sacrifice of good food!"

Large fir, spruce, witchhazel and birch — some measuring twenty-one or twenty-two inches in the top and twice as big around on the butt — were termed "dory sticks" by the Garnish woodsmen. Sticks like these close to Grand Bank had long since disappeared; most had been cut in the shipbuilding era prior to the 1880s. Timber had also been depleted several decades later when five tern schooners were built in Grand Bank:

Roberta Ray, 1917, 164 ton; *General Currie*, 1918, 162 ton;
Carl R. Tibbo 1918, 173 ton; *General Allenby*, 1919, 145 ton;
General Ironsides 1920, 157 ton;

D.J. Thornhill — Bill Henry Grandy could visualize her on the stocks and he knew what timber was necessary. He would go out in the morning to select certain trees, mark them, and assign men to get to work with the bucksaw. Two men could cut, trim, and pile around two or three logs a day. On Sunday, a day of rest, and in the late evening when the day's work was over, the Grand Bank loggers enjoyed Bill

Crowds gather in their finest in August of 1919 to witness the launching of tern schooner *General Allenby*. The wharf, although at a slightly different angle, corresponds to the western pier today, the schooner rests in the area of the bait depot/Foote's oil yard and at least two houses are recognizable: those of Curtis Forsey and John Thornhill. Thornhill's sheds and stores are between the house and the landwash.

Henry Grandy's yarns for he was known to be quite a story-teller.

After the spring thaw, two to three hundred logs were floated down Garnish River. The heavy birch and witchhazel tended to sink, but a "rampike" of fir or spruce nailed to them kept these afloat until they reached Garnish Gut. From there *Winnie*, a little schooner owned by John Tom Cluett, brought the sticks for *D.J. Thornhill's* timbers and planking to Point of Beach in Grand Bank harbour. Max Grandy, one of young men slated to work on the schooner, had cut the timber for his new house which were floated down the river at the same time.

Point of Beach, where the Grand Bank Clearwater Fish Plant now stands, was chosen as the best construction site. Master builder Hughie McKay oversaw the work. Thornhill had asked McKay's Shipyards at Shelburne, Nova Scotia, to send someone to build his schooner.

When McKay, who was in his early twenties and had boyish good looks, arrived on the coastal boat someone in Grand Bank remarked: "John Thornhill sent to Shelburne for a man to built his schooner, but look what he got, a boy!" But despite his youthful appearance, McKay proved to be a master shipwright. He, his wife, and infant daughter lived in the Thorndyke, John Thornhill's home and boarding house.

Under McKay's direction, Bill Henry Grandy was the head shipwright on the schooner. Grandy's son, Fred, worked with him as a "dubber". Both men were experts with the adze axe which had its blade at right angles to the handle and was used primarily for dressing timber. With an adze, the dubber trimmed or bevelled edges of the frame or timbers before the planks were nailed in place.

While the raw material was making its way to Grand Bank, Hughie McKay and Bill Henry were in Grand Bank preparing the bedding and slipway for the vessel. Not all those employed cutting timber built the schooner, but Chas Stone, William 'Chum' Osmond, Jake Matthews, Harry Hickman, Bob Riggs, Stephen Leonard Grandy and his son, Max, were Grand Bank men who did. Later in the spring when more labourers were needed, Bill Baker and Am Thornhill were hired.

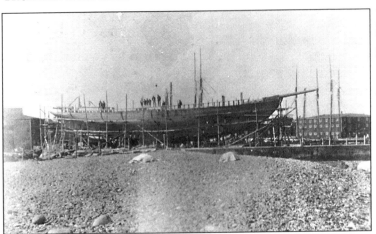

Courtesy of Otto Kelland

D.J. Thornhill on the stocks at Point of Beach in Grand Bank harbour about August/September 1935. Scaffolding surrounds the schooner as workers (standing on deck) are just completing the top of the bulwarks.

Masts of schooners in the harbour lace the skyline. Samuel Harris' fish store (later Grand Bank Fisheries) is in background right. The wall (middle right) is the wharf leading to the eastern lighthouse.

Stephen Leonard Grandy operated the band saw which McKay had shipped down from Shelburne especially for sawing planks. In the first stages, several workers prepared the groundwork for the keel and slipway while two or three men were engaged in chopping timbers with a broad axe to make a flat side to fit on the band saw. Bill Henry Grandy, well-experienced in preparing and hewing timber for plank, was in charge of this operation and gave directions:

> Now boys, whatever you do, don't under hew the timber. In other words don't cut it in under, cut it straight. If you do, you will spoil it.
> Chas Stone asked what would happen if a piece was spoiled or under hewn.
> "Well", said Bill Henry, "if you spoil a piece, look around to make sure nobody is looking at you. Carry it over and heave it in the scrap heap. Pick out another piece and start chopping that. If you can do that, without anybody seeing you, you'll do all right."

Although he was not employed building the schooner, Elic Stoodley remembered that some time during the summer, he and Bill Henry Grandy went back to Garnish woods for a couple of days. Apparently there was a certain piece of wood, perhaps for the stempost, which Grandy needed. By now it was mid-summer and they travelled by dory which could be rowed or sailed upriver with fair wind. They went deep into Garnish River watershed, crossed overland to Black River where the appropriate stick was cut and hauled out.

That summer McKay's uncle came from Shelburne to Grand Bank to visit McKay. He was at the building site for a few days and helped with shaping the counter. He, too, was very skilled with the adze. Onlookers watched him swing the tool with heavy strokes taking off the right amount with each swing.

There were no electric tools or machines used in 1935 (although electricity came to Grand Bank in 1929, six years previously). Holes through the planking and timbers for the iron or wooden bolts were bored by hand using a crank drill or auger.

Work started at seven am and finished at six in the evening with a one hour break at mid-day. The carpenters employed on *D.J. Thornhill* were paid at a rate of "a dollar a day". In those days local carpenters in their search for work would offer to build a barn or stage under the verbal contract "a dollar a day and dinner." By the 1940s, pay became a little better, rising to $1.10 per day.

All through the summer of 1935 while the schooner was under construction, Captain Thornhill lost no fishing time. He had command of *Helen Forsey*, a banker owned by William Forsey, Ltd. In between voyages, Captain Thornhill came to the work site and when the fishing season ended in September, he came every day. Although Thornhill showed impatience with McKay at times, the master shipbuilder proceeded at his own pace and no corners were cut in building the best product possible. Most likely two of Grand Bank's best caulkers — Bill and Bob Handrigan — were hired to caulk *D.J. Thornhill* before she was painted and readied for launching.

In Thornhill's bid to give his newly-built schooner every

Courtesy Otto Kelland and Hughie McKay, master builder

D.J. Thornhill on the stocks at Point of Beach in Grand Bank harbour during the fall of 1935, about a month before her launching. She has a good coat of black paint; masts, seen lying on the ground to the left, are stepped after she is launched. To the right is a pile of dry fish covered in canvas.

advantage over other fishing vessels, a forty-four Kelvin engine was installed in the months after launching making *D.J. Thornhill* an auxiliary/sail schooner. The engine bedding was installed and the drive shaft log put in place while the vessel was being built.

Most of the vessels John Thornhill owned or had shares in were named for family members. Thornhill had already decided to use D & J on this one after his wife Dinah and himself. Highest tide that fall occurred on Tuesday morning, November 26, 1935, and *D.J. Thornhill* was launched with great acclaim — a school and civic holiday was called. Under McKay's supervision, the launch went without a hitch: stern-first pointing slightly toward Grand Bank Bridge.

When the schooner slid down the ways, Bill Henry said that all their hard work had just gone out into the water and their employment was over. The same evening after the launch, McKay and his family left for Nova Scotia via Port aux Basques on the coastal boat *Portia*.

By the spring of 1936 *D.J. Thornhill* was outfitted for the fishery, the herring baiting off the Western Shore on Quero, Burgeo or Rose Blanche Banks. Because Thornhill knew where the cod were and usually brought in above average catches, he had no trouble finding a crew — most of his men having sailed with him before. *D.J. Thornhill*'s crew list for 1937 is listed in Appendix K.

Despite all her acclaim, *D.J. Thornhill*, built of softer, unseasoned local timber and badly strained from heavy cargoes and winter storms, did not last long. Less than eight years later in January 1943, she succumbed to a severe storm and sank about twenty-five or thirty miles south southeast of Halifax. At that time, *Thornhill* was under the ownership of Pelleys of Port Blandford.

Her crew — Captain Gordon "Johnny" Williams and Berkley Nurse of Pool's Cove; mate Hughie Grandy; engineer Wilson Price, Grand Bank; James Brown, born in Baine Harbour but a resident of Grand Bank; cook Winston Taylor — were rescued two days later by a passing Canadian corvette. Her crew were close to death from exposure.

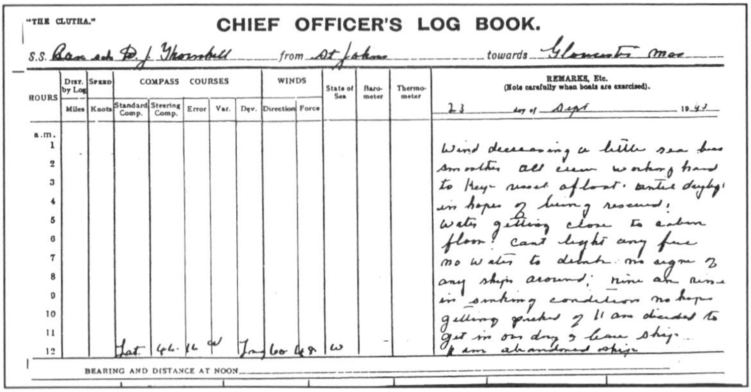

"THE CLUTHA."

CHIEF OFFICER'S LOG BOOK.

S.S. Bann sch D. J. Thornhill from St John towards Gloucester mass

HOURS	Dist. by Log (Miles)	Speed (Knots)	Compass Courses: Standard Comp.	Steering Comp.	Error	Var.	Dev.	Winds: Direction	Force	State of Sea	Barometer	Thermometer	REMARKS, Etc. (Note carefully when boats are exercised). 23 day of Sept 1943
a.m. 1													Wind decreasing a little sea has
2													smoothed all crew working hard
3													to keep vessel afloat until daylight
4													in hopes of being rescued;
5													water getting close to cabin
6													floor! can't light any fire
7													no water to drink no sign of
8													any ship around; nine am vessel
9													in sinking condition no hopes
10													getting picked off 11 am decided to
11													get in our dory & leave ship.
12			Lat. 46.16			Long 60 48				W			I am abandoned ship

BEARING AND DISTANCE AT NOON

Courtesy Ed Nurse

Capt. Gordon Williams' log of the *D.J. Thornhill* on her last voyage. All other dates read January, but, in error and through stress, the last date is pencilled Sept. The last entry reads: 23 January, 1943. Wind decreasing a little, sea has smoothed. All crew working hard to keep vessel afloat until daybreak in hopes of being rescued. Water getting close to cabin floor. Can't light any fire, no water to drink, no sign of any ship around; nine am vessel in sinking condition. No hopes of getting picked off. 11 am decided to get in our dory and leave ship. I am abandoning ship.

Harold Guy, a schooner of the same era as *D.J. Thornhill*, entering Grand Bank harbour with Lewis Hill in background. In this photo she had a bowsprit. While Sam Piercy owned *Harold Guy*, he did not remove the bowsprit although the vessel was powered by a sixty-six Kelvin engine. When the vessel was purchased by Foote's the bowsprit was taken off which improved manoeuvrability in confined harbours.

Chapter Three   Story Eleven

𝔄𝔯𝔞𝔴𝔞𝔫𝔞'𝔰 𝔇𝔞𝔶 𝔅𝔬𝔬𝔨

By the 1950s the banking schooner was nearly obsolete. Businesses in Grand Bank — Forward & Tibbos, Buffetts, Footes, Piercys and Pattens — which had once depended on their exports of salt cod now had their few remaining wooden vessels engaged in the coastal trade. This account traces the purchase, work, and eventual loss of a coasting vessel.

For a period of one hundred years (approximately 1870 to 1970), several large and small businesses in Grand Bank owned and managed hundreds of vessels. Various lists of schooners have been recorded and invariably each totals over three hundred ships owned by local people. Yet the number of logbooks, diaries of sailors, and journals of owners documenting the maritime comings and goings is relatively few. Today when such written accounts do surface, if the discoverer is aware of his find or is heritage conscious, Newfoundland history is possibly preserved, but more often than not, such artifacts disappear forever.

Not long ago the journal of a vessel owner, Howard Patten, became available. The Grand Bank business Patten managed had been in existence for several decades. His father, J.B.(John Benjamin) Patten in partnership with William Forsey, founded a codfish procuring and exporting business around 1900. In 1922 J.B. Patten separated from Forsey and, for the next forty years, sent his own bankers to the productive grounds and his coastal/trading schooners along the coast.

Patten and his sons, over a period of time, owned several vessels, including *Alsatian* (disappeared with crew, 1935); *Coral Spray* (stranded St. Shott's, 1937); *J.E. Conrad* (abandoned at sea, 1940); *Florence* (sank at sea, 1940); *M and L Lodge* (burned, 1948) and *Miss Glenburnie* (rammed and sank, 1955).

In the 1940s J.B. Patten's firm, as managed by Howard Patten, acquired two vessels: the nine-dory banker *A and R Martin* and one hundred seventy-two gross ton *Arawana*, a converted mine-sweeper employed in guarding England's coast during the war. At one hundred nineteen feet in length and twenty-three feet wide, the wooden *Arawana* had been built in 1942 in Metategen, Nova Scotia, and had a four hundred fifty h.p. Morris diesel engine. When the war ended, vessels like *Arawana* were expendable and sold.

Captain Hughie Grandy, his wife, Howard Patten, and a skeleton crew flew to England and brought *Arawana* over from Plymouth in a transatlantic journey lasting twelve days. For Captain Grandy, who had spent twenty-four years in the foreign-going trade plus thirteen years in the bank fishery, it was his first crossing of the Atlantic in a powered ship. "Quite a contrast. The *Arawana* is an excellent sea boat," he told a *Daily News* reporter in St. John's. When the vessel arrived in Newfoundland some of her oil storage tanks and passenger accommodations were removed to make more room for cargo space.

Arawana made her first trip for Patten on September 21, 1949, with a Grand Bank crew: Captain Hugh Grandy, engineers George Patten and Bill Rose, mate Ben Snook, Hubert Grandy, William J. Hatcher, John Keeping and Foote Lee. Within a month the mate left and George Hillier replaced him. Wages were paid monthly and the captain received $150, engineers $100 and deckhands $80.

The following timetable, as indicated in Patten's journal, shows the *Arawana*'s first trip beginning February 24, 1949:

Feb. 24, left Grand Bank 2:30 p.m. for Halifax, came back 5 p.m. generator trouble, left Feb. 25

Feb. 27, arrived Halifax

Mar. 4, sailing to-night for St. Pierre, 30 tons coal, 415 barrels under deck, 538 on deck for F. Robert, St. Pierre. Also *A and R Martin*'s engine, generator and sundry packages

Mar. 6, arrived St. Pierre and arrived back Mar. 7

Mar. 9, left Grand Bank towing *Martin* to St. Pierre, thence to Burin for fish meal for F. Products

Mar. 10, left Burin 5:30 p.m.

Mar. 11, arrived Burgeo this am. delayed loading due weather conditions

Mar. 14, leaving Port aux Basques for Halifax 1800 bags of meal

Apr. 20, sailed from Halifax this p.m. Barrels of flour,etc. 106 brls below deck, 621 brls on deck

Apr. 22 arrived Grand Bank, sailed this am for Rose Blanche (to) tow *Glenburnie* to Burin

For the next thirteen years, this pattern repeated with *Arawana* visiting practically every major port in Newfoundland and on Canada's eastern seaboard loading various products until September 28, 1962, when *Arawana* ran into difficulty in heavy weather. According to the day book entry for that date, she left North Sydney — after a storm delay — laden with one hundred seventy ton of coal for Greenspond, Newfoundland. Two days later, the end of *Arawana* is tersely penned in Patten's day book: "Arawana abandoned & sank 60 miles east Cape Breton. Crew rescued. (Oct. 1, 62) Men picked up by M/V Marie Stone & taken to Burin."

Most coastal vessels had high crew turnover rate and *Arawana* was no exception. When she sank, none of her crew was from her home port: Capt. Arch Broydell, Burin Bay Arm; Edgar Strowbridge, Nathan Myles, Frank May, Ernest W. May, Ernest John Walters, all of Point Rosie; Fred Grandy, Garnish, and Mike Hennebury of Lord's Cove. The shipwrecked crew arrived in Grand Bank on October second and received their wages that evening.

From 1949 to 1962, *Arawana*'s captains had changed four

11 MARCH

70TH DAY
295 DAYS TO COME
DAY OF WEEK

MARCH 12

71ST DAY
294 DAYS TO COME
DAY OF WEEK

Today is the Birthday of

July 10 - 20 @ Arawana left here
4 pm 6 days for
Rattling Brook, Lumber
to St John

July 13 Rattling Brook
July 17 Arrived loading 6 day
Sailing Now.

July 18 Arrived St Johns

22 Left Little Bay for here

23 Arrived here 2 pm
Discharged Lumber from Rattling Brook
to Horwood Lumber St John

July 24 Left here 1 pm for North Sydney
25 Arrived North Sydney
don't [know] get coal

Today is the Birthday of

July 26 Arawana sailed this
am 149 tons for North Sydney
Coal for St Bollock for day

July 29 Arrived here 7 am
July 31 Got the tow leaving to start

Aug 1 Left here 2.50 pm for
St Pierre for fish
Cannot

Aug 3 Arrived Sugg 6 pm
from St Pierre

Aug 7 Joshua Schooner
got that $120.00 /mo.

Aug 9 Left here 7 pm
for Halifax

Journal entry with *Arawana's* journeys and cargoes from July 10 to August 9, 1950, showing she left for Rattling Brook, Green Bay, with lumber for Horwood Lumber, St. John's; went to North Sydney for one hundred forty-nine tons of screened coal for Grand Bank; carried the Grand Bank soccer team to St. Pierre on August first and left on the ninth for Halifax. Note: the dates on the top of the yearbook page do not correspond with Patten's daily entries.

120

Courtesy of Blanche (Parsons) Hollett

At one thirty am on September 15, 1937, Patten's coal-laden *Coral Spray* stranded at Watering Cove, near St. Shott's on the southern Avalon Peninsula. Mate Sydney Weymouth, married and a resident of Grand Bank, drowned as he swam for the dory which had drifted off deck. Seaman Joe Price climbed ashore, secured a rope and helped the remaining four men climb to safety. For his bravery Price was later awarded a certificate from the Royal Humane Association and received it in a public ceremony in the Frazer Hall, Grand Bank.

The surviving crew as seen here standing on the deck of the S.S. *Belle Isle*, which had carried the shipwrecked crew to Nova Scotia, are: (l-r) Captain Fred Parsons, Charles Francis, Joe Price, cook Clayton Good and Don Baker.

Courtesy Mary and Russ Walters

The crew and passengers of a wrecked Grand Bank schooner. On January 11, 1957, G.& A. Buffett's coasting schooner *Merilyn Clair* grounded at Moria Gut near Sydney. She was refloated, but five years later was wrecked at Port aux Choix.

Her shipwrecked crew and passengers in 1957: (l-r) Russ Walters; passenger Tom Price; Garfield Rogers; Captain Reuben Thornhill; Don Baker; passenger Ted Riggs; Charlie Grant; unidentified sailor from Terrenceville; passenger Thomas Bartlett and Hector Rose.

times and included Hughie Grandy, Wilbert Moulton, George White and Broydell. During Patten's thirteen year tenure wages had risen significantly — captain $300, chief engineer $180, and deckhand's salary ranged from $110 to $135 monthly.

Chapter Four   Soccer: Grand Bank Style

The Early Years

For many years soccer was the only game played in Grand Bank, but recently it has had to share the resources and attention with other sports. As far back as the 1920s Newfoundland newspapers carried soccer scores not only for St. John's but for other outports like Grand Bank. Thus finding accounts of scores and players was relatively easier than determining how the game got its roots and why it was played so extensively in Grand Bank and on the Burin Peninsula.

Soccer was first introduced to Grand Bank before the turn of the century. The game, however, had been played in Europe for centuries and references have been made to it since the days of the Roman Empire. According to Fred Carberry (1973) who did a study of the sport in "A History of Football in St. John's," football or soccer as its now called, first came to Newfoundland during the second great immigration from Europe — between 1848 and 1860. In 1890, the Scots living in St. John's formed a city league. Carberry claims:

> Football must have been established on the West Coast of the island by this time also because there is a record of a Brigade team (1900) from St. John's playing a team from the Bay of Islands. There was also football in Grand Bank. Apparently football

must have started at all the seaports in the same manner. It was also strong in Grand Falls up to 1914...

The immigrant influx of Scots and Irish farmers or fishermen is probably not the reason for the rise of soccer in Grand Bank; few of the town's early settlers were from Scotland or Ireland.

Prior to the 1900s, and for some years after, many larger Newfoundland outports like Grand Bank received its educated men, i.e., clergy, merchants, teachers, government officials directly from England. These community leaders brought with them the skills, equipment, and rules of the game which they themselves learned and played in English schools and universities.

In turn they taught soccer to the youth of Newfoundland towns. In Grand Bank, from 1816 until around 1920, there was a continuous flow of English-born Wesleyan ministers (and to a lesser extent, merchants and teachers) and by the turn of the century Grand Bank soccer was well-established.

Rev. Lench, describing Grand Bank in 1912, said: "The men have an Athletic Association. They have purchased a fine piece of land and have spent much time and money in their efforts to clear and roll and bring it into line for football and other purposes. They will soon have splendid recreation grounds." This area as described by Lench preceded the football field on Marine Drive, but its exact location is unclear. In 1919, Aaron Buffett, a Grand Bank businessman, donated land on Marine Drive for a field; this was later named Stoodley Memorial Field in honour of Samuel Stoodley, a football great and an early town mayor.

Old photos, with players in uniform and wearing football boots, show the game well-organized before the 1920s. One photo, dated 1919, shows thirteen Grand Bank players with three positively identified: Clayton Camp, George and Clarence Foote.

Clarence Griffin once told me he recalled the crew of a British warship playing soccer in Grand Bank in the 1920s.

The ship had anchored off the Grand Bank bar and its crew had challenged the local eleven to a game. The British seamen walked from the waterfront to the field as a group juggling, kicking and heading the ball along the way. Laughing and joking, they seemed confident of an easy victory. A large crowd watched the game which the Grand Bank team won by a wide margin in a shutout.

Likewise Carberry, in his research, noted that all-star teams from St. John's were selected for playing against crews of battleships and other large craft. It was reported that the British warship *Hood* was in St. John's in 1906, and the ship's soccer team was defeated seven to one by the city all-star team.

Another unlikely source for a description of the early game in Grand Bank came from a Harbour Breton teacher, Ted Russell. Russell, who taught school in Harbour Breton in 1923, recalled football as a popular recreation in Harbour Breton. On one occasion Russell, as his daughter Elizabeth Russell Miller writes in her book *The Life and Times of Ted Russell* (1981), travelled by schooner across the bay to Grand Bank with the Harbour Breton football team. According to Russell, half the players were Smiths — a very athletic family in Harbour Breton. Russell, not a football player himself, went with the team saying: "On that particular occasion the team had no goaltender and asked me to go along; I agreed to go as a third goal post." Russell's brief words about local soccer in the 1920s is one of the few published accounts of inter-town play in that era.

In later years, Russell returned to Harbour Breton as a magistrate and in 1949 was elected to the Newfoundland House of Assembly. Most people remember Ted Russell as the writer of "The Chronicles of Uncle Mose," short stories many of which were later televised as the popular *Tales from Pigeon Inlet* series. Although one of his stories concerns baseball, none centre around soccer, a popular diversion in Fortune Bay.

In Harbour Breton the feats of the town's soccer team was

recorded in a folk song of which only one verse is known today:

> The game it started at half past one,
> See Phonse Smith how he did run!
> I tell you what we had some fun
> At the football match at Grand Bank.

One of the earliest Grand Bank football team pictures in which all players are identified is dated 1928 and it shows them dressed in uniform: dark (red) jerseys with a white GBAA crest, white shorts, red and white striped socks, football boots and some wear tams; tams kept long hair in place. Team members included:

> **Grand Bank Soccer Team 1928** Elic Stoodley, Robert Stoodley, Samuel Stoodley, Clarence Foote, Howard Patten, Gus Patten, Philip Forsey, Charles Francis, George Grant, Chesley Dunford, George Welsh, Reuben Forsey.

In November 1994, I located a photo of the 1931 Grand Bank soccer team. Although it is dark and taken from a distance, it became important for me to identify the fourteen people standing in front of a goal — the Grand Bank goal net in the Marine Drive field with Louis Hill in the background. The goal net mesh is wide, a clear white line on rocky ground marks the goal line and the goal frame seems to be made of two by four.

The words on the back of the photo read, "1931 Grand Bank Soccer Team Winning Team Taking the medals from St. John's, Burin, & Fortune." George Hickman, who played and eventually replaced players on that team, identified the players.

In August of following year, 1932, according to the *Daily News*, Grand Bank again won a cup. After defeating the Avalonians (St. John's) six to one, George Crosbie of St. John's presented the awards to George Welsh, Phil Forsey, C.

Grand Bank Soccer Team Burin Peninsula and All-Newfoundland Champions 1931 (front sitting) Elic Piercy, goalie; (front kneeling l-r) Sam Stoodley, Elic Stoodley, fullbacks; (second row l-r) Clarence Foote, Howard Patten, Gus Patten, halfbacks; (back row standing l-r) Reuben Forsey and Charles Francis, (both in white indicating alternates); John Penwell, George Grant (white hat), Phil Forsey, Tom Rose Sr., George Welsh, forwards; George Foote coach.
The men in white shirts and dark ties, left, may be linesmen and goal judges, the latter were used regularly up to the 1940s. Courtesy Neil Locke

Patten, Elic Piercy, John Penwell, Gus Patten, Howard Patten, Ches Dunford, Sam Stoodley, Robert Stoodley and Tom Rose, Sr. (The latter is not to be confused with another Tom Rose who played in the 1950-60 era).

In that series, games between St. John's, Fortune and Burin were played in Grand Bank during a week in mid-August and on the Friday night before the final game, all teams were feted in the Grand Bank Orange Hall with a banquet, concert and dance. The cup, won by Grand Bank, went on display at the town drugstore owned by player Howard Patten.

> **Grand Bank Soccer Team 1942** Aaron Penwell, Edward Hawkins, Morgan Matthews, William Evans, William Thomasen, Max Riggs, Max Thornhill, Samuel Evans, James Hunt, Robert Ruelokke, Eli Thornhill, Winfield Hiscock.

Courtesy George Hickman

Grand Bank team, GBAAA, in St. Pierre in 1944. (front seated) Gerald Nurse, goalie; (front kneeling l-r) George Hickman, Les Douglas; (middle row kneeling l-r) Max Thornhill, Edward Penwell, Edgar Tessier, Buff Tibbo, Sam Saunders; (back row l-r) Fred Tessier, manager/coach; George Dodman, Phil Cox, Max Riggs, Henry Lee, Edward Hawkins, George Foote coach. Edgar Tessier, who lived in Grand Bank for ten years and was Fred's brother, played in place of Jim Hunt.
Many players with longer hair wear tams which could be bought in St. Pierre for fifty cents. Players who had shin guards wore them outside the socks. The team has red shirts stylized with a deep white V, a fish logo with GBAAA initials, and white shorts. Alternate players, or "spares," as evidenced by Saunders above, often doubled as linesmen. Courtesy George Hickman

Grand Bank Soccer Team 1946 Edgar Rose, William Evans, Philip Cox, William Thomasen, Stan Grandy, Robert Ruelokke, Tom Rose, Charlie Snook, Charlie Forsey, Norman Matthews, Henry Lee.

Chapter Four   Story Two

All-Newfoundland Competition

𝔅y the 1930s and 40s, organized and scheduled football games against Fortune and St. Pierre were frequent. Newfoundland newspapers describe outcomes of St. Pierre and Grand Bank matches as the teams frequently played a home and home series. All-Newfoundland competition began in 1951 when Jack V. Rabbits became president of the St. John's League in 1950 and he saw a need for island-wide playdowns. St. Lawrence, representing the Burin Peninsula, played Holy Cross that year and Holy Cross won the first island championship.

In 1951, playdowns evolved to a three team round robin with teams representing the St. John's, the Burin Peninsula, and the Corner Brook Leagues. Rabbits sponsored and provided the J.V. Rabbits Cup for provincial competition. St. Lawrence represented the Burin Peninsula in 1951 and won the J.V. Rabbits Cup as All-Newfoundland champions, the first peninsula team to do so.

On August 18, 1951, a Burin Peninsula All-Star team played St. Lawrence and the *Daily News* reported the opposing line-up: Grand Bank — Stan Grandy, Tom Rose, Max Thornhill, Malcolm Osmond; Burin — Piercey, White, Newbury, Etchegary; Fortune — Douglas, Buffett; Lawn — L. Edwards, C. Edwards and J. Edwards. In regular season play St. Lawrence was Peninsula champs in 1951-52-53.

Soccer in Grand Bank became well-organized and more popular in the 1940 and 50s. Large crowds attended the games and, with only one town team, competition to make the line-up was intense. Many boys played pick-up games in various locations around town and a certain pride developed with the Long Shore, Cross Brook, Cownap teams.

With the development of younger players and better coaching in the 1950s, soccer under the Grand Bank Amateur Athletic Association (AAA) improved and the town won the Burin Peninsula championship in 1954. Funds to assist the team in its travels was raised in a variety concert sponsored by the Grand Bank/Fortune Lions Club under President John R. Dixon of Fortune, one of the first functions of the newly-formed club. The provincial title would be decided in St. John's that year with three teams competing: Grand Bank, St. Bon's, and Corner Brook. According to newspaper reports, the Grand Bank team was the odds-on favourites to win the provincial championship. The team included:

> **Burin Peninsula Soccer Champions 1954** goalie Gordon Grandy, fullbacks Sam Piercy, Bruce Buffett, halfbacks George Trimm, Stan Grandy, George E. Hickman, forwards Tom Rose (captain), Charles Snook, Edwin "Bud" Welsh, Jack Rogers, Waterfield Emberley, Sam Tibbo, Amiel Welsh, Max Riggs, coach George Welsh, manager Harry Welsh.

However, an All-Newfoundland title was not to be. *Daily News* sports page of September 2, 1954, told the story under this lead:

> GRAND BANK ELEVEN REGRETS INABILITY TO CONTINUE SERIES
> Grand Bank football team, who ended up in a three-way tie with St. John's and Corner Brook in the Newfoundland football playoffs, regretfully withdrew from further competition last night (Sunday). The others leave for home as their players must return for work.

Three of the Grand Bank players were on their way home last night and must report for work today. The others leave for home at 10:00 o'clock this morning and must be at work tomorrow.

"We have no complaints," said Fred Tessier, President of the Burin Peninsula AAA, last night...

The series was not expected to be played past the weekend but for some reason — probably weather or the three-way tie — it was. For several players, work on Monday morning came first and they had to return home on Sunday. The Grand Bank team withdrew, but found some consolation from the number of young players in the lineup who had played exceptionally well. Charlie Snook was voted the Most Valuable Player in the tournament, the first Grand Bank player to win the honour. In the 1950s other MVP's around the province were: 1950 Tom Turpin, St. Lawrence and Harry Ennis, Holy Cross; 1951 and 1952 Walt LeMessurier, Corner Brook; 1953 Jim Wells, Corner Brook; 1954, Snook, Grand Bank; 1955 Herbert Slaney, St. Lawrence; 1956 Hubert Wakelin, Corner Brook.

In 1956 Grand Bank vied, unsuccessfully, for the All-Newfoundland title when the series was played at Corner Brook with Corner Brook and Holy Cross of St. John's as the other two competitors. Amiel Welsh's name does not appear in the lineup; he had a knee injury in a game in August 1955 which curtailed his soccer career.

In 1957 Grand Bank again won the right to represent the Burin Peninsula in a series to be played at St. John's with Corner Brook and Guards of St. John's.

Burin Peninsula Soccer Champions 1957 goal Gord Grandy; fullbacks Bruce Buffett, Sam Piercy; halfbacks George Edward Hickman (captain), Stan Grandy, Malcolm Osmond; forwards Eli Lee, Alf White, Tom Rose, Clarence Brooks, Tom Stone (Cumben), Newman Bartlett, Allister Buffett, Richard Foote, Frank Ralph; coach George Welsh; manager Fred Rogers; executive member Fred Tessier.

For Tom Stone this was his first and last All-Newfoundland series. On August 28, during the playoffs, he broke his leg and remained behind in St. John's hospital. Back home, Stone's teammates played benefit games and raised money to offset his expenses. Although Stone recovered fully from his injury, he retired from soccer that year. Although Grand Bank did not win the series, Gordon Grandy was awarded the Most Valuable Player.

In 1958, Grand Bank again won the Burin Peninsula series and hosted the finals with the Corner Brook Royals and the St. John's Guards. Charlie Snook, who now worked in St. John's and had joined the Guard's team, returned to Grand Bank to play against his former team mates. Lloyd Stoodley, another Grand Banker, was a member of the Guards at the fullback position. The other Guards were: Gerry Smith, Roy Jenkins, Ray Wilkins, Don Winsor, Don Ash, Hobie Pike, Bill Goobie, Fred North, Gene Garland, Sterling Hoddinott, and Bob Badcock. Grand Bank was represented by these players:

> **Burin Peninsula Soccer Champions 1958:** goal Gordon Grandy, fullbacks Stan Grandy, Sam Piercy, halfbacks George Edward Hickman, Al Buffett, Malcolm Osmond, forwards Bruce Buffett, Clar Brooks, Tom Rose, Alf White, Eli Lee, Ray Stoodley, Newman Bartlett, Harold Hollett, Manuel Bolt, coach George Welsh, manager Fred Rogers.

According to the provincial newspapers Grand Bank, since they had dominated regular season play, was favoured to win, but an unexpected three-two victory by Corner Brook meant Grand Bank had to defeat Guards in the last game by at least two goals. In case of a tie in a three game round robin series, the All-Newfoundland trophy would be based on goals for and against.

In the evening of September third, over fifteen hundred fans, many incited by the seemingly rough tactics by the Guardsmen in the round robin, turned out for the final game, refereed by Louis Legentil from St. Pierre. About the twenty-seven minute mark of the second half, with Grand Bank still down a goal or two, a near riot broke out. Two Gee Bees and one Guards player were ordered off the field for rough play and several hundred spectators rushed onto the field. After order was restored the match continued, but Guards held the lead and claimed the championship. Although Grand Bank seemed to have the better team and played on home field with tremendous fan support, the Guards, sensing the fever pitch of players and spectators, played an inspired and chippy game.

Three times in the 1950s Grand Bank had advanced to the championships, but an All-Newfoundland title was still two years away.

Seeing that most teams in competition against Grand Bank —Fieldians, Guards, Laurentians, Corner Brook Humber Royals — had a distinctive name or logo, the soccer players and executive decided it would be in the team's best interest to split

A Burin Peninsula basketball trophy won by Grand Bank. The engraving reads, "Burin Peninsula Basketball 1945-46 Won by Grand Bank Seniors Donated by Coca Cola." Seven of the players on that team were: Fred Tessier, player and coach, Max Thornhill, Eli Thornhill, Morgan Matthews, Edward Hawkins, Bill Evans and Tom Wooden. Wooden also played goal in soccer for eight years.

Basketball games were low-scoring and rough. Burin won one championship in Grand Bank in 1948 by a thirteen-twelve score. Frank Pierce, a school teacher from Burin, refereed and on one occasion he had to be escorted out of town with two Ranger policemen guarding him.

In the basketball season — late fall and winter — games were played in the United Church Academy gym every second Friday night; other Fridays the team travelled, usually by Don Tibbo's taxi, to play in Burin (in Sheen's Hill Old Hall), St. Lawrence and Marystown.

from the other sport groups in town and to carry their own unique name.

In the 1940 and 50s another competitive sport in Grand Bank was basketball. Played in the United Church Academy Gym and to a lesser extent in the Frazer Hall, both men and women had separate teams. Burin Peninsula inter-town competition had been organized, and Grand Bank had won basketball cups in 1945-46 and in 1946-47. Other inter-town sports which had been organized, albeit to a lesser extent, were track and field in summer and pond hockey in winter.

But soccer dominated other competitive endeavours and had grown in the town and across the island. A local contest offering a cash award of fifty dollars would determine the name for the Grand Bank soccer team. Many entries came in including Grand Bank Kickers, Grand Bank Fish, but Gee Bees, in a likeness to the Conception Bay Cee Bees, a successful Newfoundland hockey team, was chosen. Lena (Stoodley) Fizzard had submitted the Gee Bees and won the contest.

Grand Bank's first All-Newfoundland Soccer Championship in senior men (ladies and junior titles came later) came when the town hosted the series in 1960. Gee Bees had already defeated St. Pat's in St. John's and had the right to play Corner Brook Royals in Grand Bank in a three game total goal series. On Monday evening, September 4, the teams tied one to one; on Tuesday evening the Gees Bees won seven to one; and on Wednesday evening, with Alf White and Eli Lee scoring goals, they blanked Corner Brook two to nothing.

In 1962, Grand Bank went through the season undefeated winning the provincial title on Jubilee Field in Corner Brook. A new trophy, the Colonial Broadcasting System Trophy, replaced the Rabbits Trophy which had been retired after the 1960 season.

All-Newfoundland and Burin Peninsula Soccer Champions 1962 goal Harold Hollett; fullbacks Clar Brooks, Eric Grandy; halfbacks Alf White, Al

GeeBees Cop Senior Soccer Title
Take First Crown On
2-0 Win Over Royals

This is how the *Daily News*, September 8, 1960, headlined Grand Bank's first All-Newfoundland title (excluding any titles in the 1930-40s).
All-Newfoundland and Burin Peninsula Soccer Champions 1960 goal Gord Grandy; fullbacks Ray Stoodley, Clarence Brooks; halfbacks George Edward Hickman, Al Buffett, Malcolm Osmond; forwards Eli Lee, Alf White, Tom Rose, Harold Hollett, Bruce Buffett, Max Hollett, Newman Bartlett, Manuel Bolt, coaches George Welsh, Henry Lee. Eli Lee was awarded the Most Valuable Player in the series.

Buffett, Malcolm Osmond; forwards Eli Lee, John Russell, Clar Patten, Arch Wells, Max Hollett, Frank Fizzard, George May, Charlie Crowley and William Wells. Malcolm Osmond was the Most Valuable Player in the series.

Burin Peninsula Soccer Champions 1963 Harold Hollett, Alf White, Clar Brooks, Eric Grandy, Al Buffett, Malcolm Osmond, Arch Wells, John Russell, Max Hollett, Clar Patten, Frank Fizzard, George May, Charlie Crowley.

Burin Peninsula Soccer Champions 1964 Harold Hollett, Clar Brooks, Eric Grandy, Clayton Welsh, Al Buffett, Malcolm Osmond, Frank Fizzard, George May, Max Hollett, Bill Matthews, Arch Wells, Newman Bartlett, Clar Patten.

After the mid-60s other teams, mainly from St. Lawrence and St. John's, contended with success in the local senior soccer scene. In 1961, a new league for junior players (under age twenty-one) with provincial playdowns was organized. That year Grand Bank's junior representatives were: goal Larry Osmond; fullbacks George Penwell, Eric Grandy; halfbacks Max Cox, Clar Simms, Eli Patten; forwards Max Hollett, Harold Hollett, Clar Patten, William Wells, John Russell, and Arch Wells.

This first youth team did not win, but on August 20, 1963, the Junior Gee Bees won the provincial title and the Daily News Trophy.

Junior All-Newfoundland Soccer Champions
1963 goal Keith Welsh; fullbacks Sim Hickman,
Clar Patten; halfbacks Max Cox, Clayton Welsh,
Harvey Hunt; forwards Max Hollett, John Russell,
Frank Fizzard, George May, Bill Matthews, Corey
Crewe; coach Newman Bartlett, manager Dick
Forsey
Junior Burin Peninsula Soccer Champions 1964
goal Keith Welsh, fullbacks Max Crocker, Maurice
Dodge; halfbacks Harry English, Bill Matthews,
Clayton Welsh; forwards Rex Matthews, Steve
Hiscock, Lloyd Handrigan, George May, Frank
Fizzard, Bill Hillier. Fizzard was MVP in the All-
Newfoundland series won by the St. John's
Guards.

In 1969, the Senior squad lost in the finals to the Fieldians
but, with a strong junior or feeder system, many younger
players were advancing to the senior team. The next year
Grand Bank once again advanced to provincial playdowns:

All-Newfoundland and Burin Peninsula Cham-
pions 1970 goal Norman Butt; fullbacks Clarence
Brooks, Max Crocker; halfbacks Bill Matthews,
Clayton Welsh, Harry English; forwards Max
Hollett, Frank Fizzard, John Russell, Fred Cox,
Arch Wells, Jack Cumben, Clayton Welsh, Jack
Burfitt, Wayne Rideout, coach Stan Fizzard.

It was the mid-1970s before Grand Bank again represented the Burin Peninsula in All-Newfoundland competition. By this time, the Challenge Cup playdowns had been
organized whereby teams on the Avalon and Burin Peninsula accumulated points in interlocking league play. The
provincial champions won the right to represent Newfoundland against other Canadian teams. Grand Bank went to the
Challenge Cup finals the first two years and won the right to
represent Newfoundland in the third year.

The team (below) played nationally for the Challenge Cup and went undefeated in the round robin series. The final playoff game with Ontario was a tie with Ontario winning on penalty shots.

> **Challenge Cup Representatives 1974** goal Norman Butt, Tony Cornish, Eli Hillier, Clayton Welsh, Frank Fizzard, Cecil Trimm, Jim Handrigan, Henry Keeping, Art Cluett, Harry English, Jack Cumben, Clarence Brooks, Lloyd Hillier, Max Hollett, playing coach Bill Matthews, manager Stan Fizzard.

Inter-town rivalry of three decades ago was intense, but players knew and respected each other. As well, they often played together as a Burin Peninsula unit; for example, in the 1966 Come Home Year competition in St. John's, the Burin Peninsula team was: Grand Bank coach Gordon Grandy, Harry English, Frank Fizzard, Bill Matthews, Max Hollett; Fortune George "Bow" Collier; Lawn Winston Strang; St. Lawrence Norm Kelly, Bob Slaney, Reg Farrell, Brendon Slaney, Cyril Quirk, and Wils Melloy.

In the early 1970s, a new soccer field was built on Riverside East replacing the smaller and inadequate Stoodley Pitch. By the 1980s a ladies' soccer league was organized, locally and provincially, but unlike the Grand Bank senior and junior men's teams, the ladies had to draw on the talent of two or more towns to field a competitive team.

In 1987, the local Soccer Association headed by coaches George and Judy Cooper, assembled a team of girls that achieved success. The team competed as the Burin Peninsula Ladies' Soccer Team and the Grand Bank players were: Deanne Elms, Tracey Osbourne, Tracey Keeping, Lisa Barnes, Connie Cooper, Natalie Stewart, Marjorie Prior and Michelle Cooper.

That year, after taking the provincial title, they won the Atlantic Provinces championship and in October competed unsuccessfully for the national championship in Saskatchewan.

The 1987 ladies' soccer champions for the Burin Peninsula, Newfoundland and the Atlantic provinces.
Front row (l-r) Deanne Elms, Cynthia Parsons (Fortune), Tracey Osbourne, Tracey Keeping, Lisa Barnes, Kim Kendell (Fortune), Connie Cooper
Back Row (l-r) George Cooper, Joanne Mallay (Marystown), Sherry Barnes (Fortune), Kathy Masters (Fortune), Marilyn Warren (Fortune), Natalie Stewart, Marjorie Prior, Delsey Slaney (St. Lawrence), Michelle Cooper, Donna Grandy (Garnish), Debbie Hartson (Burin) and Judy Cooper.

Grand Bank Ladies Burin Peninsula Champions 1994 Terri Blagdon, Sherri Burton, Michelle Caines, Heather Crowley, Stephanie Crowley, Carla Douglas, Nancy Douglas, Lisa Fizzard, Valerie Forsey, Pauline (Caines) Harris, Marsha Hiscock, Raelle King, Tracey (Osmond) Moores, Cynthia Parsons, Nancy Parsons, Lottie Vallis, Alison Wiseman, coach Randy Douglas

When people think of soccer in Grand Bank, one person readily comes to mind — F.M."Fred" Tessier. Although he was not a player, he was totally dedicated to the sport and earned an unofficial title around Newfoundland as "Mr. Soccer." He spent twenty-seven years as president of the Grand Bank Soccer Association. Others who succeeded him as President were: Stan Fizzard, Frank Fizzard, George Cooper and Randy Douglas. Tessier also served twenty-four terms as president of the Burin Peninsula Soccer Association.

It has been said that you do not know a people unless you

have seen them at their sports and Harry Smith, of Ontario, followed that maxim when he watched a soccer game in Grand Bank (versus Burin) in the summer of 1952. He was impressed with the happy mood of the people as they mingled with the players, visiting players included. In his book *Newfoundland Holiday* he wrote:

> The playing field has a high board fence, and you learn why when, at the gate, you part with a small piece of silver as a contribution towards expenses. There are no seats, but a rail keeps the crowd in place, and at start of the game there's little vacant space around it.
>
> Football uniforms display rugged, muscular physique and there's no lack of grace or vitality in their movements, or courtesy and goodwill between contenders. The game is a good one, smartly played and noisily encouraged by a good-humoured crowd.

Today, attendance is not as great as it once was, but the spirit of goodwill and fair play still exists, and the excitement generated by the rivalry of peninsula and island competition is still present. Many Grand Bankers like to remember summer evenings spent at the Stoodley Memorial Soccer Field on Marine Drive watching soccer in the golden years of the 1950-60s.

Chapter Five   Landmarks

Grand Bank Lighthouse: Heritage Symbol

In 1987, while in the process of searching for information related to our historic town, one story in particular intrigued me; that of the lighthouse and the damage it received from a schooner in 1923. I talked to several older residents, some of whom have since passed away, and they told me the general outline of what happened. As well, while browsing through archival newspapers I found a reference to the accident giving the date only, but no other information.

At the time, 1987, a brochure, which later became the Heritage Walk, was being planned. It was designed for the tourists expected during the town's tri-centennial. As publicity for the brochure, I submitted a story of the lighthouse to the *Southern Gazette*. This is the revised version (but probably not the final version, as other facts concerning the lighthouse may yet be uncovered) of a distinctive town feature.

Tourists visiting Grand Bank often walk along the wharf admiring and photographing the Grand Bank Lighthouse at the entrance to the harbour. Over the years it has become one of the symbols of the town's heritage.

A casual glance, however, may not reveal that the letter 'B' in BANK on the side of the lighthouse is damaged. Yet, from the western pier the hollow or dent can be easily seen. Since its construction in 1921-22, the lighthouse and its scars have weathered many storms.

Although the incident with the 'B' happened over sev-

141

Taken from a flat, calm sea this is a view of the lighthouse, with an insert of he damaged B. The bowsprit of *Frank R. Forsey* also bounced up and slightly chipped the D.

A tribute to the foresight and pride of its builders, it is, perhaps, the only lighthouse in eastern Canada with the name of a community engraved. For many years, there was no wharf out to the block on which the lighthouse stood, but only sections of rock-filled cribs. The eastern concrete wharf was built in the fifties when the fish plant was under construction.

In the 1930s and 1940s, Bert Riggs (1891-1948) tended the Grand Bank lighthouse. In addition to lighting the lamp at sundown and extinguishing it at dawn, Riggs also kept the glass clean, trimmed the wick, and filled the lamp daily with kerosene from the two barrels kept inside the lighthouse. In his log book, he recorded daily fuel consumption and weather conditions.

Riggs tended the light until 1948; by then his wages as lightkeeper were $21.63 a month. This was actual cash, paid by the Newfoundland government, in a town where very few dollars exchanged hands. Every merchant in Grand Bank — for each felt he had partial ownership in the town lighthouse — wanted Riggs to spend the money in his store. After World War II, an ex-service man looked after the light until the 1950s.

enty years ago, Clyde Forsey, carpenter/shipwright, remembered the day the bowsprit of the *Frank R. Forsey* rammed the newly-constructed lighthouse.

"I was only a young man," Forsey recalls, "before I went away to work, so it had to be in the early twenties. The *Frank R. Forsey* was coming from Oporto, Portugal, with a load of salt. The captain, Charlie Rose, whose crew at this time was mate John Vaters, his brother Phil Vaters, cook Tom Thorne and John James Hickman, apparently became confused with location of the new lighthouse in the storm, kept the vessel too far to the eastern and the bowsprit struck the lighthouse. To this day the dent in the B is visible."

According to Clarence Griffin, who kept fairly accurate records of ships and sailors of Grand Bank, there were three vessels approaching the harbour on that day to make a run into port. Griffin recalled that during a thick snowsquall, the *Vera P. Thornhill* came in

When a schooner harboured in Grand Bank with her catch, dory loads of salt bulk fish were taken from the harbour to the eastern side of the brook or past the lighthouse to Trimm's Beach. There it was washed out in fish pounds and then carried to the beaches to dry.
Even the harbour's close confines posed a danger to seamen. James Keeping of Harbour Breton drowned when his overloaded dory sank in Grand Bank harbour as he was carrying salt bulk fish to the pounds. Keeping was married to Maggie (Rose) Keeping of Harbour Breton.
Keeping's fatal accident in Grand Bank harbour was not the first to happen there: on August 2, 1921, Luke Thornhill and George Patten upset a dory near the harbour and drowned. Several years previously two Grand Bank men, John Francis and John Beavis, disappeared off Grand Bank Cape when their punt, full of fish, apparently capsized.

first followed by the *General Trenchard* and finally by the *Frank R. Forsey. Forsey* miscalculated the entrance, hit the lighthouse, breaking off her bowsprit in the bargain, and grounded near the harbour mouth.

Eric Tibbo, too, was aware on that day something exciting had happened in the harbour, when as a young man, he viewed the accident from the wharf. "The *Forsey* was aground on the eastern side of the harbour outside the lighthouse," he remembered. "It happened a short while after the lighthouse was built in 1921."

Some months after she was launched, the *Frank R. Forsey* was converted from a two-masted vessel to a tern with three masts. After the grounding, she was refloated and continued as a coasting schooner for Samuel Harris' business. She ended her days moored in St. Pierre as a salt storage vessel.

General Trenchard sank in the Western Atlantic in March of 1929; *Vera P. Thornhill*, after a few years as a banking schooner under the command of Captain John Thornhill, was sold to a company in Burin. Later her registry was transferred to the West Indies and her eventual fate is not recorded.

Chapter Five   Story Two

Fidelity Lodge and its Legacy of the Sea (1876-1936)

Several years ago I became master of the Freemasons in Grand Bank's Fidelity Lodge. At the installation ceremonies I gave a brief talk about the sea tragedies that often affected fraternal and social institutions in seafaring towns such as Grand Bank. Later, I searched for more information, expanded the ideas and sent the revised information to the *Newfoundland Quarterly*. Editor Harry Cuff accepted the article, and it appeared in the July 1990 magazine.
Some the ships mentioned in this section have already been dealt with to some measure in Chapter Three.

Just about the time when the bank fishery was establishing its hold along the South Coast, a lodge of Freemasons was established in Grand Bank. The coincidental growth of the two is not accidental. When the first schooners sailed to St. John's, Halifax, Lunenburg, and Boston delivering fish or bringing food and supplies to the emerging community, the early mariners no doubt came in contact with fraternal institutions already flourishing in those ports. In time many Grand Bank seamen joined Newfoundland Masonic Lodges in St. John's and Fortune. In 1876, when the District Grand Master, James Shannon Clift, issued the official charter to Fidelity Lodge, Grand Bank, most of the local signees were members of lodges at St. John's or Fortune.

According to Aaron Buffett's history of the town, bank fishing got its start in Grand Bank in the 1880s and the distinction of pioneering the venture belongs to "Samuel Harris who in 1881, captained his own vessel the *George C. Harris*, of about seventy tons to the offshore banks." With his fleet of foreign going vessels and banking schooners numbered in the dozens, Harris eventually became a prominent merchant and vessel owner in the town. In 1892, he became one of the first masters of the Masonic Lodge in Grand Bank.

Established in a fishing town, a vast majority of Fidelity's officers and members were closely associated with the sea; many were shipowners, merchants, captains, seamen, and fishermen. But in any town where a fleet of ships go down to the sea, earning a living, tragedy on the ocean, and death by drowning go hand in hand. Throughout the years, hundreds

Fidelity Lodge, the oldest meeting hall in Grand Bank, was built in 1904-5. The insert shows the cornerstone, laid by George R. Forsey, in 1904 and in which he placed his dedication speech. The A.L. 5904 translates into 1904, the year lodge construction began. (See Chapter 2, Story 2)
According to a lodge yearbook, the hall was built (and probably designed) by one of its members, Samuel K. Bell (1853-1930). Born in Grand Bank, Bell was a master carpenter and was recognized as the leading shipwright in Newfoundland. After his first wife died, he moved to St. John's and married into the Crosbie family. He did such a thorough repair job on the S.S. *Rotterdam* that when the ship returned to England, her owners showed off the work. In 1885, Bell helped build the St. John's dry dock and, in 1917, he was appointed to Newfoundland's Legislative Council by Prime Minister Edward P. Morris.

of wooden sailing schooners were owned in Grand Bank, and over a score disappeared at sea without a trace taking with them the early entrepreneurs and social leaders of the community.

All too frequently names in the lodge roster book are tersely appended "Lost at Sea" or "Master Mariner, presumably drowned." For many casualties prior to 1900, only the captain's name has been recorded; most crew lists have never been written down and few details of the wrecks are known.

William Buffett, who signed the original charter in December 1876, had lost a son only three months before in one of the first sea disasters to ravage the community. In early October, William Buffett (Jr.), age thirty-four, left Prince Edward Island in his own schooner the *Idol*, headed for Grand Bank with fresh produce. On October 18, the tail end of a tropical hurricane lashed across Newfoundland's South Coast without warning. The *Idol* and her crew never made port; her hulk, bottom up, drifted in Pass Island days later.

Just a few years after its initial meeting, another loss at sea hit Fidelity when the *Mikado*, a thirty-seven ton schooner, mysteriously vanished. With five crewmen and her master Thomas Alex Hickman, the *Mikado* left Grand Bank on October 15, 1897, headed for Halifax. Hickman, the paternal grandfather of Newfoundland's Supreme Court Chief Justice T. Alex Hickman, had affiliated with his hometown lodge from St. John's and was one of the first officers of the organization.

On his last voyage, it was the intention of Captain Hickman to discharge fish at Halifax and proceed to Charlottetown, Prince Edward Island, to load fresh produce for Grand Bank. The *Mikado* never reached Halifax. On the night of October 18, only three days out of port, she disappeared with her crew.

Very few written accounts of the loss are known, but one is available. Around the turn of the century, the Methodist Church in Newfoundland published a news pamphlet, *The Methodist Monthly Greeting*, and in this booklet, the Freemasons of Grand Bank expressed their sorrow:

Dear Sir, — During that memorable gale of Sunday
night, on October 18 last, one of the most respected
and honoured members of this community, Mr.
Thomas Alex Hickman, master of the schooner
MIKADO en route to Halifax, found rest from his
labours with all his crew, in the waters of the great
deep. The departed one being known to many of
your readers you will oblige by inserting the following letter of condolence sent ... by Fidelity
Lodge, of this place.

Yours truly,
W. P. Way,
Grand Bank
December 27, 1897

(There follows a copy of the letter of sympathy
written to the bereaved family.)

Fifteen years passed before the Fidelity Lodge again had
to confront the toll of the sea. By this time, many South Coast
merchants were sending their own vessels overseas to
Europe laden with dried fish. These little ships brought salt
on the return journey to the expanding salt dried cod industry. Most of the trade occurred in the harsh winter season
when schooners ran a treacherous gamut between Atlantic
storms.

During the winter of 1911-12, a series of fierce gales swept
the North Atlantic for several weeks, one storm following
another without letup. One Grand Bank vessel out in the
furious windstorm that November, beating her way to
Europe, was the *Arkansas*, a schooner of one hundred eleven
ton owned by Samuel Harris Limited. Her captain was Charles Deveaux, a young, dark haired man who had taken up
residence in Grand Bank a year or two before.

Deveaux, of French descent from Nova Scotia (most
likely Neil's Harbour), had found employment in Grand
Bank as the master of foreign going schooners. Several other

Frenchmen joined Fidelity during this period, most of them skilled in specific trades — navigators, master mariners, and sailmakers. One local lodge by-law stated that candidates for membership into Fidelity had to be a resident of the colony except for .".. seafaring men and residents of St. Pierre." Deveaux had joined in December 1909, and enjoyed the social outlet it provided for he was known to have attended lodge functions and outings with his wife and young family.

Built in the Smith and Rhuland yards, Lunenburg in 1903, *Arkansas* left Grand Bank on November 6, 1911, laden with fish destined for Portugal. After sixty-seven days, the schooner had not reached any port nor had she been seen or spoken to by other vessels. Deveaux and his five crew, mostly single men from Fortune Bay, were officially declared lost at sea. In Fidelity's minute book for 1912, an entry dated January 19, 1912 reads:

> Aaron F. Buffett, (a merchant and owner of several schooners) alluded to Bro. Charles Deveaux, a member of this Lodge, who in all probability has been lost at sea. Wor. Master and several members also made some sympathetic remarks on the same subject.

In this instance, no reference was made to contact the Deveaux's widow as was the case with the Hickman family. Presumably she had returned home to Nova Scotia some time before.

Such was the severity of gales during that long and stormy winter between November 1911 and February 1912, five vessels were reported "missing without a trace" — one from Harbour Grace, two from St. John's and two from Grand Bank, the *Arkansas* and the *Dorothy Louise*.

Dorothy Louise, a tern schooner, (locally referred to as three masters and the first of this type owned in Grand Bank) was built in Allendale, Nova Scotia, in 1910 and was jointly owned by Jos. Sellers, Samson Hiscock and George C. Harris. On her final voyage, the *Dorothy Louise* sailed from Portugal on November 20, 1911, headed to Newfoundland. She had taken fish from Seller's premises in St. John's to Portugal and had left Oporto deeply laden with fishery salt for Newfoundland.

Since she was relatively new, larger and sturdier, this one hundred twenty-five ton schooner was believed for some time to have survived the succession of storms. But after seventy-two days without a word, the tern and her crew of five men were officially declared lost at sea. Captain Samson Hiscock of Grand Bank, age twenty-nine, had joined Fidelity in October 1910, a year before.

In the lodge minute book, dated March 1, 1912, two months after the previous reference to the disappearance of Captain Deveaux, the following entry appears: "Aaron F. Buffett called attention to the probable loss of Bro. Samson Hiscock in the *Dorothy Louise* and suggested that a message of sympathy should be sent to his parents and family."

Samuel Harris, a prominent businessman, fish exporter of Grand Bank and a former master of Fidelity Lodge, owned a fleet of tern schooners used primarily in the European-West Indies trade. (see Harris' biography in Chapter 2, Story 3)

One of his terns was the *General Plumer*, named for Herbert Charles Plumer (1857-1932), who commanded the British Second Army in France during the Great War. Built in Allendale, Nova Scotia, in 1911, the *Plumer* netted one hundred forty-nine ton and measured one hundred two foot long. Her master was Lionel Hickman of Grand Bank, age fifty-two, and a ten-year member of the lodge.

To give his men time to spend at home on New Year's Day, Captain Hickman postponed sailing to the Caribbean until January 1, 1930. After the tern arrived in the Indies and discharged her fish cargo, she had a lengthy delay in Barbados trying to obtain a load of molasses destined for St. John's. According to port authorities in Barbados, some of the heavy puncheons were stacked on deck which may have affected the schooner's stability in turbulent weather.

While south some of the Grand Bank crew had heard about the disastrous fire in their hometown which broke out

Workers sift through the rubble and old anchors after a 1930 waterfront fire. The structures in the background: l-r George C. Harris' home; Patten's drugstore; Cyrus Patten store/garage; the two-storey peaked roof house (right) is the home of Aaron Forsey, the author's great-grandfather. The edge of the building far right is the Bank of Nova Scotia. Courtesy of Neil Locke

during the night of March 1, 1930. It had destroyed ten stores and sheds along the waterfront and caused $250,000 damage. One of *Plumer's* crewmen, mate George Hickman, had written home saying how anxious he was to view the ruins. But somewhere in the Atlantic between Barbados and Newfoundland in a frequent Atlantic storm, the *General Plumer* disappeared with Captain Hickman and his five crewmen.

The procession of marine casualties seemed to reach its peak in 1936 when two schooners were lost within months of each other; both captains were veterans of the sea and long in service to their society.

Owned by Samuel Harris of Grand Bank, the *General Gough* netted two hundred and thirty-six tons and was built in Essex, Massachusetts. Harris, as was his custom in appending names of British generals to his foreign-going fleet of schooners, had this tern schooner christened *General Gough* in honour of World War One General Hubert Gough (1868-1945). Planked with white oak and copper fastened, she was considered, because of her size, superb construction and timbers of white oak, to be the flagship of Harris' foreign

The *General Plumer*, heavily burdened with molasses, disappeared somewhere between Barbados and Newfoundland. Her crew: Captain Lionel Hickman, mate George Hickman, cook Charles Belbin, Bill Snook all of Grand Bank and two young men of Grand Beach, Walter Follett and Tom Tibbo.

going fleet. The *General Gough* left Portugal in the fall of 1935 with fishery salt in her holds for Grand Bank Fisheries Limited.

Other schooners making the transatlantic run at the same time reported mountainous seas and terrific head winds; for the people of Grand Bank these stories aroused concern and fear for the overdue *Gough*. After three months without any reports of the missing vessel, the March 14, 1935, edition of the *Evening Telegram* declared: "All hope has been abandoned for the *General Gough* which has not been reported since leaving Lisbon on November 22...her captain and crew were residents of Grand Bank."

With his crew of five — mate Randell Hickman, cook Richard Riggs, seamen Robert Gillard, Ron Pardy and Charlie Anstey — the *Gough* was under the command of Amiel Welsh, an experienced sea captain and a member of the lodge since 1927.

His wife Charlotte often recalled those dark days of looking out to sea waiting for the tall sails of her husband's schooner to appear.[1] She would take her family of two young boys with her, walk slowly through the streets of Grand Bank and to the top of Grand Bank Cape. There, on a clear day, the view reached across Fortune Bay and beyond to the ocean off St. Pierre. Tall white sails could easily be spotted in the distance, but the Welsh family returned from their lonely vigil, disappointed and empty.

That same spring, the sea claimed another ship. The banking schooner *Partanna*, under the command of Charles Anstey with his full complement of twenty-five men, was wrecked off the southern Avalon Peninsula. Debris — one or two broken dories, trawl tubs, a smashed spar and sail and a partial nameplate — suggested the schooner had driven upon the rocks, most likely St. Mary's Keys.

Earlier in his sea career, Captain Anstey was a part owner of schooners and had sailed the *Castle Carey* and the *Electric Flash* across the Atlantic several times. It was during these years, he became a member of Fidelity Lodge, joining in October 1909.

As the age of sail drew to a close in the 1940s, the litany of wasted men and material tapered off. Since that time two vessels whose masters were members of Fidelity were lost. The *Administratrix* was run down off Cape Race in April 1948, resulting in the death of Captain Chesley Forsey and Mate Harvey Keating, both Masons. Although equipped with modern navigational aids and the latest communication devices, the trawler *Blue Wave* succumbed to winter icing conditions in February 1959 taking Captain Charles Walters and his crew with her.

Nearly a quarter century has passed since a vessel from Grand Bank has gone down with major loss of life. Traffic by sea from the harbour has virtually stopped; certainly none by sail. With the exception of one or two preserved in mainland ports, schooners are on the bottom of the Atlantic. It is not likely social organizations in the town will again feel the anguish that was once endured in the past. (Appendix F lists the Fidelity Lodge masters since its formation)

Endnote:

1. Few Grand Bank sea stories and loss of life at sea have elements of ghosts or tokens, but the disappearance of *General Gough* does. Since this article first appeared, a story of spiritualism and tokens was related to me.

Charlotte Welsh, who was a fine and stately lady in her nineties when I spoke with her in the Grand Bank Blue Crest Senior Citizen's Home in 1987, had a portent that her husband's ship and his crew were lost. Such a length of time had passed and no word had been heard from *General Gough* that most people in Grand Bank had given up hope of seeing the ship again.

In her long, lonely vigils at night wondering and waiting, she heard a sound in the kitchen. She waited to make sure. It was the rocking chair in motion, the chair her lifemate had often used.

Knowing then her husband would not be returning, she got up and pulled down all window blinds, a symbol of death in the house.

Chapter Five   Story Three

Ties with History — Frazer Park

In May 1987 Frazer Park was named and dedicated to the memory of George C. Frazer, a man who came out from England to Newfoundland to minister to Methodists.

George C. Frazer was born at North Shields, England, on October 20, 1854, and came to Newfoundland in 1883 with nine other Englishmen. He was sent to Petites on the South Coast for two years and was then appointed to St. John's. On June 27, 1887, he was received into full commission with the Methodist Church and ordained for the work of the ministry. Following his ordination he served with the Bonavista, Exploits, Trinity, Grand Bank (1894-97), Blackhead and Twillingate circuits.

On June 5, 1902, Rev. Frazer died at age forty-seven. The Rev. Charles Lench, in his book on Grand Bank, said of George Frazer: "His preparation was most painstaking and thorough and he was ranked among the best preachers among the conference." Something of the truth of this statement is perhaps born out by the fact that the two towns in which he served — Grand Bank and Twillingate —chose to name their church halls Frazer Hall. When the Methodist congregation of Grand Bank built their church hall in 1903-04, they dedicated it to Reverend George Frazer.

Frazer Hall became one of the several distinctive buildings of Grand Bank. It was more than a church hall, but rather a community centre for sixty years. Often the affairs of the town were discussed and decided there before Grand Bank

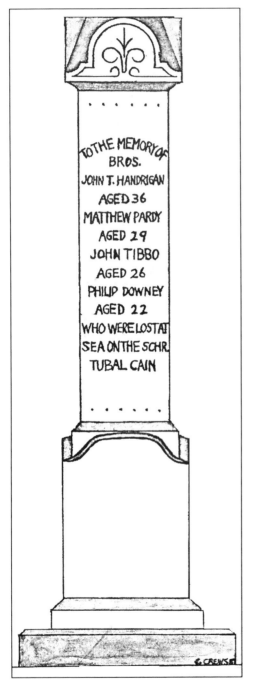

TO THE MEMORY OF
BROS.
JOHN T. HANDRIGAN
AGED 36
MATTHEW PARDY
AGED 29
JOHN TIBBO
AGED 26
PHILIP DOWNEY
AGED 22
WHO WERE LOST AT
SEA ON THE SCHR.
TUBAL CAIN

had elected municipal representation. In the Frazer Hall, patriotic crowds gathered during two World Wars, and local concerts were performed in the hall by various school classes and organizations. Visiting artists, particularly from Mount Allison University, a Canadian university with strong connections with the town, often performed there.

The Frazer Hall became underutilized when the new United Church with its kitchen, stage, and congregation/comm unity seating facilities in basement, was built in 1965. Considered too expensive to maintain, the hall was dismantled in 1979.

Dedicated to Grand Bank's lost seamen, the Tubal Cain monument in Frazer Park lists crewmen and ages on one face while the other face details the Orange Lodge connection. Line drawing by Gerald Crews

According to town oral tradition, Frazer Park was the site of the first Methodist Church, built in the winter of 1816-17. Known as the "Little Chapel," it was used for thirty years until a second church was built in 1846 near the location of the present day United Church.

In Frazer Park, stands the only monument Grand Bank has erected to the memory of men and ships lost from the community. The initiative to raise money and to place a memorial stone there belongs to Grand Bank Loyal Orange Lodge.

In January 1907, the schooner *Tubal Cain*, owned by businessman Simeon Tibbo of Grand Bank, disappeared with all hands en route from Halifax to Grand Bank with a full load of coal and lumber. Of the eight crew members who lost their lives in the tragic misadventure were four Orangemen: Captain John T. Handrigan, Philip Downey, Matthew Pardy, and John Tibbo. The other men, some of whom were captains journeying home on the schooner, were: William Rogers, Robert Forsey, Aaron Forsey, and William Strowbridge.

A folk song, handed down orally through the years and preserved in Newfoundland song collections, details the circumstances of the tragic loss of the *Tubal Cain*. The sixty-five ton schooner had been built in Grand Bank in the winter of 1902-03 making her a little over three years old when she disappeared. The folksong poem "The Loss of the *Tubal Cain*" claims four of the crew were married and left sixteen orphans. Newspapers of the day determine the date the schooner left Halifax, but the exact day and location of her loss may never be known.

That year, 1907, Grand Bank hosted Newfoundland's session of the Orange Lodge, the first time the town had done so. Rankin Loyal Orange Lodge #10 of Grand Bank, with the co-operation of the Provincial Grand Lodge and the many delegates assembled at Grand Bank, collected the necessary funds to erect a monument dedicated to lost seamen.

Grand Master Captain Abraham Kean and Deputy Grand Master T.W. Gushue were two officers in the delega-

This is how the *Daily News* of February 4, 1907, reported the loss of the *Tubal Cain*. The other disaster referred to is that of *Nellie Harris*, which disappeared with Grand Bank crewmen some months previously.

```
                                          Grand Bank, Nfld.
   PATTEN & FORSEY.                        March 18 1907.
     General Dealers.


Mrs Pardy,
   Grand Bank.

   We, the members of the Loyal Orange Lodge of Grand Bank
do offer to you our deep sympathy in your sad bereavement.
We have no words to express our brotherly sorrow, but can
assure you our sorrow is sincere that you should have lost
so kind an affectionate husband but assured that trusting
in the Divine love of Him that doeth all things well you will
be strengthened to drink the bitter cup, and we pray that God
will bless you and your house in this the hour of your
affliction.
                                   William Forsey W. M.

                                   Leonard Forsey   R. S.
```

A letter in the possession of David Benson, the great-grandson of Matthew Pardy, showing the notification of *Tubal Cain*'s loss and the condolences from the Orange Lodge. Letter is signed by the W.M. (Worshipful Master, William Forsey) and R.S. (Recording Secretary, Leonard Forsey).

tion. Captain Kean, a successful sealing captain, came to Grand Bank on the coastal steamer *Glencoe* with the other Newfoundland lodge delegates.

The monument site in the southeastern corner near Church Street was selected and approved. The Importers Association of Grand Bank, made up of Grand Bank's four chief merchant houses, set in place a public holiday for July 12 of that year when the monument was unveiled.

The Tubal Cain memorial stone has since been since to the northwest corner and today Frazer Park is a public rest area with picnic tables. Many outdoor community events happen there: Light-Up for Christmas and the Community Christmas Tree; outdoor sing-alongs, drama, and picnics.

A 1907 Poem on Grand Bank

When Kean, T.W. Gushue and the other Grand Lodge delegates went back to the Avalon Peninsula from Provincial Sessions, one of the group wrote a poem about the visit. It appeared in the March 2, 1907 edition of the *Daily News*:

The P.G. Lodge Session

Twas a fine day in February,
When ten of our rank,
Left St. John's in the morning
To go to Grand Bank
To the 36th Session
We were outward bound
And a better outport
Could never be found.

On reaching Brigus Junction
Our surprise was to hear
The train had broken down
Coming up from Carbonear,
This delayed us two hours,
But sure 'twas alright
For down in Placentia
We spent a good night.

On board the *Glencoe*
As she lay at the pier,
Loaded with Orange-men
Everywhere
Telling tales and old yarns
Enjoying the fun
As she swung to her anchors
Till rise of the sun.

The next morning at eight
We let go the line,
And to say it was blowing
was cutting it fine;
The ocean was boiling
With a gale from Sou' Wes'
And all hands on board
were sick more or less.

One o'clock the bell sounded
Calling to dinner,
Not one soul responded
Either saint or a sinner,
Some were hugging the rail,
Others took to the bed,
And lay like a corpse
'Till we rounded the head.

Land ho! was the cry
and Burin was near,
And a rush to the table
Filled up every chair,
All forgot their sea-sickness,
And took a good haul
Of roast beef and fried codfish
Prepared for us all.

St. Lawrence and Fortune
Were next ports of call,
And the nice little harbours
Were well viewed by all,
Our stay there was short,
So we bid them adieu,
And set sail for Grand Bank
Already in view.

Grand Bank is reached
On a Saturday morn,
What a crowd did assemble
At the blow of the horn,
The orange, the purple,
The red and the blue,
Were down at the pier
To welcome the crew.

We reached terra firma
And marched to the hall,
Where an address of welcome
Was read out to all,
Bro. Lench, the Grand Chaplin
Gave the reply,
In a nice fitting speech,
Which none can deny.

Our church parade
Was second to none,
And the sermon on twelve stones
Surprised everyone,
Delivered by our Grand Chaplin
The Rev. Lench,
Will inspire every Orangeman
Never to flinch.

The Grand Lodge session
Went through with a swing,
And the Election of Officers
Made a new ring,
Capt. Kean at the helm
The old ship to steer,
And lead on to victory
Everywhere.

Our second in command
Is Brother Gushue,
Who for faithful service
Is one of the few,
The rest of the branches
Of the old orange tree
Are jolly good fellows
Hip! pip! one two three.

To wind up the session
The ladies took part.
In a sumptuous spread
To the joy of our heart,
The people of Grand Bank
Will ne'er be forgot,
That town on the West Coast
That dear little spot.

Good bye dear old Grand Bank
Kind people good bye,
As we board the *Glencoe*
With tears in our eyes,
We hope for the pleasure
To meet you once more,
If not on this earth
On the bright happy shore. J.W.P.

As a branch of the Orange Lodge, the Royal Black Preceptory's charter was issued in 1907, the same year the national
conference was held in Grand Bank. The Preceptory minute
books are lost from 1907 to 1919 but, since then statistics and
records were kept. From those a representative year, 1920,
was chosen when the preceptory officers were:

W. Preceptor — John Nicholle   1st Censer — James Hollett
D. Preceptor — Henry Lee   2nd Censer — Bob Handrigan
Chaplain — John H. Matthews   1st Standard
Registrar — John Camp   Bearer — Henry Stoodley
Treasurer — Sam Rose   2nd Standard
1st Lecturer — Harold Patten   Bearer — Angus Brown
2nd Lecturer — George Diamond   Pursuivant — Jacob Penwell
Tyler — Robert Hickman

Chapter Five   Story Four

Two Schools Close

As in any town, schools are built, grow, become out-
dated, close, and are torn down. Below are some of the
chronicles of two Grand Bank schools within recent memory.

In 1976 and in 1988, two of Grand Bank's educational
institutions, the United Church (Methodist) Academy and
the Salvation Army School, were closed and taken down.
Between them, the years of educating Grand Bank youth
amounted to one hundred twelve; forty-seven years for the
Salvation Army school and sixty-five for the Academy.

Built in 1922 with eight rooms, the United Church Academy soon expanded into a ten-room school with overflow
classes in the basement and in the "Gym." When the John
Burke Regional High School opened in the fall of 1961,
grades nine, ten, and eleven attended the new school and this
relieved overcrowding.

In 1969, the Burin Peninsula Integrated School Board was
formed and the Academy became the Grand Bank Primary
School. With the opening of Partanna Academy in 1972 and
the extending of classrooms in John Burke High School a few
years later, there was no further need of the U.C. Academy. It
closed its doors in 1987. The next year, after the property was
sold to the town, the school was demolished.

During its early years, United Church Academy Christmas concerts were an annual and social event: a highlight of

the holiday season. Unlike today, when the whole school participates in one concert, in those days each class organized an event selling home-made ice cream and fundraising for the school. For example, in the Frazer Hall on December 6, 1932, Miss Alice Lacey's class had a concert.

The program:

Chorus	— "We're Mighty Glad You're Here"
Recitation	— "Tight Times" by Harry Welsh
Exercise	— "Upside Down Drill"
Trio	— "Bothersome Brothers" by Jean Matthews, Rose Nicholle, and Alfreda Smith
Dialogue	— "Pulling Sam's Tooth" by Gilbert Rogers, Harry Welsh, George Foote, Mary Tibbo, and Jean Matthews
Exercise	— "Mother Goose Party"
Flag Drill	
Chorus	— "Buy a Broom"
Dialogue	— "A Sudden Discovery" by Carrie Hillier, Max Thornhill, and Willie Handrigan
Duet	— "The Tin Soldier" and "The Doll from France" by Mary Tibbo and Willie Forsey
Recitation	— "A Queer Hole" by Hubert Tibbo
Chorus	— "Keep Smiling"
National Anthem	

On December 22, 1932, a Friday night, another class program; this time from Miss Betty Collins' room (probably Grade One or Two):

Chorus	— "Welcome"
Recitation	— "Mixed Up Welcomes" by Ivy White and Gordon Williams
Exercise	— "Bear Hunting" by Johnnie Burke and Charlie Patten
Recitation	— by Alex Hickman[1]
Dialogue	— "Tenna's Dream" by Maude Douglas, Ivy White, Tom Belben, Violet Rogers, Ellen Smith, Frank Grandy
Chorus	— "Santa in his Aeroplane"
Exercise	— "When I'm a Woman" by twelve girls
Exercise	— "When I'm a Man" by twelve boys
Recitation	— by Charlie Patten
Fairy Drill	— Mary Hickman, Jane Forsey, Ellen Smith, Eva Fox, Mary Camp, Lucy Thornhill, Dinah Patten, Mary Forsey, May Thornhill

Doll Show	— Emma Riggs, Mabel French, May Thornhill, Eva Fox, Ivy White, Mary Camp, Mary Hickman
Play	— "Christmas Controversy" by Wilson Foote, Eva Fox, Johnnie Burke, May Forsey, Bobby Carr
Recitation	— by Fred Moulton
Chorus	
National Anthem	

In 1961, the last grade eleven class of the U.C. Academy graduated:

Alice Parsons, Anita Thornhill, Ruby Thornhill, Viola Melbourne, Shirley White, Maria May, Joyce Emberley, Olive Keeping, Alice Douglas, Les Fox, George Mayo, Corey Crewe, Clarence Patten, Ida Farewell, and Gerard Vallee — a student from St. Pierre.

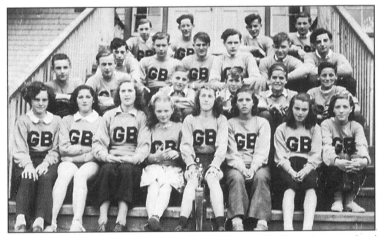

Over the years both Salvation Army and United Church schools combined to send strong track and field teams to inter-town competition in the Burin Peninsula Schools Sports Day. In 1947, the team wearing Grand Bank colours are: (front row l-r) Belle Murphy, Helen Brooks, Maria White, Vera Piercy, Margaret Brooks, Myrtle Melloy, Margaret Riggs and Martha Lee;
(second row l-r) Charlie Snook, Max Baker, Tom Buffett, Carl Williams, Bruce Buffett, Bert Gillard;
(third row l-r) Max Stoodley, Harold Thornhill, Wilfred Follett, Frank Tibbo, Roy Grandy, Don Brown;
(top row l-r) George Hickman, Edward Penwell, Harold Piercy, Tom Rose.
The Peninsula Sports Day Championship Trophy is in front of Margaret Brooks, a star short-distance runner. Courtesy Tom Rose

By 1925, the two-room Salvation Army school built in 1907 on Hawkins Street/Citadel Road, was considered inadequate and plans were made for a three-room school. According to *Memoirs* (1992) this opened in 1926 with two classrooms downstairs, one upstairs, and a multi-purpose Junior Hall in the basement.

Two extensions were added later — one in 1948-50 and a larger section in 1960. This gave the school its characteristic L-shape. The *Atlantic Guardian* of January 1949 reported the Salvation Army school had seven rooms (no classes were held in the basement where coal was stored) with a staff of six teachers, and a pupil registration of two hundred fifty-two.

With the formation of the Burin Peninsula Integrated School Board in 1969, the school housed grades four to eight of all denominations. The last class attended the Salvation Army School in June of 1972, and when Partanna Academy opened that fall, the school ceased to function. In 1976, it was taken down.

Nineteen sixty-one was the last year the school operated under the Salvation Army Board with pupils ranging from Kindergarten to Grade Eleven. That spring, as it had for many years, the school held its Annual Sports Day. The date was June seventh; the *Evening Telegram* (June 23 edition) carried the results:

Kindergarten Race (Boys)
   1st Place Lloyd Hillier
   2nd Place Stephen Tapper
   3rd Place Harold Cumben

Kindergarten Race (Girls)
   1st Doreen Bennett
   2nd Brenda Hatcher
   3rd Marilyn Thompson

Grade 1 Race (Boys)
   1st Frank Newport
   2nd Keith Hillier
   3rd Wilson Price

Grade 1 Race (Girls)
 1st Joy Wyatt
 2nd Elizabeth Baker
 3rd Marilyn Snook

Grade 2 Race (Boys)
 1st Bruce Warren
 2nd Jim Samms
 3rd Chesley Matthews

Grade 2 Race (Girls)
 1st Ellen Hatcher
 2nd Merina Downey
 3rd Joyce Cumben

Grade 3 Race (Boys)
 1st Jack Royle
 2nd Jack Williams
 3rd William Baker

Grade 3 Race (Girls)
 1st Esther Hatcher
 2nd Charlotte Snook
 3rd Winnie Snook

Broad Jump (Senior)
 1st Larry Osmond
 2nd John Russell
 3rd Bob Parsons

Broad Jump (Junior)
 1st Max Crocker
 2nd John Greene
 3rd Frank Bennett

High Jump (Senior)
 1st Everett Sampson
 2nd Larry Osmond
 3rd Bob Parsons

High Jump (Junior)
   1st Max Crocker
   2nd Albert Handrigan
   3rd Tom Anstey

Sack Race (Girls)
   1st Nancy Hatcher
   2nd Gladys Hatcher
   3rd Jean Williams/Jessie Downey

Sack Race (Boys)
   1st Max Grandy
   2nd Percy Warren
   3rd Wayne Bungay

Pole Vault (Senior)
   1st Tom Grandy
   2nd Everett Sampson
   3rd Jack Bungay

Pole Vault (Junior)
   1st Bruce Forsey
   2nd Norman Butt
   3rd Charlie Matthews

Mile Run
   1st Gordon Lee
   2nd Bob Parsons
   3rd Charlie Rogers

Slow Bicycle (Girls)
   1st Doreen Oakley
   2nd Emily Prior
   3rd Carletta Warren

Slow Bicycle (Boys)
   1st Bill Tapper
   2nd Wayne Oakley
   3rd Bob Lee

Potato Race (Senior)
  1st Freda Brooks
  2nd Jean Williams
  3rd Annie Grandy

Potato Race (Junior)
  1st Doreen Oakley
  2nd Edwina Vallis
  3rd Shirley Noseworthy

100 Yard Dash (Jr. Boys)
  1st Max Crocker
  2nd Frank Bennett
  3rd Maurice Dodge

100 Yard Dash (Jr. Girls)
  1st Nora Clarke
  2nd Mary Rogers
  3rd Sarah Keeping

100 Yard Dash (Sr. Boys)
  1st John Russell
  2nd Everett Sampson
  3rd Bob Parsons/William Welsh (tie)

100 Yard Dash (Sr. Girls)
  1st Freda Brooks
  2nd Bertha Anstey
  3rd Phyllis Warren

220 Yard Dash (Sr. Boys)
  1st John Russell
  2nd Everett Sampson
  3rd Bob Parsons

220 Yard Dash (Sr. Girls)
  1st Freda Brooks
  2nd Bertha Anstey
  3rd Velma Hickman/Phyllis Warren (tie)

Tug of War Won by Red Team 2-1

Judges for the Sports Day: RCMP Officer Jay and Town Peace Officer Russell Thornhill. Scorekeeper Clarence Brooks

Endnote:

1. Born in Grand Bank on October 19, 1925, Thomas Alexander Hickman attended and graduated from the U.C. Academy, studied law and was admitted to the Newfoundland Bar in 1948. He served as M.H.A. for Burin from 1966 to 1975, for Grand Bank district from 1975 to 1979 and was Minister of Justice and Attorney General for about ten years. In 1979, following his retirement from political life, he was appointed Chief Justice (Trial Division). Since becoming Chief Justice, he has chaired two of the most important public enquiries in Canadian history: the 1982 sinking of the oil rig *Ocean Ranger*, and an enquiry into the administration of justice in Nova Scotia following the wrongful conviction for murder of Donald Marshall.

METHODIST COLLEGE

Grand Bank, Newfoundland
1922—1923

MARIA A. FORSEY, Teacher

"The time is short."

"Safe in the arms of Jesus, Safe on His gentle breast."

PUPILS DECEASED DURING YEAR

Emily J. Kelland   George W. Rose
Robert R. Thornhill

With Jesus, "Till we all meet at home in the morning."

PUPILS IN ATTENDANCE AT CLOSING JUNE 22, 1923

BOYS

Lawson F. Mullins	Ronald M. Noseworthy
Stanley D. Handrig	Robert R. Thornhill
Frank R. Forsey	Ira G. Harris
Gilbert R. Tibbo	Harvey Keating
Richard B. Noseworthy	S. Noel Tibbo
Clarence W. Handrigan	Ambrose F. Matthews
Walter C. P. Forsey	John H. Skinner
Claude Matthews	Allan D. Snook
William H. Grandy	Wilson Bellman
Matthew English	

GIRLS

Myrtle Piercy	Ellen M. Evans
Violet Evans	Jessie J. Baker
Frances I. Evans	Georgie R. Hyde
Beatrice M. G. Laurence	Dorothy M. Camp
Margaret J. Patten	Louisa L. Parsons
Rebecca H. Rogers	Rose L. Penwell
Emma C. French	Henrietta Rogers
Maggie B. Royal	Jessie E. Fox
Maria Poole	Martha Bambury
Emeline Noseworthy	Maud Thornhill
Bessie Piercy	

SCHOOL BOARD

Rev. Charles Howse, Chairman
S. Merrill Libbo, Esq., Secretary
H. G. Harris, Esq., Treasurer

Robert F. Dunford, Esq.	F. G. Tibbo, Esq.
A. F. Buffett, Esq.	J. Rose, Esq.
A. F. Foote, Esq.	G. E. Tibbo, Esq.

John Burke High School regularly produces a yearbook with names and photos of its students. Early John Burke yearbooks go back to 1964; so Grand Bank school yearbooks seem to be a convention that goes back at least thirty years. Thirty years? Maria Forsey, who taught in the United Church Academy (Methodist College) after the turn of the century, produced annual pamphlets with pictures and names.

This reproduction of a page from the school yearbook of 1922-23 shows nineteen boys and twenty-one girls registered. It is dedicated to Max and Robert Thornhill: Max, a victim of diphtheria, and Robert died in 1923 from a head injury. Their father John Thornhill, a schooner master and owner, named a vessel *Robert Max* after his two boys.

The Salvation Army School as it appeared in 1961, the last year it housed Kindergarten to Grade Eleven.

Chapter Five   Story Five

The Beach Bonnet: Its Heritage

As a type of uniform attire or costume for Grand Bank's tri-centennial and Come Home Year festivities in 1987, many businesses adopted as a "costume" the beach bonnet and long dress once worn by beach women of the town. The apparel became a frequent sight around Grand Bank that summer. As a preamble or introduction to the idea of using the beach bonnet as a town promotional item, I talked to Harriet Welsh and wrote this piece (with some subsequent information added) which appeared in the *Southern Gazette* on May 20, 1987.

When the economy of Grand Bank relied on the curing of salt fish between 1880 and 1950, the town's prosperity depended not only on the bank fishermen, but also on the working women —the beach women. Each woman had her sunbonnet, long dress, and white apron ready for work when she looked for a "chance" on some merchant's beach making fish. The term used by local workers was "making fish" since the wet, heavy salted cod was made or turned into a dry product ready for the foreign markets of Spain, Portugal or Greece. In those days, many women worked long hours for little pay. The few dollars coming in supplemented a meagre income earned by the men at sea. In terms of real dollars, income was low or non-existent dependant upon the credit accumulated at the company store or shop.

At the end of the fishing season when accounts were

Receipt for goods bought at S. Piercy's business illustrates the credit system. It reads: Balance $32.58; Oct. 18th 1 lb. of Tip Tops 20 cents; 1 lb. peanut butter 25 cents; Oct 21st 1 shirt 40 cents; 1 pair bloomers 50 cents; 1 brassier 38 cents; Nov. 27th cash to balance $10.00. Total owed $44.31; Credit by making fish $56.77
When this worker/customer "settled up" in the fall, Piercy had to pay him/her $12.46.
One man took a casual approach to the problem. When summoned by the local merchant to his store, he was asked, "What are you going to do about your bills?"
"Well, it's this way," he said. "The big bills I can't pay and the little ones I don't bother with."

settled up, many families who depended on the fishery for a living owed the merchant money especially if the fishing voyage had been poor.

Harriet Welsh, better known in Grand Bank as 'Sis' Welsh, worked on the beaches with the generation of the 1940s working women. Like hundreds preceding her, she

Date on the back of this postcard reads July 5, 1911. There are large fish stores on the beach (right) and wooden fish flakes on Trimm's Beach. The round rock-like features, centre, are piles of drying fish.

Dr. Nigel Rusted, the chief medical officer of the floating hospital ship *Lady Anderson* assigned to the South Coast in 1935, wrote a book of his experiences, *It's Devil Deep Down There*. In the spring of 1935 he toured the coast by boat and said of Grand Bank: "As we passed Grand Bank, we saw on the beach what appeared to be a large flock of sheep, but with our binoculars we found it was numerous large piles of fish covered with white canvas. This was the work of (women) whose source of income was to look after the drying of fish caught by the bankers. Ashore I noted that the forearm muscles of the women rippled as those of men."

175

spread fish "face up" in the morning and turned it "back up" in the evening. Although her tenure was a short one in comparison to those who spent twenty to thirty years making fish, Sis has vivid memories of her days on the Patten, Buffett, or Piercy beaches. The beaches are gone now; only remnants of the vast cobblestone beaches remain, barely visible near the Seamen's Museum, opposite Malcolm Boulevard, on Marine Drive and surrounding Mistywave Crescent.

Sis recalls her times at the beaches which was her first job at age fourteen when she earned twenty-eight dollars, enough to buy her first pair of eye glasses; and she remembers her toils. A season's work lasted from April to November. Working from Monday to Saturday, the women started at seven am and kept spreading, turning, or piling fish until dusk. If there was much fish, they often started at sun-up, around five or six am, and worked after dark; often using flashlights.

"On Patten's beach where I worked," Sis recalls, "there were over fifty women, ten or eleven in a group and their bosses — Betty Shute, Sarah Lovell, Dinah Lee, Kitty Parsons, Edie Breon and others. We had a daily routine."

Work included unloading the saltbulk fish brought to the beach, spreading, and faggoting (bundling) the drying product. Each day around dinner time, fish had to be turned over. About three o'clock in the evening, the women took up 'yaffles' or armfuls of fish for piling into a large round pile much like a 'pook' of hay.

Fish drying beaches had been used in Grand Bank probably since the inception of the off-shore fishery, but by the 1900s the successful banks fishery meant the creation of additional beaches. Merchants employed men, usually some of the crew from a schooner in the off-season, to build or extend a drying beach. Cobblestones were hauled by horse and cart from Admiral's Cove or L'Anse au Paul onto existent land.

Today these beaches — Trimm's Beach, Buffett's Beach and others —are litter-strewn, but in Sis's time the beaches and rocks for drying fish would be spotless. "There was no garbage from people's homes because there was no left-over material. Everything suitable that could be burned would be burned; there were no chip bags or pop cans. People carried bread with molasses and tea in a bottle for a 'mug up', so there was nothing to throw down to make a mess."

Sis recalled one strange event from her working days on the beach. Through some source, now long forgotten, the women of the community learned that this day was the end of the world, and that the final hour of existence was at three o'clock in the evening. Dinah Lee, the piling boss, convinced them not to work. There was no sense piling fish or spreading it in the sun to dry if the world was in its final hours. Somehow, foreman George Tibbo heard the news and, in a rage, strode onto the beach ordering them back to work in no uncertain terms. Sis and her would-be rebels worked twice as hard that evening and well up into the night using flashlights to see and made up for lost time. These were the hard times, but to Sis it was the good old days.

Each group of women would be responsible for the fish of one schooner, and the boss women would be in charge of timing the various stages. She had to judge weather conditions so that the fish was neither burnt by the sun nor soaked by rain. If rain threatened, fish was piled into a large stack or "pook" and covered with a canvas sail. Work on the beaches was not continuous; there were frequent breaks daily while the fish dried. Then the women could dash home and fulfil other domestic obligations. Sis recalled the hard work: "We used to come off the beach and go up in the garden and spread hay and take it up. And then we have to on to the beach perhaps around two or three o'clock. We'd take up the fish and then we came back and go at the hay again. And then, like when you had a lot of children, it was washing everyday."

In essence, the women who cured the fish brought in from the Newfoundland banks made the system profitable. The prosperity of salt fish business houses depended on the beach women's industriousness. Harold Horwood, in his book *Newfoundland*, tells of the Grand Bank merchant who gave praise — even if he couldn't offer higher wages — to the women.

The merchant remarked, "All the bank fish was made by women, every cod's tail, and a hundred women might share a thousand dollars between them. It was a wonder that kind of thing lasted as long as it did. All that had to happen was for the women to refuse to go on the beach day after day for that backbreaking work and the bank fishery would have come to an end right there... But it's over now, of course. Today, you've got to stand in line in Grand Bank to buy a salt fish when a bit of it arrives at the store."

Sis was part of that economy for five years until she married at age nineteen. By then, 1946, wages had risen to around seventy-five dollars a season. But tragedy, as it often does in a seafaring town, touched Sis. On April 29, 1948, when the motor vessel *Administratrix* was cut down off Cape

Trimm's Beach in the 1940s facing east. A "pook" of fish is on the left; some fish are spread near it. A group of women prepares to spread the fish 'heads and tails' on the cobblestone beach. The house in the background, which still stands, was once owned by Captain George Lee. At least two other buildings once stood there: the homes of William Trimm, and Hester Belbin.

The area was known, in later years at least, as Trimm's Beach because Trimm families lived near there. Archie Trimm, lost on the *Alsatian* in 1935, resided with his father, William, at the end of present-day Beach Road. William Trimm had an extensive garden, the land of which has since been re-claimed by the sea. Courtesy Seamen's Museum

Race by the Norwegian freighter *Lovdal*, she learned her husband, Arch Rose, was among the five crewmen lost. Sis was left with an infant baby.

Those who wore the beach bonnet and long dress on the fish drying beaches remember their past work experiences which were governed by backbreaking labour and long hours. At home, housework was long and hard, but their additional beachwork represented extra income. Thinking back on that time, workers like Sis recall the beach bonnets with a mixture of sadness for an era which can never come back, but they also remember with an honest evaluation of those years as good and bad.

Chapter Five   Story Six

☰lar ⸭lemorials: Keeping the ⸭lemory Alive

One of the most impressive monuments to be found on the Burin Peninsula stands on a grassy plot of land that separates College Street from Main Street in Grand Bank. The bronze soldier and the epitaph are dedicated to the memory of Grand Bank men who made the supreme sacrifice in World War One. The names of the war victims are written on the bronze tablets, and those of the WWII are on tablets in the Memorial Library.

Prior to the Great War, Newfoundland had not been extensively involved in war except for the several battles between the French and English fought on Newfoundland soil centuries before. There had been an Imperial Garrison in St. John's, but it was withdrawn in 1870 and thereafter, as it had done for centuries, the Royal Navy kept a watchful eye upon the island's defence. When war broke out in 1914, the only military establishment in Newfoundland consisted of a naval reserve made up of fishermen who had received four weeks of training each year. They responded to the call to a man.

At the same time, the British Government accepted the undertaking of the Newfoundland Government to recruit and maintain an infantry regiment for overseas service. In all, more than six thousand young men were accepted while

180

another two thousand enlisted for naval service. Both forces served with great gallantry and suffered heavy casualties. The Newfoundland Regiment distinguished itself at Gallipoli and served with epic heroism in France where twenty per cent of all who served were lost in action or died of wounds. Of the seventy-eight Grand Bank men who went overseas to serve, fourteen (or nineteen percent) were killed.

In the 1920s, War Memorials, dedicated by a proud and sorrowful people to the enduring memory of slain Newfoundlanders, were erected in many Newfoundland towns such as Carbonear, Fortune, St. John's, and Harbour Grace.

The campaign to erect a war memorial in Grand Bank was spearheaded by the Loyal Orange Association. On December 17, 1918, a little over a month after the war ended, the following men served on a committee to obtain a monument for the war dead: Joseph Hiscock, Joseph Evans,(Jr.), Joshua Belbin, Bert Riggs, J.M. Howell, and Henry Lee. Before the committee's work was finished Henry Lee was drowned on the *Jean and Mary* on December 5, 1921.

By 1923, basic groundwork was finished. A telegram sent on March 23 of that year to Charles Forward, who at the time was in Toronto, stated:

Memorial committee want you to look up bronze soldier statue that can be erected in local concrete base. Statue of Newfoundland Infantry Man and life size. Also bronze tablet to set in front concrete base to subscribe names of dead. Have manufacturers send diagram designs, statue and tablet with prices not to exceed two thousand dollars.

Several days later the committee decided to order the monument. J.G. Tickell and Sons on King Street in Toronto sent the statue to North Sydney on August 14, 1923, in care of Salter and Sons. The schooner *Millie Louise* brought the statue from North Sydney to Grand Bank.

G.& A. Buffett donated the land on which the monument first stood, a little to the northwest of the present day Memo-

Courtesy Rosalind Downey

Grand Bank War Memorial. On January 23, 1995 the flags flew at half-staff to mark the passing of Frances (Drake) Breon. She was one of two Grand Bank women who had served in the Armed Forces (Air Force) in World War II; the other was Olive Warren.

rial Library. The concrete base was made by a local carpenter and lodge member, William Courtney. By 1924 the war memorial was ready for unveiling. Sir Richard Squires, a former Prime Minister of Newfoundland, had unveiled other monuments throughout the country, but he was unavailable. Although the exact day and details are not recorded, it is likely J.B. Patten and/or the resident magistrate did the unveiling. The bronze statue was valued at $1,750.00 and the tablets two hundred dollars which was within the budget. Up to 1954 sisters of the LOBA looked after the monument. Since that time, maintenance has been done by the Royal Canadian Legion or the Grand Bank Town Council.

Fourteen names are inscribed on the war memorial tablets:

George M. Clarke, Corporal in the Newfoundland Regiment and son of merchant Lionel B. and Sarah Clarke. George was killed in the trenches in France April 18, 1918, and buried in Neuve-Eglise. He was twenty.

Andrew Douglas, Newfoundland Regiment. This name is inscribed in error and should read Aaron (Andrew was his father's name). Aaron Keeping Douglas, age twenty-four, lived on Brunette Island and came to Grand Bank to enlist. Hostilities in Europe where Aaron served had ended, but on September 29, 1918, an errant or discarded shell in or near a mess hall exploded killing him and several others. He is buried at Kieberg Ridge.

In January 1919, when the Grand Bank Orange Lodge solicited funds to erect the monument, they canvassed Douglas' hometown of Brunette, as well as Grand Beach, the hometown of Albert Follett.

Albert Follett, Newfoundland Regiment, was born in 1896 at Grand Beach, enlisted in Grand Bank and died in Europe April 14, 1917. He is buried at Monchey-le Preux. Albert had six brothers: William

T., Garfield, George, who became a well-known fishing captain in Grand Bank, Edward "Ned," lost on the *John McRea* in December 1917, Charles, lost on the *Jean and Mary* in December 1921, and Walter, lost on the *General Plumer* in March 1930.

George Forsey, Canadian Service, son of Joshua and Hester Forsey.

Charles F. Hickman, Canadian Service, son of James and Harriet Hickman. Charles died at Vimy Ridge on April 12, 1917, while bringing in a wounded comrade to hospital services. Age twenty-three.

Wilson J. Hickman, Canadian Service, brother of Ralph Hickman who once resided on Church Street.

Edward Nicholle, born in 1892, received his early education at the Methodist Academy and was a salesman by profession. He enlisted in the Royal Newfoundland Regiment at the outbreak of hostilities, rose to the rank of Company Quarter Master Sergeant and was mentioned with distinction in Field Marshall Earl Haig's despatches from the front lines. Nicholle was killed in action at Broembeek, Belgium on October 10, 1917. He was a member of Grand Bank Masonic Lodge.

Reuben Osborne, Newfoundland Regiment, brother of blacksmith Wilson Osborne. Osborne was thirteen years old when he and his parents came to live in Grand Bank from Hoop Cove, Fortune Bay in 1911. He was killed in action on September 28, 1918; age twenty.

Eli Patten, Canadian Service, Corporal in the 102nd Battalion, became the first Grand Bank causality of the Great War. Older brother of Grace (Patten) Sparkes, Eli was born in 1893. He finished school in the Methodist Academy, completed a business course in a Toronto college and worked in the Maple Leaf Milling Company as an accountant. He enlisted in 1915, rose to Corporal, but in late August 1916, while on a reconnaissance mission, he was hit by a sniper's bullet and died September 1st. He was 23.

When word of his death reached the Patten home in Grand Bank, younger members of his family pulled down blinds to show their grief. Eli's father, John B. Patten, asked to have them put back up saying that it was dark enough around the home already.

Evan W. Pugh, Canadian Service, 85th Battalion. Pugh enlisted October 2, 1917, and was killed August 22, 1918. For many years his stone, purchased by grandparents John and Matilda Matthews, was attached to a wall in the Grand Bank Salvation Army Citadel until it was relocated several years ago to the S.A. Cemetery.

Lyman Stoodley, private in the Newfoundland Regiment. Stoodley was killed in France on August 18, 1917, age twenty. A memorial stone dedicated to him is mounted in the vestibule next to the choir room in the Grand Bank United Church.

Joseph Thorne, Newfoundland Regiment, number 3149, was a private who died on December 19, 1917, age nineteen.

Robert Wooden age twenty-one, Canadian Service, was killed while driving a tank at Bramshott, England, on October 28, 1918, just two weeks before the war ended. His brother George, also a soldier in the Great War, survived to return home, but died in the 1918-1919 Spanish influenza epidemic that followed the war.

Benjamin Woundy, at age twenty-three and a cadet in the Royal Air Force, Woundy died overseas November 29, 1918, from the Spanish influenza epidemic. He was the son of James and Elizabeth (Lawrence) Woundy.

World War II

An equal number of names, fourteen, as on the war memorial are inscribed on bronze tablets in the Grand Bank Memorial Library:

Bertram Baker, Newfoundland Regiment. On the night of December 12, 1942, Private Bert Baker, identification number 955, was in the Knights of Columbus Hostel in St. John's. The hostel's auditorium was full of servicemen and civilians attending a Barn Dance when a fire broke out. Ninety-nine people were burned to death or killed. Baker was one of the victims.

William Barnes, Merchant Navy, unmarried brother of Jacob, George and Samuel Barnes. According to most sources he left home, joined a ship, probably in a convoy, and was lost at sea. The date and circumstances are obscure.

James Brown, Merchant Navy. Brown was born in Baine Harbour, Placentia Bay, but lived in Grand Bank practically all his life. When he married a girl from Little Bay East, he moved there.

In 1943, James Brown was employed on a foreign-going steamer running from Barbados to Newfoundland. Brown and a companion were standing on the stern of the ship when both were washed overboard. Their caps were seen floating on the water, but both men disappeared. He was survived by three children; now living in Ontario. His wife had predeceased him.

John Edwin Cornish, Royal Artillery. He saw his final action in the battle of Monte Casino in the Italian campaign. When an enemy mortar hit his artillery piece, Cornish was struck with debris and shrapnel. He died instantly. Edwin Street on Grand Bank's Riverside East is named for Gunner Edwin Cornish.

Thomas E. Evans, Merchant Navy. After his schooner *Alhambia* sank on a transatlantic voyage, Captain Tom Evans signed on the British merchant ship, *Claudius Magus*. He died a natural death on December 5, 1942 and was buried in Blyth, England, on the shores of the North Sea near North Shields. He was thirty-seven and was survived by his wife and four children — Janet, Thomas, Margaret, and John. Evans had been a veteran seaman and captain all his life sailing on the *R.L. Borden* and had been shipmates with Captain Charles Anstey.

Albert Follett, Sergeant Royal Air Force. Albert enlisted at Halifax in 1942, trained in Quebec as an aircraft tail gunner and crossed overseas on the *Queen Mary* in August. On November 7, 1943, while returning to home base in England after a sortie with German aircraft, his plane was shot down. He is interred at Oxford, England. Age twenty. His uncle, Albert Follett, had lost his life in World War One.

Reginald Grandy, Royal Navy, was born in Garnish on July 22, 1919, but resided in Grand Bank. A leading seaman, No. V349, Grandy was reported missing when the destroyer HMCS *St. Croix* was torpedoed by an enemy U-boat on September 20, 1943. Son of Mr. Hubert and Edith Grandy. Age twenty-four.

Cecil Hardiman, Merchant Navy. On Wednesday, May 19, 1943, Cecil Hardiman, Grand Bank; and four men from Belleoram, mate Arthur Holmans; his twenty-year-old son Alexander; John Hillier and Clarence Mullins and five other seamen were forced from the Canadian barquentine *Angelus* by a German sub. *Angelus*, bringing supplies from the West Indies to Canada, was sunk; the ten crew put into a lifeboat. In the five day row to land, only two men survived, Arthur Holmans and Walter Boudreau of New Brunswick. Hardiman died, probably of exposure, on May 23. He was twenty-five.

Hubert Hawse, Royal Navy, son of Elias Hawse. Hawse's ship, probably the *King George V*, was torpedoed in the Atlantic and he died in action. His body was recovered and is buried in Halifax. At that time it was considered too expensive to ship his body home.

George Lambert, Newfoundland Regiment. Private Lambert, number 995, also died in the 1942 K of C Hostel fire with his friend Bert Baker (above). There was no satisfactory explanation to the cause of the fire although German sabotage was widely speculated. As well as military personnel, several civilians perished in the fire including two women from Grand Bank — Emma Hickman and Rose Thorne.

Edward Lee, Merchant Navy, age forty, was an able seaman on the British steamship *T.J. Williams* when she was torpedoed September 19, 1941. He and thirty-nine other crew left Sydney, Nova Scotia, in convoy to England when a U-boat torpedoed the *Williams*. The ship was abandoned and Edward Lee and James Monster of Fortune were two of the seventeen who lost their lives. Lee left a wife and three children, Emma, Henry and six-month-old Eli.

Leslie Rogers, Merchant Navy. On September 6, 1942, enemy U-boat 514, intercepted the Grand Bank schooner *Helen Forsey* between Bermuda and Newfoundland. As the Germans shelled the unarmed vessel two men, Arthur Bond of Frenchman's Cove and Leslie Rogers of Grand Bank, were struck by shrapnel or debris and died on the deck of the *Helen Forsey*. Rogers was seventeen.

Captain John Ralph and his remaining crew, Jacob Penwell, William Keating, and Thomas Bolt, all of Grand Bank, escaped and rowed to Bermuda.

Henry (Harry) Thornhill, Merchant Navy, was asked to navigate a Portuguese vessel, *Catalina*, from Fortune to St. John's. There *Catalina* would pick up her sick captain, but Harry Thornhill and the Portuguese steamer never made it. According to enemy records examined after the war, a German sub intercepted the vessel, which was sailing in enemy waters and carrying goods from an enemy nation. *Catalina* went down with no survivors.

During the first World War Thornhill spent two years in Portugal as a fish purchasing agent. He spoke Portuguese fluently, and when schooners from Portugal came to Grand Bank, he often invited the crew to his home. At the time of his death at age fifty-six, he owned and ran a small business on Hickman Street. Thornhill was a veteran of the sea and had captained fishing vessels such as *Christie and Eleanor*, a one hundred forty-three ton banking schooner owned by William Forsey, and the schooner *Dorothy P. Sarty* of Fortune. (See picture in Chapter 3 Story 10)

Carl R. Tibbo, A flight Sergeant in the Royal Air Force, son of George Tibbo and Jennie (Bell) Tibbo, was killed in action 1944.

Other young men, non-residents, who worked and lived in Grand Bank were quick to answer Newfoundland's call to arms in both wars. Bill Norman, a bank clerk in Grand Bank, was one of these.

Born in Bay Roberts on July 14, 1894, William H. Norman attended Bay Roberts Academy and worked as a clerk in two Bay Roberts grocery stores — C. & A. Dawe and John Parsons. In 1913, he joined the Bank of Nova Scotia transferring to St. John's and then to Grand Bank in 1915.

In December 1915, he resigned from the Grand Bank branch to enlist for overseas duty. He sailed from Newfoundland as a Lance Corporal in the 1st Newfoundland Regiment, but was killed in action on April 15, 1917. During his year in Grand Bank, he was

GVI   RI

This scroll commemorates

E. Lee, Able Seaman
Merchant Navy

held in honour as one who served King and Country in the world war of 1939-1945 and gave his life to save mankind from tyranny. May his sacrifice help to bring the peace and freedom for which he died.

Commemorative scroll from the Royal Family for Edward Lee, casualty of World War II. Courtesy Henry Lee

well known around the town and very popular with bank
customers.

Photo courtesy of RCL and Rosalind Downey

Around 1949, Grand Bank formed Branch Twenty-Four of the Royal Canadian Legion. First meetings
were held in a school and later in the basement of the library. In time the legionnaires purchased an
old salt store, pulled it to Evans Street and through volunteer labour transformed it into the town's legion
hall.
First members and executive, above are: (front row l-r) George Bungay, George Riggs, Curtis Forsey,
visiting official Lieutenant Governor Sir Leonard Outerbridge, Newton Blagdon, John Ben Anstey, and
Thomas Burfitt; (back row l-r) Rudell Nurse, George Brown, Gordon Weymouth, Samuel Anstey,
George Nurse, and Max Matthews. All were veterans of World War One or Two.

Chapter Five   Story Seven

The Grandy Dory on Canada's Quarter

When I first saw the set of Canadian quarters issued in 1992 and realized the Grand Bank-built dory was used to symbolize and represent Newfoundland, I thought it would be important to talk to the men who built the fine little craft and to record details of its construction.

This account appeared in Spring 1996 issue of *The Newfoundland Quarterly* as "The Dory on the Coin."

In 1992, as part of Canada's celebration of its one hundred twenty-fifth anniversary, a commemorative set of Canadian coins of the quarter denomination was issued. The coin for each province and territory had its own distinctive design based on natural landscapes, cultural or historical structures; for example Prince Edward Island featured Cavendish Beach; Nova Scotia, Peggy's Cove Lighthouse; Manitoba, Fort Garry and the N.W. Territories' quarter showed an inukshuk.

The Newfoundland coin, designed by Mount Pearl artist/designer Christopher Newhook, was released in March 1992 and shows the Grandy dory, one of the most commonly used small craft in Newfoundland. The Grandy craftsmen in Grand Bank manufactured over three thousand dories in a period of about thirty years, 1940-1970. To put that number in perspective, it would have been sufficient to outfit approximately three hundred schooners at ten dories each or to employ 6000 inshore fishermen, two to a boat.

188 Vignettes of a Small Town

One of the first writers to recognize the unique design of the Grandy dory was author Otto Kelland who, in his book *Dories and Dorymen*, wrote, "The Grandy was always recognized as a good carrier and an excellent seaboat...the builders would make instructors, par excellence, in the rather intricate business of dory building." It was Kelland who first researched Grandy's method, the numbers of dories built and appended the name "Grandy" onto the unique style as he wrote about dories and dorymen in the 1970s.

Dories had been built in Grand Bank since the turn of the century when the bank fishery was in its heyday. Production could not keep up with demand and dories were brought to the South Coast from Lunenburg and Shelburne, Nova Scotia. For example, the *Shelburne Gazette and Coast Guard* of January 16, 1919, lists the cargo of the recently-launched tern schooner *General Smuts*, loaded for her initial trip from Shelburne to Grand Bank, as: lumber from the McGill Shipbuilding Company, spars from J.M. Jordan spar yard, two engines from Etherington's Gas Engines Ltd. and several boats from the John Etherington dory shop.

In addition to the importation of scores of dories, many were manufactured in Grand Bank. In the early 1900s shipwright Eli Harris, the brother of businessman Samuel Harris of Harris Export Company, operated a dory factory near the waterfront on a site which is today the parking lot between the Bank of Nova Scotia and the former Grand Bank Fisheries Building. When Harris closed out his shop in the 1930s, G.& A. Buffett Ltd. continued the business and contracted to sell dories to fishermen along the South Coast and other parts of Newfoundland.

One of the four men hired by G.& A. Buffett to build dories was Steven Leonard Grandy (1884-1960) who was born in Garnish and moved to Grand Bank as a young man. Working under contract Steven Leonard sold a dory for twelve dollars which amounted to three dollars for each of the four workers. During his tenure as builder with Buffett, Grandy studied the design of other dories and gradually perfected his own idea of a craft suitable for Newfoundland's weather conditions and fishing industry. As a testament to its seaworthiness and its ability to stay afloat on the wild Atlantic, some fishermen claimed it had "three bottoms."

In time Grandy opened his own workshop and with his three sons, Max, Roy, Leonard, and another skilled carpenter, Frank Riggs, the Grandy dories were built in a shed on Riverside West and later in Patten's store (which once stood between Buffett's coal shed and the Grand Bank bridge). Most Grandy dories were made in the latter location but, in later years when demand lessened, the operation relocated to Point of Beach on the eastern side of the harbour. As the dory-building industry came to a close, several were built in Grandy's shipyard in Fortune.

In the nineteen forties and fifties, with the hook and line, banking schooner enterprise still operating around Newfoundland, the demand for dependable dories continued. The Grandy dory workshop met a production quota of two dories per day; each sold for ninety dollars. The dory builders worked six days a week for ten hours a day, from seven am to six pm with an hour off for dinner.

When an order came for a banker's fleet or a set of eleven or twelve dories, the men would spend a week or so getting material or stock together for twice that number. By the time the workers were ready to start, other orders would have come in and excess dories were quickly sold to inshore fishermen.

The method of dory assembly was as follows: they would make up around twenty-five dory bottoms — generally fifteen foot long, thirty-seven inches wide, one inch thick — and stack them in the workshop. The four planks for bottom pieces (of white pine) were shaped, clamped together and nailed with strips. All other timber necessary for manufacture was then sawn and dressed: twenty-five sets of gunnels, cappings, and timbers; twenty-five counters, counterpieces, stem pieces and so on. These were sawn out using a mould and stacked on racks overhead in the work area.

After all preparatory work was complete, the workers could pull down each part, board or plank as needed from

the port and starboard side and, using galvanized boat nails
or clinch nails, the craft was nailed together. When finished,
the dory was turned bottom up in order to finish nailing the
bottom and to cut off any excess wood. Occasionally a piece
of board would crack, but work went on. One of the workers
would return after supper to take out the defective wood and
replace it.

Daily two dories were pulled up by block and tackle to an
overhead storage space to a painter (Charlie Royle for many
years) who gave each craft two coats of yellow paint with a
trim of green on the gunnels. During peak production, scores
of dories were turned out; in one season, from November to
March, one hundred fifty-three were produced. Throughout
the remaining months others were built, but at a slower rate.
The carpenters, also first-rate small boat builders and repair

Roy Grandy standing by one of his Grandy dories. By the late 1940s the Grandy workplace produced
fewer banking dories, but more inshore and motor dories. These took longer to build because size and
special requirements varied.

men, were frequently employed in the local ship building/repair business.

Quality of workmanship by the Grandys was high and no faulty material went into the dory. Generally Bay d'Espoir timber was used, but if a particular piece of timber was doubtful, one of the workers would test it out. In the work shed was a high wooden stool with a length of railway iron on it; the questionable piece would be swung against the iron. If the board broke or cracked, it was thrown into the scrap heap.

The Grandy dory is not radically different from any other type of dory. Owing to the way they were nested or fitted into each other on the deck of a schooner, each small boat, of necessity, had to have the same flare and measurements. Based on what was needed by local fishermen, the Grandy dory evolved from the Shelburne and Lunenburg-style dories produced by Eli Harris' factory in Grand Bank in the 1920-30s.

In 1995, when I discussed the uniqueness of the Grandy dory with Otto Kelland (for years he made and still makes model dories and analyzed small craft construction), he claimed it had "the same bottom length as the Shelburne or Lunenburger, the rake fore and aft is similar, but the Grandy dory has a raised gunnel forward and an extended rubber on the banking style dory." The rubber, or rub rail, bevelled on the lower side, was on the outside of the gunnel to protect the hull when the bobbing dory was being unloaded near a schooner.

Today the large-scale manufacture of inshore and banking dory, as featured on the 1992 Canadian quarter, is no more. Like the talents of shipbuilding once possessed by our great-grandfathers, the craftsmanship of turning out dories is fast becoming a lost skill. To see or photograph a Grandy dory, one must go to the South Coast Seamen's Museum where a single representative of a by-gone era sits complete with its small sail, oars and various pieces of bank fishing technology. Apart from that one, and the design on the coin, few can be seen today.

Several large dories being towed by Steven Leonard Grandy's motor boat to the coastal steamer in Grand Bank harbour. Designed for the inshore cod trap fishery, this batch is a special order headed for Rose Blanche. The frames (or bins) that can be seen on the side of each dory number six or seven, higher than the usual five. This photo faces east showing, in the background, the inshore fishermens' stages and the fish-drying beaches of Trimm's Beach.

Chapter Five　　Story Eight

The E.J. Pratt Connection

> While E.J. Pratt was not born in Grand Bank, it is intriguing to think of the areas, roads, church and homes he frequented as a young man when he lived in and visited this town.

Rev. John Pratt, the father of poet E.J. Pratt, like most Methodist parsons, was assigned to several parishes throughout Newfoundland including Bonavista; Brigus; Western Bay; Fortune, 1895-1898; Bay Roberts, 1898-1900; Grand Bank, 1900-1904. John and Fanny Pratt had eight children — Charlotte, Floss, William, Arthur, James, Calvert, Nellie, and Edwin John who was born in 1882 in Western Bay, Newfoundland.

E.J. Pratt grew up in several Newfoundland outports. His years in Grand Bank and Fortune, as described in David Pitt's book *E.J. Pratt The Truant Years* (1984), were different from the more contented times he had spent in St. John's and in other Newfoundland outports. Compared to St. John's and Carbonear, Fortune was smaller, more isolated and a typical sea-governed outport. In 1895-98 Fortune, like Grand Bank its neighbour four miles further east, was "forever associated with constantly recurring disasters at sea." As Pitt relates it, clergyman John Pratt often had the hard task of breaking the news when crews were lost at sea.

During his father's tenure in Fortune, E.J. Pratt was thirteen years old. In the summer months, like most outport boys, he spent many hours swimming and diving from the wharf and schooners. He is known to have, at least once, climbed up a schooner's rigging, stood on the crosstrees and dived or jumped into the harbour. According to Pitt:

> Pratt's last year at school in Fortune (1896-7) was, it seems, a troublesome one for both him and his parents...He was unable to settle down to his studies, and was soon getting into problems with the schoolmaster, 'a bit of a martinet'. It is not unlikely that, a precocious boy, he was simply bored by the repetitious, uninspired academic routine, and the dreary textbooks and subject-matter fed him day after day.

By the time Rev. Pratt was posted to Grand Bank in 1900, Edwin was eighteen years old, finished grade school and had been working in a drapery store in St. John's. After his parents moved to Grand Bank, E.J. Pratt went there for a short time. Pitt claims that what happened at Grand Bank "during that time is of crucial importance" to Pratt's life. E.J. Pratt decided to commit himself to the Methodist ministry. His work in a St. John's store was not to his liking, and in September, he attended the St. John's Methodist College.

In the summer of 1903, E.J. Pratt again came to Grand Bank to visit his parents. According to his sister, Floss, it was at Grand Bank, with his father in the audience, that E.J. Pratt gave his first sermon. At the time of E.J.'s visit to Grand Bank, his father was very sick and died the next year. That fall, Pratt returned to his teaching position at Morton's Harbour.

When his father passed away in March 1904, E.J. could not reach Grand Bank in time to attend the funeral service but travelled to St. John's to be present at the burial.

Pratt again visited the Burin Peninsula in 1925; by then he was a professor in Victoria College, Toronto, and was establishing himself as a successful poet. According to Pitt, he came to see a long-time friend Chester Harris, an amateur

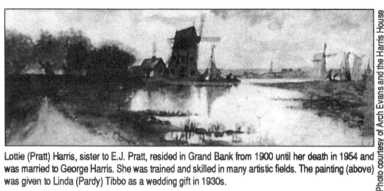

Photo courtesy of Arch Evans and the Harris House

Lottie (Pratt) Harris, sister to E.J. Pratt, resided in Grand Bank from 1900 until her death in 1954 and was married to George Harris. She was trained and skilled in many artistic fields. The painting (above) was given to Linda (Pardy) Tibbo as a wedding gift in 1930s.

poet and a medical doctor practising in Marystown. Chester Harris' brother, George, had married E.J. Pratt's sister Charlotte (Lottie). Lottie and her husband resided in Grand Bank on Water Street in what is now the George C. Harris Heritage House. (See Chapter 2, Story 6)

In 1900 Rev. John Pratt would have preached (and the single sermon given by E.J.) in the church left which was built in 1876. Its replacement (right) was constructed in 1964-5. John and Tillie Stoodley's peak-roofed house is dwarfed between the two. The long two-storey house, centre, was that of J.B. and Elizabeth Patten[1].

Endnote:

1. Although I digress a little from E.J. Pratt, yet I must for this person is a unique artist in her own right.

One of J.B. and Elizabeth's daughters was Grace (Patten) Sparkes, born in Grand Bank in 1908. She has had a long and interesting career in various fields in Newfoundland and married dentist Gerry Sparkes.

After she completing her grade school years in the Grand Bank United Church Academy, she attended university at Mount Allison and Memorial. In the 1930s, she taught school in Twillingate, ran in provincial (the first woman ever to run in Newfoundland provincial politics) and federal elections and in the mid-fifties was a journalist with the *Daily News*. She returned to teaching and finished her career at Prince of Wales Collegiate in 1972.

Grace Sparkes had always been active in charitable organizations and voluntary work. She served on the Board of Regents and chaired committees at Memorial University. She did voluntary work with the Canadian Red Cross and YWCA and was named to the provincial curling hall of fame for her work in organizing curling in high schools. Memorial University awards an entrance scholarship in music in Sparkes' name, and she has two honourary doctor of law degrees, from Memorial and from Mount Allison. Today she lives in St. John's and has played the role of Grandma Walcott on CBC's production of *Tales from Pigeon Inlet*, a popular TV series of the late 1980s and based on Ted Russell's Newfoundland stories.

Chapter Six   Local Tales and Trivia

The Policemen on the Bridge

Nineteen ninety-three marked the fiftieth anniversary of Grand Bank's incorporation as a municipality. Perhaps more momentous were the events that closely following incorporation —a resistance to authority, tantamount to civil disobedience which, in 1944, was so foreign and distasteful to our Newfoundland forebearers.

Civil unrest; all work at a standstill; the general populace, in a foul and ugly mood, gather on the town bridge shouting threats; reports of light poles being sawn down or planned arson of government buildings; jail sentences and fines; over fifty policemen take back the town bridge and parade through the narrow streets in a show of power. This scene doesn't ring true for a small Newfoundland town of fifty years ago; but it was the situation in Grand Bank in the summer of 1944.

In his book *The Newfoundland Constabulary*, author Arthur Fox makes reference to a disturbance at Grand Bank in July 1944. According to Fox, on the fourteenth of July the general population openly expressed their opposition to the newly-formed town council. On that day three Grand Bank business firms and two taximen were convicted in court for breaches of council regulations. Many people became indignant, defied authorities and interfered with the efforts of local police, the Rangers, doing their duty.

Public discontent began on December 28th of the pre-

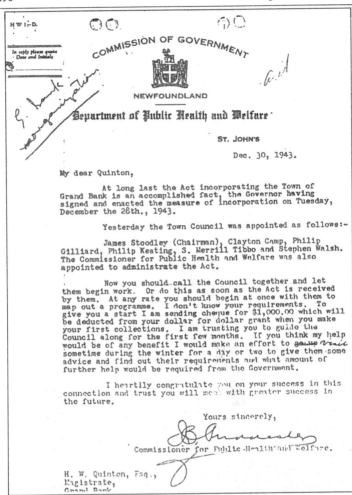

On recommendation from Quinton as outlined in Sir John Puddister's letter, the appointed members of Grand Bank's first council were: James Stoodley, Clayton Camp, Philip Gilliard, Philip Keating, Merrill Tibbo and Stephen Welsh. James Stoodley is an error on Puddister's missive and must refer to Samuel Stoodley who eventually became mayor. Not all of those appointed served. At least one, Steve Welsh, fearing a boycott of his place of business, served for only a week or so.
Puddister's department sent the council a thousand dollar advance in addition to the government's dollar-for-dollar grant.

vious year when Newfoundland's Commission of Government (Division of Public Health and Welfare), supported by a petition from Magistrate Herman Quinton and several townspeople, approved a request to incorporate Grand Bank thus giving the town council legal status.

Many Grand Bankers, for fear of increased taxation, were opposed to the new council. Those who met on street corners and at work not only grumbled and cursed, but openly planned forums of public protest. Some months later a counter-petition signed by one hundred and eleven citizens was sent to Quinton who rejected their petition outright. "Too many signed with no name, merely marked with an X," he said. These people were unable to write.

At this point, the spring of 1944, perhaps a better selling job or a public education campaign would have changed the views of opponents, but it was not to be. Commission of Goverment had decided to use Grand Bank, a self-sufficient and industrious town, as a test case. Local government came in, literally and figuratively, with a shove and a push.

In June, Sir John Puddister, Commissioner of Public Health and Welfare, came to the divided Grand Bank to incorporate it as a municipality. As the June tenth *Evening Telegram* reported, "The antis are still active and the Commissioner's visit, it is understood, is for the purpose of allaying the fears of those who oppose the measure because of the taxation involved."

Fears of the working class townspeople were not put to rest. Several citizens refused to pay town taxes and were cheered by supporters as they paid small fines and left the courthouse. To crush this blatant show of resistance and to assist the two Rangers stationed at Grand Bank (Nathan Penney and another policeman), Sergeant Ian Glendinning, who was also in Grand Bank assessing the situation, requested that a squad of fifty Newfoundland Constabulary be sent from St. John's to restore peace. By July nineteenth, the fifty Constabulary, lead by District Inspector William Case, had arrived along with Ranger reinforcements from St. Lawrence and Lamaline.

Years before, Case had lived in Grand Bank as a young police officer, some of his children were born in Grand Bank. Case enjoyed his term there. Knowing the quiet, law-abiding people, Case couldn't understand why they were rioting and was determined to find out who or what was causing the problem.

Feelings still ran deep among those who felt local government would impose restrictions and levy unnecessary taxes. Many opponents of the council had already refused to pay taxes and, to show their resentment of the arrival of the police, a general strike was called for July twentieth.

In essence, the labourers or general workers were in complete control of the town's economy. Women cured the fish on the beaches, men brought the salt bulk fish to them, carried the dried product to the fish stores where inside workers culled, pressed and packaged the finished product into barrels for overseas markets. Hundreds of quintals of fish representing thousands of dollars and weeks of toil on the fishing grounds were left unattended on the beaches. In those days there were no unions, but the power of the people could not be underestimated. Each worker convinced others that if work stopped, the town and the emerging council would be on the brink of economic collapse.

A group of three well-known businessmen were self-appointed leaders of the opposition — brothers Don and Fred Tibbo, who ran a taxi operation, and Howard Patten. In a gentlemen's agreement, all three planned to resist authority and to refuse to pay any taxes. Both Tibbos were convicted and served a short time in the Burin holding cell. When Don and Fred Tibbo found out Patten had recanted, both immediately paid any fines and were released.

Druggist Patten, a vocal dissenter and community leader, had considerable holdings and thus would be taxed heavily. He promised to deliver an anti-council speech on the Grand Bank bridge around seven o'clock that evening.

Fred Hancock, a young policeman stationed in St. John's, was one of the fifty who arrived on the S.S. *Home*. Now retired from the Constabulary and living near St. John's, he vividly remembers those unsettled days in Grand Bank.

We left St. John's by train, arrived in Argentia and travelled to Grand Bank by steamer. I remember

we went in the harbour in the evening and I
thought the town was a compact place — the
houses were near together and the streets so narrow. Ken Moore and I stayed at Buffett's — Aaron
Buffett's house. Others were all scattered around;
some in the Harris' homes and some at the Thorndyke Hotel. Case stayed in the Ranger's home
(once located near present-day Warren's Store).

By the evening of the nineteenth, news filtered down to
Inspector Case that more trouble was brewing. Case decided
to wait it out for twenty-four hours; perhaps by overnight
cooler heads would prevail. But the next day practically all
work in the fish stores and on the fish curing beaches ceased.
Workers, men and women, milled around the waterfront
and main streets discussing and damming the state of affairs
"higher-ups" in St. John's and Grand Bank had gotten them

Grand Bank Bridge in 1931. First opened for traffic in mid-July, 1927, the bridge had an eighteen-foot
wide roadway, was one hundred seventy-eight foot long with five spans and the whole bridge contained
twenty thousand cubic foot of concrete. Designed by Newfoundland government engineer T. A. Hall,
it was constructed under the supervision of a Mr. Thomas and three Grand Bank men who worked on
it were Clayton Brown, Clyde Riggs and Samuel Riggs.
     This was the second bridge across Grand Bank Brook: up to 1863 or 1864 those who cured fish on
the eastern side crossed the brook in dories. Around 1864 a wooden bridge was built which lasted until
1927 when it was taken down and its wide beams (probably 10" by 10") were used to make the L'Anse
au Loup Bridge.
     In 1927 the bridge in the photo was constructed; in 1983-84 this was demolished for a more modern
structure — the Frederick M. Tessier Bridge.
     The bridge above became the focal point for a clash between those who wanted local government
and its opponents. Inspector Case stood on the concrete railing (left) to address the hundreds of
dissatisfied townspeople. Photo courtesy Neil Locke.

into. After supper nearly everyone in town was along Water Street or on Grand Bank bridge hoping to hear Patten's analysis of the burdens of taxation and the drawbacks of local government.

Meanwhile all that day, Case knew what was about to happen. He assembled his detachment in front of the Sons of Temperance Hall, which once stood a little east of the town library. Hancock was there and remembered special instructions:

> Inspector Case said, 'Now I want everybody in full uniform by the courthouse at six o'clock.' He gave us a speech outside the courthouse on how to manage a mob scene. At seven o'clock that night the people were going to have this meeting on the bridge. We had to turn up with our batons and handcuffs and everything like that. The only ammunition we had was tear gas which, as it turned out, we didn't have to use.

> We marched in pairs up to the bridge and there Case stood on the rail and addressed the crowd. He made a wonderful job of it — he could handle a situation like that — and reproached the people.

> Case, realizing World War Two was still being fought, used patriotism as part of his speech. I don't remember all his words, but in essence he said to the hundreds of people gathered, 'You're helping the enemy by refusing to make fish. The fish is needed; the food is needed to feed our people, our soldiers and sailors overseas. Go back to your homes or your place of businesses. The law of your town's incorporation is passed which says you have to pay your taxes. If you don't you will be punished.

> I will give you ten minutes to leave the area for this is an unlawful assembly. You can't assemble in large numbers without the written consent of the magistrate. It becomes an unlawful assembly so I

require of you to go back to your homes. You have ten minutes and if you don't move willingly, you'll be moved forcibly. Anyone who refuses to go will be arrested.'

Case, Glendinning, Penney, Hancock, Moore, William Costigan, Carter, Lethbridge, Legrow and some fifty other police lined up shoulder to shoulder along the street on both sides leading up to the bridge, securing the roadway and any access to the bridge. When Case's ten minutes expired, he gave the order to move the crowd and clear the streets. Hancock recalled the rush:

> Well, people went in all directions. As we pushed along the road, they'd fill up a front yard there, and fill up a lane or an alleyway somewhere else. Anyway we cleared the roads and we kept marching back and forth. By and by darkness set in. We kept on parading back and forth there until nightfall and people gradually went to their homes.

Businessman Patten, who had refused to pay his taxes and who had planned to lecture on the bridge, was arrested and brought before Magistrate Beaton Abbott the next day. Constable Hancock was there, as were all police gathered in or around the Temperance Hall which had been converted into a temporary courthouse. They would prevent any large crowds from gathering and obstructing justice.

While he stood guard outside the courthouse, Hancock recalled an elderly lady (Maggie Stone), incensed over the arrests and frustrations of those against the council, grabbed up a large rock and threatened to strike one of the policemen. She too was arrested and came before court that day. She refused to answer any questions fired at her by Abbott and would only reply, "I'm not going to say." After a stern lecture Magistrate Abbott fined her $25.00. "I don't care what it is," she fumed. "I'm not paying a cent!"

When Patten's case came up, as Hancock remembered it,

he was fined $70.00 and the magistrate explained to him that this was a fine for disobeying the law and for not paying town taxes. Abbott meaning business, fined Patten, but gave him an alternative — time in jail. Sometime that day, when Patten learned the prison term would be served in St. John's, he recanted, apologized and paid the fine as well as his taxes. He also talked to Mrs. Stone, paid her fine and she was released.

Patten's change of heart and reversal of fortunes was also related to a simple matter of business and the bottom line of a ledger sheet. He was the only druggist in the area served by the Grand Bank Cottage Hospital, an area encompassing the towns from Lamaline to Garnish; thus, his services (and his potential loss of income) were significant.

For two days during the protest the fish had been left unattended on the beaches and during those two days the weather remained sunny and clear. If it had rained, thousands of quintals of fish would have spoiled and the economic losses to several businesses would have been disastrous.

Within a week the tension subsided; work resumed and tardy taxpayers visited the newly-formed council. Most of the constabulary returned to St. John's, but about twenty remained for an extra week or so. Each day around noon they had to go out on patrol until dark. Hancock was one who stayed on after the situation returned to normal.

On a Saturday the Buffett family invited us to go down to their summer home at Famine, outside of

Serious Disturbance In Grand Bank

THE OPPPOSITION that has been facing the Town Council of Grand Bank ever since that South Coast town was incorporated as a municipality last year flared into violence last week when an angry mob interfered with the local Rangers in the performance of their duty.

This is how the newspaper of the day reported the result of the town protest of incorporation.

Grand Bank. Moore and I thought it over. Everything fell quiet: court cases were over, Patten paid his fine and turned over. As I recall Famine was a beautiful place. We also went to Lamaline, down to Piercey's Brook trouting right out near the salt water.

Now while we were in Grand Bank an old gentleman, I think his name was Foote, a retired captain, passed away (July 21). None of us saw him because he was in bed, but he died while we were there. We went to his funeral with all hands marching in procession.

One morning after we were all back in St. John's, we assembled in the drill hall in Fort Townshend. The inspector read us a letter from the townspeople of Grand Bank. It was in appreciation for our services.

Attending the burial services of Thomas Foote and also Sarah Forsey (d. July 23, 1944), became a public gesture which helped reconcile the town towards the intrusion of police, plus the realization of council benefits which convinced the striking workers to go back to work. When outstanding taxes were paid and the newly-appointed council members transacted the town's business, the public expression of dissatisfaction quietly ended.

The first council meeting was held in the Newfoundland Rangers' headquarters, a building which once stood near present-day Warren's Store. The headquarters measured thirty-six feet long and contained three prisoners' cells — suitable for short confinement i.e. those arrested during the council riot. Later the building was purchased by Onslow Brown who sold it to businessman Harold Warren. It was taken down in 1947.

Ironically, a few years after the council riot Howard Patten, to complete a turnaround in belief, ran in a Grand Bank municipal election and won a seat lending credence to the old maxim, "If you can't beat 'em, join 'em." After retirement from the constabulary, William Case was superintendent in the Newfoundland Penitentiary and also established the Salmonier Prison Farm, a novel concept in Canada's prison system.

Fifty years ago. Fifty policemen. A summer of discontent when Grand Bank became the third municipality in Newfoundland after Windsor and Corner Brook East to become incorporated[1] and to enjoy the benefits of local government. Appendix K lists Grand Bank councillors from the 1950s to 1995.

Endnote:

1. The 1943 Act of Incorporation defined the Grand Bank town boundaries as: commencing on the shore at L'Anse L'Eau Point and proceeding inland in a straight line to Lewis Hill, thence in a straight line to Bowbridge's Hill, thence in a straight line to Thornhill's Hill, thence in a straight line to Gravelly Napp, thence in a straight line to Bennett's Hill, thence in a straight line to Eternity Rock, thence in a straight line to the shore at a point where L'Anse Paul Brook enters the sea.

   As well it is interesting to note the proposed expenditure budget for 1944, as suggested by the Act:

1. Office rental	$60.00
2. Light	$12.00
3. Coal or other fuel	$20.00
4. Office equipment	$100.00
5. Stationary and printing	$100.00
6. Secretary to Board	$300.00
7. Balance expended on public works,	
roads, bridges, etc.	$1,695.00
Total	$2,288.00

   In comparison the total expenditure budget for 1994, fifty years after that initial budget was prepared, was $1,938,333.00, a little less than two million dollars.

Afterword

In 1994, I sent a shorter version of this event to the *Southern Gazette* where it appeared in the December 27 edition. Two years later I re-wrote the story, added detail and submitted the "The Policemen on the Bridge" as an entry in the Newfoundland Arts and Letters Competition Non-Fictional Prose category. It placed second.

Chapter Six   Story Two

𝔅𝔞𝔠𝔨 𝔥𝔬𝔪𝔢 𝔬𝔯 𝔈𝔩𝔰𝔢!

While searching for another historical item in archival newspapers, I inadvertently found reference to this singular event of Grand Bank's history. It lay in a collection of unused material until I spoke to one of our fishermen, now in his eighties, about the occasion. He remembered the great ship that anchored off the Grand Bank wharf and his subsequent trip to Greenland. I then compared his brief story to the newspaper account.

This is a version of what happened based on a personal interview (the source requested anonymity) and that lone newspaper clipping.

"I remember when she anchored off the (Grand Bank) bar; I'd say the biggest ship ever off there," the man said. "A British company wanted deckhands and halibut dorymen. We all signed on with Forward & Tibbo and the foreign company paid us good money." For this crewman, it augured well, but the rest of his story indicated less than ideal conditions.

Perhaps the biggest employment scam or breach of trust that fishermen from the town of Grand Bank and other South Coast fishing communities had happen to them occurred in 1933. Although jobs and steady wages in the Depression years were hard to come by, when the hardworking fishermen arrived at the place of employment (off the shores of Greenland) and realized the conditions under which they had to work, they rebelled. These law abiding Grand Bank workers were not about to be conned into something they didn't agree with.

This brief account is a tribute to them.

The men, some of them deckhands on the mother ship and some dory fishermen, had been signed on by Grand Bank business Forward & Tibbo for an English firm to fish for halibut off Greenland. Apparently St. John's business-man/politician and former Prime Minister of Newfound-land Albert E. Hickman, a native Grand Banker, had made contacts with the English company and arranged for the shorthanded ships to use Newfoundland crewmen. Forward & Tibbo recruited the men and supplied the list of names.

In April of 1933 a large vessel, the S.S. *Arctic Prince* under the command of Captain Myra, came to various South Coast ports including Grand Bank to pick up the recruits. Several veteran seamen alive today still remember when *Arctic Prince* anchored on the bar off Grand Bank. At that time she was perhaps the largest vessel that had ever anchored off the town and was described as "looking like the *Queen Mary*." *Arctic Prince* had every modern convenience including a large general store and her own hospital with at least two doctors.

In the terms of the contract, each man was to be paid $42 a month for six months work while off Greenland catching or processing halibut. An excerpt of the *Evening Telegram* story of May 15, 1933, outlines what happened:

Twenty South Coast fishermen who were shipped on the S.S. *Arctic Prince* were sent back to their homes from Sydney, Nova Scotia, on the gulf ferry. These fishermen left the *Arctic Prince* at Sydney because they did not find conditions as they ex-pected. Twenty or more others demanded that they be paid off and unless their demands were complied with they would refuse to work.

Yesterday morning the trawlers S.S. *Yorich*, Capt. Himmelman and S.S. *Gaul*, Capt Conrad, arrived in port (St. John's) to receive coal and water supplies also to land nine other Newfoundlanders from each of the steamers who with their fishing captains were paid off and will proceed to their homes at the first opportunity.

Arctic Prince was the mother ship of the fleet, while the *Yorick* and *Gaul* were smaller trawlers supplying the larger vessel.

Several stories are current as to the actual cause of the disturbance aboard the S.S. *Arctic Prince*. Some of the fishermen aboard the S.S. *Gaul* but who were formerly attached to the *Arctic Prince*, assert that the trouble originated because of the treatment of Captain Myra to the men, which started about a week after leaving Newfoundland shores and began when a sick fishermen was pulled out of his bunk and kicked because he did not respond to the call for work. (The Newfoundland fishermen) resent very much the statement that they did not want to work and that they would sooner be at home and living on the dole. The majority of these men, all of them belong to Grand Bank, Belleoram and the West Coast never received dole.

Some one hundred and fifty fishermen were enlisted to prosecute the halibut fishery voyage on the Grand Banks six weeks ago. When the fishery at the Banks was over they would continue the voyage in Greenland waters.

Steady wages and good pay which meant real cash in the lean years — the "Dirty Thirties." But working conditions for the fishermen were terrible. As the story goes the South Coast fishermen were virtual slaves, confined eight or ten to a room and forced to work. But what their superiors underestimated was that they were compatriots and friends and each, with his personal pride and dignity, was more than willing to help another in a stressful situation. It became a case of "All for one, and one for all."

Such were their demands to be returned to home and family, employers considered it a mutiny and slapped one or two of the men into irons. Whether these were leg irons, handcuffs or a ship board cell is not clear but, as a cover-up for mistreatment of the fishermen, officers of the English vessels exaggerated reports of drunkenness and disturbances.

Not all returned home. Several Burin Peninsula (including a few from Grand Bank) deckhands on the British vessels did not find conditions as stressful and stayed on to finish the terms of their work commitment.

Eventually, the South Coast men who were part of the crew of *Arctic Prince* were put aboard the two smaller trawlers, *Yorick* and *Gaul*, and returned to Sydney, Nova Scotia, and St. John's, Newfoundland. The discontented fishermen

Grand Bank harbour, late 1950s. Buffett's *Pauline C. Winters* (right). On Saturday January 22, 1955, Clyde Welsh of Grand Bank, aged twenty-five, was washed overboard while *Pauline C. Winters*, skipper Philip Poole, was off St. Pierre. Welsh, the second engineer, was in the pilot house with Ben Welsh when a sea smashed the door and window and swept through the house. His body was not recovered. *Mabel Dorothy* (left) was lost with crew near the Horse Islands on November 3 or 4, 1955, while en route from Roddickton to Sydney: Captain John Ralph, engineer Willoughby Riggs, cook Tom Bolt of Grand Bank, Garfield Lawrence and Henry Howse of Bay L'Argent and Thomas Jensen of Harbour Breton.

were free to join their families; the government vessel *Malak-off* brought them to their South Coast homes.

The townspeople of Grand Bank and the other Burin Peninsula towns involved considered the treatment of the men to be a terrible injustice. Some of *Arctic Prince*'s men were: John Dolimount, Sam Hickman, Charles Anstey, George Douglas, Eli Pardy, George Pardy, Gabriel Vincent, Clarence Hickman, Philip Downey, Joe English and Ambrose Matthews of Grand Bank; John Ben Rideout, Hubert Grandy and Joe Grandy of Frenchman's Cove; Gord Noseworthy and Bob Oram of Fortune; Charles Morgan Grandy of Garnish; Albert Hiscock of Grand Beach; Harry Emberley and Edward King belonged to Lamaline.

Chapter Six   Story Three

Time of Change

One June evening, on the day school closed for summer vacation, I walked up to Admiral's Cove Beach to see if the capelin were rolling. My youngest son, who at that time was about four or five, jumped for joy when he saw the capelin had put in an appearance. We rushed back home to get a net and a fishing pole. Alas, by the time we arrived back at the beach, there was no sign of the capelin. Some time later I thought: "What if I had tried to videotape capelin scull that day." This slightly fictionalized article appeared in the November 1992 issue of *Decks Awash*.

Capelin Scull

Last week I saw those two words in a foldup tourist brochure at the Oxford travel agency, and Lord, how they take me back. Back about twelve years ago, I suppose, I was there with my Camcorder whirring away, standing on a crest of cobblestones above a narrow sandy beach. In my stack of VCR memories there are a dozen people transfixed between land and water, forever videotaped in a five minute clip. I stayed on the beach long after everyone else had gone. I was caught up, captivated; how was I to know I'd never see it again.

Captivated by that wind-blown June day and by that shadow of life that appeared, shimmered and disappeared in the drifting wisp of afternoon fog. Oldtimers called the weather capelin scull. No one knew if the capelin brought the weather or if the weather lured the capelin. And who knew or even cared where the word scull came from.

Things were changing. Back then news of the fish stocks and Hibernia droned on and on; Kiks Country radio played Simani's *Music and Friends* and a song about a ghost ship with her jib flapping into the wind. But these were fading too and would soon be a memory.

That time for me was June 12. Admiral's Beach was scrubbed clean by a recent storm. It had rained the day before and I could smell the heavy sea — everyone knew the grunion-like capelin would soon follow. The fog came in grey and insubstantial, not on little cat feet as Sandberg once said, but clumsily, driven by tides and wind. A little past noon ghost-like fingers had lifted over the cape, drifted past First and Second Rock and settled nearer the beach.

Not long after the grey fog brought the silvery fish with iridescent green backs, snuggling and struggling to procreate and continue life. Like a last will and testament, my Camcorder recorded their sacrifice as they tumbled on the beach. And, as if to authenticate and witness the event, other people were there: two fishermen, professional and confident, filled a cast net with every throw, teenagers used dip nets or buckets, young boys walked just over the tops of their black Hoods and felt the icy finger of the Atlantic touch their skin. One fellow had different ideas. He pinned a capelin to a feathery jigger and flung a monofilament line from an expensive Shakespeare rod beyond the capelin hoping to hook a fighting pollack or mackerel. Herring gulls and saddlebacks dipped and dipped against a silvery sea.

After a few minutes I clicked off the record button and walked around the shore near the cape to a spring of water called Duschene's Well. From there I could shoot the whole scene wide angle, and like I had done in my youth, get a drink of the cool sweet water that ran from the brown slate. There was just enough room to cup my hand under the trickle. From where I stood at the Well, I saw, just beyond the lip of the hill, faint outlines of abandoned potato gardens, grassed over and lonely. In that shadowy, muffled world I felt that other people had once stood here. They, too, had refreshed themselves with spring water and saw the ocean pulse with life at capelin scull time. An eerie silence brought me back to the present — the thoughts of other people disappearing like Dickens' Ghost of Christmas Past.

Now the fog had mutated, drifted by the cape, over the abandoned gardens and spread through the ramparts of stunted fir trees. Almost as though it had a mind of its own, the ocean mist surrounded me making any attempt at recording this eerie spot useless. I could see nothing beyond a few feet — the shifting shadows were in charge. It was at that moment the world of capelin scull changed for me. I listened for talk and laughter from Admiral's Beach, but the silence told me the people and the tiny fish they gathered had gone.

Within a few minutes I was back at the beach; only the lop, lop, lop of lonely waves greeted me. With their backs turned to the sea-blown fog, I saw two boys walking away from Admiral's Beach and down Christian's Road.

In later springs I often visited the beach hoping to recapture nature's annual ritual. I walked the ridge of cobblestones

Western End of Admiral's Cove, as taken in the 1930s when capelin rolled on the beach, showing First and Second Rocks. Duschene's Well would be (left) behind the photographer. Those in photo are (l-r): Wes Crowley, Miss Snelgrove and Miss Shelley(?).

and stopped at the Well, listening for voices long gone, looking across at the narrow strip of sand. But the scull had ceased. The capelin no longer came in prolific numbers and never again did I see the rolling, tumbling fish as I had witnessed them in other times.

Someone once wrote about Silent Spring and I went to the local library to read the book, looking for capelin scull, but it wasn't there. Oldtimers around here are strangely silent too, when you ask them about it. Quietly, with half-knowing smiles, they only nod as if they knew all along the end was coming.

Chapter Seven   Odds and Ends

Major Grand Bank Fires

Some of the major fires in Grand Bank over years, as taken from archival newspapers and as tabulated by *The Grand Bank Fire Department 40th Anniversary Book* (1987), were:

1. **Waterfront Fire March 1, 1930.** In the early hours of March 1, 1930 fire broke out in the store of G. & A. Buffett. With no fire fighting apparatus, men did their best by bringing water from the harbour in buckets. Patten's store and Forsey's business were soon ablaze; then, the buildings on the other side of the road were smouldering although they did not catch. The coastal boat *Glencoe* turned its hose on the blaze

Courtesy of Neil Locke

View of 1930 fire taken from Point of Beach. The square rigged schooner to the left is the *General Wood* which received extensive damage. In centre, temporary shelters of sail and canvas protect the fishery salt from rain.

    Every available man in town fought the blaze. It is said that William Hatcher, who at that time lived in Molliers and came up to Grand Bank with other Molliers' men to help out, died from eating pork damaged in the fire.

and this helped bring it under control. Estimates of $250,000 damage were quoted. Buffett's relocated to Main Street.

The great cement chimney stood for many years despite many attempts to pull it down. It still exists today, inside what was once the Buffett warehouse and is now the Brumac building.

2. **The Mount Pleasant Fire June 3, 1940.** A fire broke out at Mrs. Mary (Polly) Miller's house on what is now the south side of Elizabeth Avenue, near today's Pleasant Street. There was no fire fighting equipment and a bucket brigade from local wells was the only means of extinguishing the flames. When it was seen other homes would be set afire, a long brigade was formed to Admiral's Cove Pond. Horses and carts carried barrels and puncheons of water to the scene. Two homes in the row were saved, but seven were destroyed: Mary Miller, Sarah Hickman, Edward Hollett, William Evans, Luke Keating, Capt. James Belbin, and James Dolimount. There was no loss of life.

New homes (some of which have since been taken down) were built on the sites of those destroyed by the fire. The site of Polly Miller's house is now occupied by the home of Bruce Green.

3. **Grand Bank Cottage Hospital.** At six pm on May 8, 1963, fire was discovered in the new wing (completed less than year previous) of the Grand Bank Cottage Hospital which caused $100,000 damage and totally destroyed the inside. The staff of sixteen helped evacuate twenty patients without any injury; the latter were moved into people's homes and later transferred to Burin and St. John's.

Dr. James Gough, the medical officer in charge, praised the volunteer fire brigade who controlled the fire within two hours. At that time the older part of the hospital could accommodate twenty to thirty patients and there was to be an extra fifty beds in the new section. Within a few months workmen had rebuilt the interior.

4. *Newfoundland Eagle* **April 17, 1970.** In the early hours of

the morning, smoke could be seen coming from the wheelhouse of the trawler while she was tied to the Bonavista Cold Storage wharf. The fire had been reported by the crew of another trawler *Grand Prince* as she entered port around two fifteen am.

Newfoundland Eagle, an eight hundred thirty-five ton, one hundred sixty-nine foot steel trawler, was ablaze in the upper bridge, the captain's cabin and washroom. Plant watchmen and engineers could not handle the flames and smoke and called the town fire brigade. After several hours, the fire was extinguished.

In terms of loss of life, this fire was major: Captain Michael Puddister, age thirty-six, of Bay Bulls had been asleep in the captain's cabin and died in the mishap. As far as could be determined, Puddister fell asleep while smoking and the bed clothes were set afire. Estimates of cost of damages ranged from two to three hundred thousand dollars.

Fortune Star burns behind the Irving Oil tanks. On April 16, 1967 she caught fire while tied to her berth by the Bonavista Cold Storage fish plant. The *Badger Bay* towed her out of the harbour to burn out as she grounded about one hundred yards east of the lighthouse. Her remains mingle with those of schooners lost in the same area: *Ariminta,* 1925; *Adolph Roberts,* 1943 and *Isabel Corkum,* 1948.

5. The John Burke High School Fire February 14, 1976.
Apparently one of the two furnaces located in the crawl space
underneath the school gym misfired, and around four am the
fire was reported coming from the gymnasium area. High
winds carried the flames to the classroom area and soon the
whole school was a mass of flames. The fire could not be
contained in the high winds and efforts were directed on
saving the homes and two lumber yards nearby. By mid-
morning on Valentine's Day, all that remained of the high
school were twisted pipes and the concrete foundations of
the basement. There were no injuries.

Directory of Banking Schooners — Various Years

In the course of research I located seven newspaper articles which gave statistics of the Grand Bank fishing fleet. These were dated: November 25, 1898; June 16, 1917; November 14, 1933; 1934; 1935; 1938; and 1940. Four, because of their concise information and relevancy, are tabled below.

Evening Telegram November 25, 1898 The following are the catches of the Grand Bank schooners prosecuting the Bank fishery this year:

Pointer	Capt. Henry Courtney	2100 qtls
Ida	Capt. G. Hiscock	1800 qtls
Ruby	Capt. Joshua Matthews	1700 qtls
Julia	Capt. George Hyde	1650 qtls
Myrtle	Capt. Walter Patten	1650 qtls
Violet	Capt. William Courtney	1500 qtls
Mary Harris	Capt. Sam Piercy	1500 qtls
Emily Harris	Capt. G. Patten	1500 qtls
George Harris	Capt. Robert Forsey	1350 qtls
S.J. Foote	Capt. S. Forsey	1300 qtls
George Tibbo	Capt. W.H. Tibbo	1300 qtls
Quero	Capt. Jas. Forsey	1250 qtls
Vidette	Capt. John.B. Patten	1200 qtls
Watersprite	Capt. Samuel Bradley	1100 qtls
Royal Charlie	Capt. W. Riggs	800 qtls
Chester Harris	Capt. R. Rogers	900 qtls
Selina Forsey	*Capt.* Joshua Forsey	800 qtls

Drowned Capt. Rogers, of the *Chester*, was drowned on the last trip of the Banks. He, with three of his crew, set out in dories to overhaul their trawls and were all lost. The names of the others were: Ernest Rose, 20, Grand Bank; George Janes, married[1], Grand Bank; and J. Spencer of Harbour Breton.

J.R. Matthews, of Grand Bank, was lost during the summer, from the schooner *Selina Forsey*. He had thrown out a bucket when the schooner was under sail and it pulled him overboard. Peter Handrigan, of Grand Bank, fell overboard when all were below, and they had not time to reach him when the crew were aware of the accident. Capt. Joshua Forsey died the first week in October, after being sick all the summer; his brother Robert then took charge.

The young man reported some time ago as being drowned from Foote's smack in Fortune Bay was named Philip Forsey, son of Mr. Robert Forsey. He was standing near the wheel when a "tack" was being made, and when the boom swung round it knocked him overboard. A boat was hurriedly put out, but before the unfortunate man was reached he had sunk. The body was found next day, and the funeral took place at Grand Bank, the Temperance Society marching in processional order.

1. Mrs. Ursula Squires, daughter of George Janes, related her version of the incident: although the weather was stormy and seas high, Captain Rogers, not wanting to lose a trawl or a cable, volunteered to row out and asked for some men to accompany him. Three men — Janes, Spencer and Rose — stepped forward, but at sea the dory upset.

Daily News June 16, 1917 These returns show the fleet has done remarkably well, with the *Dorothy Melita*, Capt. Thornhill highliner with 3,000 quintals. The schooners, owners, and catches follow:

Patten & Forsey

Dorothy Melita winter and spring trip	95 tons	23 men	3000 qtls
Mary F. Hyde spring trip	78 tons	20 men	1100 qtls

Theresa Maud winter and spring trip	78 tons	23 men	1900 qtls
Edith Pardy winter and spring trip	79 tons	18 men	1430 qtls

S. Harris Ltd.

Bessie McDonald spring trip	79 tons	18 men	750 qtls
Maud Thornhill winter and spring trip	79 tons	20 men	1000 qtls
Belbina P. Domingoes spring trip	71 tons	20 men	1300 qtls
Garfield spring trip	73 tons	18 men	750 qtls
Chesley Raymond spring trip	79 tons	20 men	800 qtls
Blanche Forsey spring trip	75 tons	18 men	1800 qtls
Minnie Harris spring trip	91 tons	19 men	1600 qtls
Electric Flash winter and spring trip	80 tons	22 men	2300 qtls
Oregon winter and spring trip	79 tons	18 men	1850 qtls
Castle Carey winter and spring trip	79 tons	18 men	1450 qtls
L.C. Norman winter and spring trip	49 tons	12 men	1490 qtls

G. & A. Buffett

Helen Vair spring trip	79 tons	18 men	950 qtls
Preceptor spring trip	75 tons	23 men	1200 qtls

S. Tibbo & Sons

Linda Tibbo spring trip	76 tons	18 men	600 qtls
Admiral Dewey spring trip	92 tons	22 men	1000 qtls
Thomas A. Cromwell spring trip	98 tons	23 men	900 qtls
Prospector spring trip	75 tons	18 men	600 qtls

Note: These twenty-one schooners employed four hundred nine men; although not all were residents of Grand Bank. None of the schooners listed in 1898 was still active. As well, there were more schooners owned in Grand Bank in 1917 than the above record indicates: some may not have been involved in the fishery; some were under repair; others were smaller coasting schooners. In this decade, as well, each of the four major businesses owned tern schooners and was engaged in taking the salt dry fish overseas.

The *Daily News* of February 24, 1911, recorded the crew who went to Boston to bring down Simeon Tibbo's banker *Admiral Dewey*. Philip Johnson, Philip Harris, G. Buffett, William Riggs, and George Harris left St. John's by the S.S. *Rosalind* for New York en route to Boston. The *Admiral Dewey*, built in Gloucester, was loading coal, timber, and general cargo but, according to American legislation, had to leave the United States under an American captain. In 1932, she was sold to Hardy's of Jersey Harbour and wrecked in St. Pierre harbour on September tenth the same year.

Daily News November 14, 1933 BANKING VOYAGE COMPLETED The banking voyage for another season has been completed and on the whole is better than last year. The schooners are being cleaned and made ready to be taken to the safe harbours of the Bay to be moored for the winter.

All the fishermen have great cause for thankfulness, while the women who have found employment through curing the fish, have earned upwards of $13,000 (this figure would be divided by the total number of women working on the beaches).

The following is a list of the Grand Bank fleet with the captains' names and the amount caught for the season.

S. Harris Export Ltd.

James & Stanley	Harry Hynes	4078 qtls
Robert Max	John Thornhill	4005 qtls
Partanna	Charles Anstey	3349 qtls
Paloma	William Banfield	2607 qtls
Laverna	Thomas Snook	1856 qtls

J.B. Patten & Sons

J.E. Conrad	Reuben Elms	3400 qtls
Coral Spray	Jim Lawrence	2600 qtls
Dorothy Melita	Parmineas Banfield	1320 qtls
Alsatian	Parmineas Banfield	990 qtls

G. & A. Buffett Ltd.

Freda M	George Follett	3350 qtls
Nina W. Corkum	John Smith	3110 qtls
Pauline Winters	Sidney Harris	2900 qtls

William Forsey

Helen Forsey	Alec Smith	4000 qtls
Christie and Eleanor	Tom Bill Welsh	2600 qtls

J.B. Foote Sons Ltd.

Antoine C. Santos	Tom Harris	3400 qtls
Mackenzie King	George Newport	2800 qtls

Forward & Tibbo

Irene Corkum	Will Thornhill	3900 qtls

Sam Piercy

Flores	Frank Thornhill	1700 qtls

Note: The only banking schooner still fishing from the 1917 fleet was the *Dorothy Melita,* captained in 1933 by "Min" Banfield. In May of that same year, she struck an iceberg and sank with the loss of one man, Chesley Grandy of Bay L'Argent. To replace her Patten's business brought down the ill-fated *Alsatian* from Lunenburg that summer. She was to disappear with Captain Jim Lawrence and crew, including two Grand Bankers, in March of 1935.

The *James & Stanley* was highliner, having brought home the largest catch, with John Thornhill's *Robert Max* close behind.

Fall 1940 (Source and Newspaper unavailable)

G. & A. Buffett

Freda M	George Follett	25 men	6267 qtls
Nina W. Corkum	Alec Smith	25 men	5612 qtls
Pauline C. Winters	Sidney Harris	25 men	5451 qtls
L.A. Dunton	Clarence Williams	23 men	4598 qtls

Forward & Tibbo

Mabel Dorothy	Reuben Thornhill	25 men	4970 qtls
Eva U. Colp	William Thornhill	24 men	5351 qtls

J.B. Foote & Sons

Maxwell F. Corkum	Thomas Harris	25 men	5730 qtls
Antoine C. Santos	Jacob Thornhill	23 men	3900 qtls

Grand Bank Fisheries

Adolph Roberts	Victor Fiander	19 men	2283 qtls
D.J. Thornhill	John Thornhill	23 men	5095 qtls

Sam Piercy

Harold Guy	Frank Thornhill	23 men	4833 qtls

J.B. Patten & Sons

Florence	Arch Thornhill	23 men	3200 qtls

Courtesy of Neil Locke

In the 1940s, two schooners moored near Forward & Tibbo's premises on Point of Beach while a horse and cart waits between the two fish stores. Over fifty years later, the storage store to the left still stands today, although it has been moved to become the watch house on the Bonavista Cold Storage (now Clearwater) plant.

Rhodes Scholars Born in Grand Bank

*I*s *That You, Bill?* Bill Rowe of VOCM's Open Line Show? Rhodes Scholar William Neil Rowe has had varied and interesting careers: lawyer, MHA, novelist, radio talk show host and he recently wrote a book *Is That You, Bill?* on his radio on-air experiences. He was born in Grand Bank in 1942, (a statement he has often made on his open-line talk show) son of teacher Fred Rowe who himself became a noted Newfoundland historian and politician. Fred Rowe, who taught at the United Church Academy, spent a short time in Grand Bank before moving to St. John's.

Bill Rowe graduated from Memorial University and was awarded the Rhodes Scholarship in 1964 to continue his education at Oxford University in England.

In the ninety or so years that the Rhodes Scholarship (founded by British Statesman Cecil John Rhodes) has been awarded two men born in Grand Bank have merited the distinctive honour and monetary benefits that accompany it. Rhodes Scholars are not selected on academic ability alone; each recipient must show leadership, integrity, interest, and respect for others. Newfoundland representatives have been among the brightest and the most dedicated graduates of Canadian and American universities.

In 1912, Pierson V. Curtis graduated from the Methodist College in St. John's and went on as Newfoundland's Rhodes Scholar to Oxford. Curtis was born in Grand Bank; son of clergyman Rev. Levi Curtis who was stationed in Grand Bank in 1891-94.

Haddon's Map of 1894

About twenty-five years ago, I bought an old home in Grand Bank which once belonged to Captain Ab and Alice (Camp) Bellman. After initial move in and clean-up, I rummaged through the attic. Not much there except a few items to discard and a rolled piece of paper tied in string. Spreading the paper out in the living room sometime later, I recognized a map of Grand Bank and read the writing in the lower right hand corner: **Grand Bank, surveyed by J. Haddon, August 1894**; the names of the property owners on the left hand side.

A few weeks later (early 1972), I brought it to my father's house where he and I studied the names and streets. From that time the map disappeared as far as I was concerned; I had no idea where I had stored it or if I had misplaced it. In 1989 I sold my home, cleaned out the trash and moved to another residence in Grand Bank. But the map was still missing. As time passed, I thought it must have been thrown out prior to or at the time of moving.

In 1991 it reappeared. I had left it at my father's home where someone had unwittingly put it away and there it was again —a one-hundred-year old cadastral map of Grand Bank, my home town.

In *McAlpine's Newfoundland Directory* of 1898 under the heading "Fortune" there is an entry for Henry J. Haddon, Land Surveyor; he must be the map-maker. Quite an interesting life he had in Fortune — teacher, architect, surveyor, Justice of the Peace, and one of the founders of Fortune's Freemasons. There's a street named for him and up to a few years ago the Fortune school bore the name Haddon Academy. Haddon, in his work, probably surveyed other towns around the peninsula making cadastral maps.

According to the Oxford dictionary, cadastral means, "of or showing the ownership of land for taxation, __survey". Most likely Haddon was commissioned or paid by the local Grand Bank businessmen to produce a community survey map. To my knowledge, no map of its likeness has turned up for Fortune where Haddon lived, nor any other Peninsula community.

The copy I have measures about 62 inches by 36 inches and is on heavy brown paper, the ink and paper remarkably well-preserved after one hundred years; it had been kept in a cool, dry attic. The numbered land lots correspond to the list of owners on the side, in flourished handwriting; thus the chance of occasionally mistaking an I or a J, etc.

In numbered order with spellings (or misspellings) as they appear on the survey map, the names are:

1. —	19. T. Walsh	36. James Belbin
2. R. Rose	20. —	37. " "
3. T. Rose	21. —	38. " "
4. Ann Rose	22. Mrs. Riggs	39. Bradley
5. T. Hickman	23. Ben Diamond	40. R. Studley
6. S. Harris	24. Jo Francis	41. B. Matthews
7. S. Harris	24. Jo Francis	42. Sam Tibbo
8. G.R. Forsey	25. B. Francis	43. " "
9. G. Buffett	26. W. Fox	44. Jon Evans
10. —	27. John Francis	45. Wm. Evans
11. —	28. Thom Francis	46. George Rose
12. —	29. Sol. Francis	47. Ben Buffett
13. Wines & Hick-man	30. —	48. Thos Riggs
14. Grant	31. R. Riggs	49. W. Matthews
15. Nich Handrigan	32. Mary Matthews	50. John Parsons
16. W. Riggs	33. Chas Pardy	51. John Matthews
17. Sam Patten	34. " "	52. H. Matthews
18. John B. Patten	35. Morgan Matthews	53. W. Evans
		54. P. Nichole

55. G. Butt
56.   "   "
57. John Forsey
58. —
59. G. Buffett
60. Charles Patten
61. —
62. Mrs. Foote
63. Tibbo & Brothers
64. Sam Harris
65. —
66. —
67. Edward Evans
68.   "   "
69. J. & C. Hickman
70. Jabez Hickman
71. Hickman
72. Forsey
73. Forward
74. Lovell
75. Jon Tibbo
76. Jon Hiscock
77. John Hickman
78. Henry Hickman
79. Forsey
80. J. Hickman
81. Buffett & Harris
82. Sarah Forsey
83. Wood
84. Lou Tibbo
85.   "   "
86. Thos Foote
87.   "   "
88. John Foote
89. John Foote
90. Mrs. Foote
91. Simms

92. W. Tibbo
93. H. Hickman
94. —
95. —
96. Mrs. Lovell
97. Mrs. Lovell
98. " "
99. Dr. Macdonald
100. Phil Patten
101. Ben Patten
102. —
103. —
104. —
105. Ed. Nichole
106. Jane Hickman
107. —
108. R. Forsey
109. John Riggs
110. Morgan Riggs
111. Wilson Rose
112. R. Noseworthy
113. R. Rose
114. John Forsey
115. George Bell
116. Edward Evans
117. George Hickman
118. Charles Hickman
119. Wilson Hickman
120. Wm Tibbo
121. D & S Tibbo
122. —
123. S. Dunford
124. Sam Deer
125. Jon Hickman
126. Edward Walsh

127. —
128. Jacob Weymouth
129. Aaron Forsey
130.   "   "
131. G. Hickman
132. —
133. —
134. G. Hiscock
135. B. Buffett
136. Sam Harris
137. John Rose
138. Mrs. T. Grandy
139. Sam Harris
140. G. E. Forsey
141. G. Lovell
142.   "   "
143. Simeon Tibbo
144. —
145. H. Evans
146. John R. Hickman
147. Ed. Forward
148. Am Forward
149. —
150. Sam Tibbo
151. —
152. James Rose
153. Jon Tibbo
154. George Foote
155. W. Tibbo
156. H. Hickman
157. Walter Patten
158. John Grant
159.   "   "
160. G.A. Buffett
161. Mrs. Courtney

162. James Hickman
163. Frank Hiscock
164. Jon Hickman
165. —
166. Mrs. Simms
167. Jon Tibbo
168. Sam Emberley
169. Mrs. Hyde
170. Joseph Hiscock
171. James Hickman
172. Mrs. Evans
173. Joshua Hickman
174. Mrs. Kendle
175. —
176. —
177. G. Grandy
178. T. A. Hickman
179. Ben Bennett
180. Saml Hickman
181. Mrs. Evans
182. __
183. Sarah Lawrence
184. Thos Studley
185. Geo Tibbo
186. Aaron Grandy
187. John H. Hickman
188. Morgan Hickman
189. Ed. Hawkins
190. Mrs. Hudson
191. Isaac Hynes
192. Robt. Hanlon
193. Geo. R. Forsey

194. Mrs. Studley
195. Ben Wadden
196. W. Bond
197. Ben Hollett
198. S. Harris
199. Orange Hall
200. Temperance Hall
201. M. Parsonage
202. G. R. Forsey
203. J. Penwell
204. Joseph Evans
205. Joseph Evans
206. —
207. John Forsey
208. —
209. —
210. G. Camp
211. Aaron Forsey
212. James Forsey
213. Mrs. Patten
214. Saml Harris
215. Mrs. Pool
216. —
217. —
218. Rogers
219. —
220. John Walsh
221. Sam Studley
222. Meth. Church
223. W. Penwell
224. Court House
225. Patten & Courtney
226. C. Dodman
227. Joshua Walsh
228. —
229. John Williams

230. —
231. P. Nichole
232. W. Evans
233. A. Warren
234. H. Wynes
235. W. Osmond
236. S. Anstey
237. Thornhill
238. —
239. Osmond
240. John Grant
241. Sam Tibbo
242. Ambrose Forward
243. Downey
244. R. Ralf
245. Jo. Hiscock
246. P. Keating
247. R. Keating
248. W. French
249. Esther Foote
250. Patten
251. Meth. Schools
252. Alex Bethune
253. —
254. Bethune
255. ?
256. Barnes
257. Harding
258. S.A. Barracks
259. Harding
260. Thos. Foote
261. Geo. Hiscock
262 "
263. Amb. Evans
264. Dunford
265. John Camp

Haddon has written in several streets; however small side lanes (which have a name today) are omitted probably due to space limitations on his map. The streets shown on Haddon's map are: Water Street; Jellicoe Street; Mystery Street; Hickman Street; Church Street; George Street; Circular Road; Blackburn Road; Walsh's Road; Fortune Road; Cownap Street; Hospital Street; Foote's Street, and College Street. The latter extends westward to include Road to Shore (Admiral's Cove).

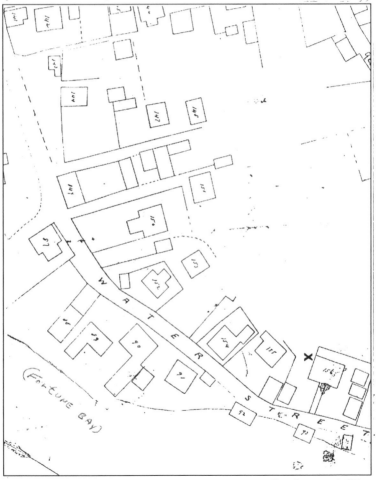

A section of Haddon's Map of land lots 143-156; the 156 (marked by the X) on the west end of Water Street the family property of Albert E. Hickman, who later became Prime Minister of Newfoundland.

Several of these roads bear comment based on their map location: Jellicoe Street corresponds to Chilcott Street. It is likely Haddon mistook the pronunciation of Chilcott, writing it as Jellicoe. Mystery Street seems to be today's Butt Street; Walsh's Avenue is a shorter road but receives the title Avenue and this today is Ralph Street. Cownap Street has the name Citadel Road today — in time the Salvation Army Citadel was built there, but on Haddon's map the S.A. Citadel is located on Point Bouilli. Likewise the hospital was on the extension to Atlantic Avenue; in 1894 the lane was called Hospital Street. Foote's Street corresponds to today's Fairview Street. No streets, roads or houses are shown east of the bridge. The town boundaries is the area enclosed between Riverside West to Butt Street and Citadel Road to Camp Street.

In 1992 another "Haddon" Grand Bank map, this one drawn on oilcloth, was donated to the Newfoundland and Labrador Provincial Archives, St. John's, by a former Grand Banker now living in Toronto.

Courtesy of Mrs. June Russell

The first (outdoor pool) summer swim team that competed against Gander, Grand Falls, Buchans, and Baie Verte in 1970: (back row l-r) Gail Vincent, Robert Parsons coach, Carolanne Anstey, Lucy Warren, Maxine Scott, Marguerite Grandy, Hazen Russell, Michael Large, Charlie Thomasen, Marvin Welsh, Joan Prior and Janet Russell (front row l-r) Daisy Matthews, Colleen Grandy, Wendy Squires, Roy Fox, Frank Thornhill, Murray Moulton, Sean Large, and Paul Vincent.

Of the nineteen young people in this photograph only two now live in Grand Bank. Because of limited employment opportunities, the others sought work elsewhere. This out-migration shows why many Newfoundland towns have an older and declining population today.

The Harbour Changes Again

Grand Bank harbour on August 18, 1994: far left, pleasure craft; a small scallop dragger; background *Melissa Desgagnes*, a salt boat delivering highway salt to trucks; to the right *Endeavour I*, a scallop dragger and (far right) *Atlantic Surf*, a Clearwater scallop dragger.

A newer breed of vessel now frequents the harbour as scallop draggers bring shellfish from Fortune Bay and the St. Pierre Bank. This change in species and technology marks the fourth time Grand Bank people have adapted to economic and natural setbacks: early settlers depended on the inshore fishery and supplying bait to foreigners. After the 1887-8 Bait Act, which prevented Newfoundlanders from selling bait fish to St. Pierre and the United States, the schooner fishery had its beginnings and that phase lasted until the 1940s. A third great fishing enterprise lasted for over three decades 1955-1991 as Grand Bank's economy hinged on the fresh frozen fishery wih steel side and stern trawlers landing catches in this port.

Today, scallop draggers scour the grounds off St. Pierre and Fortune Bay for up to ten days returning to offload their catch at Clearwater Fine Foods (at the site of the former Bonavista Cold Storage Plant) or at Grand Oceans Fishing Company, once the site of Samuel Harris/Grand Bank Fisheries building. Scallops shucked at sea are valued around seven dollars a pound; market value may more than triple that.

Chapter Eight   A Backward Look

𝔚𝔥𝔞𝔱 𝔦𝔰 𝔊𝔯𝔞𝔫𝔡 𝔅𝔞𝔫𝔨?

by Les Stoodley

In August of 1987, at the State Dinner for Grand Bank's tri-centennial celebrations, two former Grand Bankers gave an after dinner speech: Dr. Eugene Forsey spoke of the Meech Lake Accord and its potential effects on Newfoundland. Les Stoodley delivered a highly thought-provoking and informative talk on his feelings as a Grand Banker. Forsey's talk, although erudite and forceful, was not appropriate for this book, but Les's memories — of events in the 1950s in a small town — are more relevant.

The several endnotes are added for those readers who did not have the privilege of growing up in Grand Bank; hence, may not be familiar with the events, folkways, and language of the town.

Les Stoodley lived on Riverside West, moved away for a career as a radio announcer, first at CKCM in 1962 where he did his first play-by-play hockey broadcast with Bob Cole (now of Hockey Night in Canada). Les subsequently moved to CBC Gander, CBC TV Corner Brook, and CBC Radio and TV, Halifax in 1969. He presently lives in Bridgewater, Nova Scotia.

𝔊rand Bank is more than houses and streets, ships and services, rain or snow, fog or sunshine, Grand Bank is people — a different kind of people.

Grand Bank is the memory that sweeps back to your

youth and you know that Grand Bank is people. People whose contribution to you is life lasting.

Grand Bank is or was knowing that everyone was safe as long as Fred Tessier was mayor.[1] It was the sense of security that you had in your education with teachers like Lilly Noseworthy, Christie Bradley, and Gar Fizzard.[2] It was being scared to death when Dr. Reynolds preached, or the wonderful sound of the male choir singing on New Years' Eve,[3] ring out the old and ring in the new. Watching the faces and hearing the incredible sounds on a Sunday night at the Barracks when the Salvationists sang as only Grand Bank Salvationists[4] can sing.

It was the pain in the pit of your stomach when you saw the messenger boy's bike stuck in the fence by your house.[5]

Grand Bank was calling men like Clyde and Hub Grandy "Uncle" when you knew there was no blood relation. Catching your glimpse of Phil Riggs' *Time* magazine when you needed an essay for Civics.

Grand Bank was hearing the putt putt of a dozen four horse power Acadia engines echo out of the cove and the cape[6] on lazy summer evenings when you and four buddies got a chance to go to the salmon net.

Grand Bank was the Frazer Hall on Friday night when Mr. George Foote was the scout master and you thrilled to the prospect of ten days in Main Brook.[7]

It was the pride of the town when Eli Price, Max Patten, Clayt Handrigan, Eugene Nurse, Gar Fizzard, and yes Les Stoodley went to the 8th World Jamboree and represented the first Grand Bank Troop.[8]

Grand Bank was the defiance and confidence of Bruce Buffett waving his fist at the football field saying, "We'll see you in the All-Newfoundland Cockie, and we will win," and win the Gee Bees did.[9] It was the knowing smile of one hundred old timers when Tommy Rose outsmarted Martin Dutan when the Frenchmen played[10] or the catty play of Don and Charlie Snook or the bullet drive from right wing by Eli Lee or the grunt of Stan Grandy when he shouldered Bob Slaney off the ball.[11]

Grand Bank was George Grandy and the Friday night dances at the theatre[12] or the sound of the Salvation Army Band on Easter Sunday morning when the knee drill became wake up to a new spring and fishery;[13] Captain Harry Thomasen bringing home the crew of the *Student Prince*[14] and taking his baton on Sunday night as the band played with new meaning and fervour "O Boundless Salvation."

Grand Bank was like mornings of February 9, 1959, when sixteen men didn't come home and you knew never would come home again.[15] Grand Bank was the support, understanding and compassion that friends displayed on days after mornings like that. When you rushed home from Halifax and you feel the calloused hands of workers gripping when they expressed their sadness and grief at the death of your father. When an aging Dr. John Burke[16] allows tears to roll down his wrinkled sleepless cheeks as he stands over your mother's casket.

Grand Bank was the reception you got when you came home after being on the radio and Uncle Jim Crowley, now blind, held your hand as you tried to describe what broadcasting was all about.

Grand Bank was the laughter of the white jackets,[17] the LOBA tea,[18] the heated discussion over the WAR in Levi Bungay's barber shop,[19] buying a two-cent cigarette, a ten-cent slice of baloney and bottle of Coke at Steve Welsh's[20] while the discussion on the last Leaf game made you an instant expert.

It was rushing into Patten's Drug Store[21] for a copy of the *Star Weekly* with Harry Lumley's picture on the back cover. It was using your father's handcat and sliding down the pinch or Dicky Butt's Hill and cleaning out three or four palings.[22]

Grand Bank was the frightful night the bank burned down,[23] the day Skipper Ben Snook lost a schooner[24], the Christmas concert in the Junior Hall when Santy Claus came,[25] walking into Mr. Charlie Forward's office[26] with your cap in your hand because you were told you had to do so. The wonderful day we turned on the water and the hoop and the water buckets rotted on the fence.[27]

Grand Bank the town of widows, the little dot on the toe
of the Burin Peninsula[28] — HOME — PEOPLE.
People with a fire in their hearts to try again when the
tragedies came. People with the keenest sense of community
I've ever known. People who shared their soup and their
sorrow, their births and their deaths, weddings and their
wakes, people who cared about each other. That's the Grand
Bank I knew and the Grand Bank that was, but I believe the
Grand Bank that still is. Filled with a vault of memories, filled
with a spirit of tomorrow, Grand Bank and Grand Banker.
Home - the best of people.

Endnotes:
1. Fred Mainwaring Tessier (1915-1992) was first elected mayor of Grand
   Bank in 1953, a position he held until 1981. In those early years of
   municipal government, with financial help from provincial and federal
   sources, Grand Bank had a water and sewer system installed, as well as
   street lighting, town policing, fire protection, improved athletic facilities and, in later years, street paving. In various interviews in newspapers and magazines, Tessier often quoted these as important
   achievements of his mayoral leadership. In the same vein, he jokingly
   told of failures including the purchase of a large street cleaning machine
   in the early 1970s. A virtual "white elephant," Grand Bank was able to
   sell it, at a substantial loss, to another town.
      Tessier was active in many sports, although soccer was his great
   love, and was inducted into the Newfoundland and Labrador Sports
   Hall of Fame. This came as a result of his twenty-seven years as
   president of the Grand Bank Soccer Association along with his service
   as president of the Provincial Soccer Association.
      He was also awarded membership into the Order of Canada.
2. Lilly Noseworthy taught in the Salvation Army schools for around three
   decades, 1940s-1960s.
      Christina B. Bradley taught and exhorted many students to excel
   academically and morally for forty years. Most of her career was spent
   in the Grand Bank United Church Academy or John Burke High School.
   She retired in 1968.
      Garfield Fizzard, born in Anderson's Cove, moved to Grand Bank
   as a young man and graduated from the United Church Academy in
   1950. He returned to teach there from 1953-55. In the early 1960s, he
   became a professor at Memorial University of Newfoundland. He has
   written two books for the Grand Bank Heritage Society — *Unto the Sea*
   and *Master of his Craft.*
3. Dr. Jesse Reynolds (1888-1964), a United Church minister, had a long
   term of service in Grand Bank, 1944-1959. Born in Broad Cove, Bay de
   Verde, Reynolds was ordained in 1923 and served in Little Bay Islands,

Lewisporte, Carbonear, Bay Roberts, and Grand Bank where he ended his ministry.

The AOTS (As One That Serves), a United Church men's service group, often sang at special occasions; for example, when the new church was dedicated on May 10, 1965, the AOTS sang, performed skits, and sponsored a poetry contest.

4. The Salvation Army came to Grand Bank in 1887. They built their first church, referred to as the Barracks or Citadel, on Point Bouilli in 1888. Other subsequent Barracks were built: in 1903 on the corner of Hawkins Street and Citadel Road; the third on the corner of Hickman Street and Citadel Road (facing Hickman Street) and today their fine church, their fourth, built in 1978 and opened in 1979, stands on Citadel Road.

5. In the days before telephones, the primary source of communication was the telegraph. Messages were sent and received at the Telegraph Office where the messenger boy delivered a telegram to the house or business. Telegrams of shipping disasters or marine mishaps put a fearful dread into women whose men had gone to sea.

Some messenger boys were: Johnny Penwell, who later became the Post Master; Howard Francis in the 1930s; Charlie Forsey; Fred Riggs; Herb Riggs; William Anstey, and Stanley Melloy. Melloy, born in Grand Bank in 1921, received his early education at the Salvation Army school and served with distinction in the RAF overseas in WWII. He was employed with the I.A.C.; later becoming one of the founders and president of the Continental Bank of Canada.

The standard uniform sported by messenger boys, although it was not worn by all, was the black uniform with brass buttons. From 1886, when the telegraph office was set up in Grand Bank, up to the 1930s or 40s, the messenger boy walked. Later, as bikes became affordable, this became the mode of transport.

6. Before 1950, Grand Bank relied primarily on the offshore bank fishery, but a few fishermen pursued the inshore cod as well as the seasonal salmon and lobster. Some of the men who gillnetted, trapped, or jigged cod in their Acadia-driven yellow dories were: Charles Rose and his son Ab, George (Traps) Rose, Albert Riggs, Morgan Francis, Dave Grant, Billy Vaters, Eugene Weymouth, Jim Crowley and his son Wes, Phil Riggs, and Phil Stoodley.

In an earlier era, inshore fishermen found good grounds at Dantzig Cove and Point aux Gaul. Not long ago, Hedley Parsons of Grand Bank, who now lives in Red Deer, Alberta, wrote to tell me about his fishing experiences in the 1930s at Dantzig, near Garden Joe. In those years men who fished and lived in their Dantzig summer fishing houses were: Phil Keating (Sr.), George Miller, and Caleb Penwell. Uncle Dave Keating and his sons lived in the dwelling next to Hedley Parsons.

Many Grand Bank fishing families summered in Point aux Gaul in the 1920s; for example Wilson Rose, Benny George Riggs, Jabez Hickman, and Will Green Handrigan. The Tidal Wave of November 18, 1929, destroyed twenty-three fishing premises in Point aux Gaul including many owned by Grand Bank fishermen.

7. Frazer Hall, a church hall located on the corner of Circular Road and

Church Street, was the meeting place for many United Church and community groups.

Ten days were happily spent in the Main Brook scout camp living in canvas tents under the leadership of George Foote. The camp was located on the southern side of Main Brook.

In the late 1980s, through the initiative of Oscar Elms, a long time church youth and scout leader, a permanent hut was built at Main Brook. On August 11, 1990, opening/dedication day for the George Foote Camp, over fifty people came to honour George Foote who attended the event with his daughter Joan and son Tom.

8. The eighth Boy Scout Jamboree was held at Niagara-on-the-Lake, Ontario, in mid-August, 1955. Ten thousand scouts gathered from all parts of the world including a large contingent from France and Japan. Over five thousand tents withstood all that Hurricane Dianne threw at them.

World Jamborees are usually held every four years but, in a break with tradition and to celebrate 100 years of scouting, it convened again 1957 in England, scouting founder Baden Powell's birthplace. Grand Bank's Harold Tibbo attended this jamboree.

9. Gee Bees was Grand Bank's Senior Soccer Team. Prior to the logo GeeBees, the soccer team wore GBAA (Grand Bank Athletic Association) on the front of the red or red/white jerseys. In 1960, the GeeBees won their first of three All-Newfoundland Senior Soccer championships.

Bruce Buffett was a key member of teams that "brought home the bacon." When the victorious motorcade passed through Grand Bank, a side of bacon hung from a car window.

10. The Frenchmen were the teams from St. Pierre — ASIA and ASSP. Arrival of these teams was tantamount to a town holiday. Everyone rushed through chores and finished work early to take in the match.

Dutan was a centre forward from St. Pierre; other teammates were: Rene Arrossamena, August Audoux and Andre Rouille. St. Pierre soccer players were noted for their controlled game, short sharp passing and fancy footwork. Peninsula teams were usually equal with large fan support, running endurance and team play.

11. Brothers Don and Charlie Snook played in the 1950s. In 1954, Charlie Snook was the first Grand Bank player to receive the Most Valuable Player award issued for Newfoundland soccer. Eli Lee played mostly in the early sixties and is remembered for his hard shot. Stan Grandy was of an earlier team, the mid-fifties and played with the Snook brothers. Bob Slaney played for St. Lawrence.

12. Grandy's theatre on Evans' Street is now an apartment building. The theatre was operated by businessman Harry Grandy from July 1947 until it closed in 1964. The show (movie) played every Saturday afternoon and on weeknights except Sunday, but after the movie on Saturday nights, an adult dance attracted crowds. Popular local performers, like Hughie Vallis and George Grandy's Band, played there. Grandy's theatre also hosted other attractions: Wilf Carter and his family put off

a show in the 1950s, magicians, and the Lions Annual Christmas Party for children were community events.

13. Knee drill, a soldier's field training, is a military term adopted by the Salvation Army. It was their custom to hold a march and service at dawn on Sunday morning to pray for the day's spiritual work. The band played Easter hymns and members of the congregation following along and sang. In the spring, or at Easter, it heralded a new season of work, and prayers for safety and prosperity in the upcoming fishing season were offered. Once common in Grand Bank and in other parts of Newfoundland, knee drill is now practised to a lesser extent.

14. The *Student Prince II* sank on her way home from the West Indies on January 5, 1955. Caught in a tropical storm, the two hundred eighty-five ton freighter's seams opened and the vessel, owned by G. & A. Buffett, took on water faster than it could be pumped out.

The *Queen of Bermuda*, a luxury passenger liner, responded to a distress call and rescued the men from the sinking *Student Prince*. Grand Bank crew were: Captain Harry Thomasen, engineers Fred Broydell and Ray Hardiman, cook Sam Butler, mate Levi Warren, Cecil Warren, and Hector Rose.

Captain Harry A. Thomasen (1897-1994), who came to Grand Bank from Denmark as a young man, was for many years a band master in the Grand Bank Salvation Army Band.

15. The dragger *Blue Wave* sank with crew in a severe winter storm about one hundred miles south of Grand Bank on February 9, 1959. Her crew: Captain Charles Walters, mate Herbert Price, cook John Walters, Arthur Kearley, Otto Dodge, Garfield Prior, John Hillier, Reginald Baker, John Sam Barnes, Abe John Barnes, Samuel Dodge, Philip Fizzard, George T. Miller, Michael Price, James Fizzard, and Roy Baker.

Seven years later in 1966, tragedy in the deep sea dragger fleet came again. The *Blue Mist II*, on February 17, disappeared with crew, again with mostly Grand Bank crew: Captain Stewart Price, Angus Hillier, John Miller, Max Miller, Clyde Vincent, Clarence Power, William

Courtesy of Chesley Tibbo

Grand Bank fish plant in the early sixties. Two side trawlers, (left) the ill-fated *Blue Mist II* and on the right probably *Luckimee*. *Luckimee*, a side dragger that spent fourteen years operating out of Grand Bank and Fortune, was sold in 1974 to American interests. Postcard courtesy Chesley Tibbo.

Myles, Percival Myles, Absolom Dodge, George Mayo, George Banfield, Graham Rogers, and James Pardy. All except Pardy lived in
Grand Bank.

16. Born in Carbonear Dr. John Burke (1889-1977), after whom John Burke
High School is named, came to Grand Bank in 1919 and spent forty-two
years practising medicine in the Grand Bank. Since Grand Bank had a
regional facility, Burke was often called to homes from Garnish to
Lamaline to Brunette Island and usually travelled with electrical
line/repairman George French. At the hospital, Burke performed every
kind of medical service, both major and minor surgeries.

On July 5, 1948, Dr. Burke was awarded CBE (Commander, Order
of the British Empire) in recognition of his years of service as a doctor
and surgeon. At the same ceremony, Mabel Forsey, a long time post-
mistress and telegraph operator, was presented with a MBE (Member,
Order of the British Empire). Miss Forsey had previously been given the
King's Coronation Medal for service to the public.

In 1938, Elizabeth Rose of Grand Bank, in recognition of her years
and service as a teacher, was awarded the MBE.

17. The Whitejacket concert was organized by the Salvation Army men
although local performers from other denominations, especially those
talented in acting, singing or playing an instrument, would take part.
Their soup supper concerts and variety shows were held in the Citadel's Junior Hall and were always well attended. There would be
locally composed songs, kitchen table parodies on town events, past
and present, "poking fun," and great singing.

18. LOBA, Loyal Orange Benevolent Association, had teas as a fund raiser.
These social events were a soup, pie, and tea supper, an auction, variety
show, games for the young and films. In the 1950s, short films were
good fund-raisers and many remember the "shows" in the Frazer Hall,
the Orange Lodge, and in the
basement of the library where
the Canadian Legion charged a
nickle or a dime.

19. Barber shops have always been
a gathering place for those who
discussed local or world news.
Levi Bungay's barbershop
which was later owned by barber Lyman Crowley, was lo-
cated at the foot of the hill a little
south of J.B. Patten's store. In the
1970s, it was moved to Warren's
property on Christians Road
where it still stands. Today,
these groups of men congregate
on the wharf and the tradition
continues.

20. Steve Welsh's candy store was

Steve Welsh's candy store on "the bank" in 1964.
Originally owned by merchant William P. Evans,
small stores like those of Welsh and Ray French
were gathering places for those who had the time
to stand around and discuss hockey, social issues,
and small town news.

Courtesy Lucy Welsh

located directly across from the present day Bank of Nova Scotia.

21. In Howard Patten's Drugstore, once located on the corner of Water Street and Chilcott Street, one could buy magazines like the *Star Weekly* which could have coloured pictures of popular hockey stars. CBC Radio from Toronto was the broadcasting centre making the Toronto Maple Leafs a popular team.

    Howard Patten began his work in Grand Bank as a druggist in June 1929 and finished July 31, 1966. He also owned J. B. Patten and Sons, a general store established by his father, and he operated several vessels. (see also Chapter 6 Story 2)

22. A handcat is a home-made wooden slide used to bring wood or water barrels. The Pinch is the hill on the northwestern end of Riverside West. Roads like Dicky Butt's Hill were narrow and steep; the handcat was hard to control and striking a wooden fence was common. Palings (wooden pickets) were often broken off.

23. The Bank of Nova Scotia burned to the ground June 27, 1952, apparently started by faulty wiring. Merrill Tibbo's store and Grand Bank Fisheries warehouse received some fire damage. At this time the Fire Department, which had been organized in 1947 and housed in the fire hall/council office located on the corner of Riverside West and Water Street, owned a 1941 Dodge fire truck. It wouldn't start and had to be pushed out of the fire hall, up over Patten's Hill to the scene of the fire. Residents of the area, including the family of Thomas Burfitt, had to be evacuated. Fred Rogers, an employee of Grand Bank Fisheries, broke his leg helping fight the fire, but there was no loss of life.

    In June 1953, the new bank opened on the same site. The present day building is the fourth bank to be located there.

24. This schooner, Patten's *A & R Martin*, grounded while entering Lamaline on a stormy evening December 12, 1951. Captain Ben Snook and his crew — Ambrose Murphy, Maurice Snook, Frank Barnes, cook Charlie Fizzard, and passenger Clyde Warren — were rescued by residents of Allen's Island who rowed out to the stranded schooner and took the men off. The schooner and cargo of coal were lost.

25. Located in the basement of the Salvation Army Citadel (Barracks), the chief purposes of the Junior Hall were for Sunday school, social gatherings, concerts and teas. On the night of the Christmas concert, a huge fir tree loaded with gifts stood near the stage. When Santa came during the singing of the closing carol, usually "Here Comes Santa Claus," the goodies were distributed.

    In 1958-59, due to overcrowding in the S.A. school, the Grade Eight class with teacher William Thomasen, was taught in the Hall.

26. Charles Forward (1875-1972) was one of the owners and managing directors of Forward & Tibbo's business. Courtesy and respect to elders, especially a merchant who employed a considerable labour force, dictated social graces such as taking off your cap or not speaking until spoken to. A young boy would want to get a few hours' work shovelling coal out of a schooner's hold and into the coal buckets, or shovelling salt for the Grand Bank schooners. The arrival of the Portuguese salt boat often meant skipping school and asking the foreman on

the wharf for a job or going to see the merchant — in this case Forward, Eric Tibbo, or one of the other principal merchants in town.

27. The Grand Bank water and sewage system, for most areas of the town, was completed in 1953-54. Homes down around the brook and nearer the pump house were the first to turn on the water.

Up to that time, water came from two main sources: wells and Grand Bank Brook water. Nearly everyone had a well which necessitated buckets and hoops; the latter kept the buckets off from the body to avoid spilling and make carrying easier.

Brook water could be delivered by horse and cart or by sleigh in winter. One carter in recent memory is Edgar "Nigger" Ralph whose horse, it is said, knew routine so well it stopped by the proper customers' houses without being reined in. Ralph would take the water barrels and the canvas to cover them to a dip in the brook a little east of today's town hall. Ralph, Morgan Francis and his son Earl charged fifteen cents a barrel which rose to twenty-five cents a barrel in the fifties.

28. Over twenty-five Grand Bank vessels had been lost with crew in a one-hundred-year span, 1860-1966. Most early vessels had five or six crew; banking schooners had twenty to twenty-five crew for an average of seven to eight men per vessel. In that time frame then, approximately two hundred men were lost through wrecked or missing vessels. Needless to say, not all were residents of the community. For example, in 1907 the *Orion*, owned by G.& A. Buffett, disappeared with seventeen crew. Only three, Captain Edward Evans, mate Charles Bungay and Richard Dunford, belonged to Grand Bank, and twelve were residents of Mortier Bay. In the two communities affected by the tragedy, ten wives and thirty-one children were left without support.

Scores of Grand Bank men were drowned other shipping and marine accidents.

The little town on the toe of the Burin Peninsula became the third largest bank fishing centre in North America, next to Gloucester and Lunenburg. After 1900, as the fleets declined in the latter two centres, many large one hundred to one hundred fifty ton bankers were purchased by Grand Bank until the bank fishery also declined in Newfoundland.

In the 1970s, fishing technology on many draggers had changed to the mid-water trawl and sophisticated fish-finding equipment. As evidenced by these photos, tremendous catches of redfish (ocean perch) were brought to South Coast fish plants to be processed.

Tricentennial Cake

1 cup minced salt pork
1 cup hot strong coffee
¼ cup butter
1 cup granulated sugar
3 eggs
¼ cup sherry
1 tsp almond flavouring
1 tsp vanilla
2/3 cup molasses - 1 tsp soda added
¼ cup raspberry jam

Sift together the following:
4 cups flour
1 tsp allspice
1 tsp nutmeg
1 tsp cloves
1 tsp cinnamon
1 tsp mace
1 tsp baking powder
2 tsps ginger

Mix and sprinkle with ¼ cup flour, the following:
2 cups raisins
1 cup currants
2 cups mixed fruit
1 cup citron peel
1 cup dates
1 cup brazil nuts
1 cup walnuts

Method: Pour hot coffee over pork - let stand until cold. Cream butter, sugar, add eggs, beat well. Add jam, sherry, molasses and flavouring. Add pork and coffee, then sifted dry ingredients. Lastly add floured fruit and nuts. Pour into pan lined with waxed paper. Bake at 275 degrees for 3 hours.

Recipe by: Mrs. Doris Evans,
Main Street, Grand Bank, NF.

COMPLIMENTS OF GRAND BANK LUMBER CO. LTD.

Courtesy Grand Bank Lumber and Doris Evans

At every place setting at the tri-centennial state banquet held on August 11, 1987, there appeared a complimentary copy (made available by Grand Bank Lumber Co. Ltd.) of a recipe of a dark fruit cake used by Doris Evans.

For years Doris and Arthur Evans owned and operated a restaurant on Grand Bank's Main Street that, chiefly through its pot-luck dinners, became widely-known throughout Newfoundland and eastern Canada. But main courses were not the only treats the Evans' prepared, as this delightful cake recipe verifies.

APPENDIX A

Frazer Park Gravestones

𝕿he Frazer Park stones have all been relocated from the eastern end of the property. They were first moved in 1903-4 when the Frazer Hall was being built and placed behind the Hall near the centre of the park; a few years after the Frazer Hall was taken down (1979), they were again moved to their present location in the northwestern end. The earliest stone is dated 1816; the latest, 1916. Only two are dated in the 1900s. Note the early spelling of Foot(e).

Marker Number:

12—**Blackburn, Josiah** A stipendiary magistrate for 31 years d. Jan 12, 1868, age 69 (Note: Blackburn's place of birth has not been recorded, and he left no descendants in Grand Bank. Blackburn Road is named after him.)

9—**Buffett, Benjamin** Native of Grand Bank, d. 1865, age 86

17—**Buffett, Frederick Walter** Son of Thomas and Hannah Buffett, d. Nov. 17, 1877, age 7

4—**Chillcott, Robert Banks** d. May 19, 1817. Age 58

18—**Evans, Thomas** Infant son of Edward and Caroline Evans, b. Mar. 13, d. April 2, 1871

16—**Evans, James** Drowned at Lamaline, Sept. 6, 1871. Age 30

24—**Evans, William** Born in Devonshire, England, d. June 16, 1845. Age 76

26—**Foot, George William** Husband of Hesther Foot, d. April 4, 1868. Age 38

7—**Foot, Thomas** Age 1 year; **Foot, Eleanor**; age 1 month, children of George and (H)Esther and George; **George Forsey**. Age 5 months; **Amelia**. Age 1 year

8—**Forsey, Amelia** Wife of George Forsey, d. Nov. 23, 1865. Age 37

6—**Forsey, George** d. June 7, 1863

36—**Forsey, George** d. Sept. 18, 1847. Age 59

1—**Forsey, George Robert** Stipendiary Magistrate, d. July 14, 1916 Age 72; also **Eugene** who died in Mexico City, Nov. 28, 1904 Age 35; And of his son **Raymond** who rests in Edmonton, Alberta, d. Jan. 15, 1912. Age 32

31—**Forsey, Harriet** Wife of John Forsey, d. May 26, 1855. Age 35

11—**Forsey, Jane** d. June 14, 1863. Age 6 months and **Robert** d. Age 13 days and **Amelia J** d. July 14, 1866. Age 12 days. Children of Elizabeth Forsey

23—**Forsey, John** Husband of Charlotte, d. July 21, 1845

14—**Forsey, Joseph B** d. Aug. 9, 1864. Age 49

27—**Forsey, Thomas** d. February 13, 1842. Age 5

29—**Forward, Frances** d. 1842

13—**Forward, John A** d. Sept. 17, 1869. Age 73

15—**Forward, Sarah** Wife of John A. Forward, d. Aug. 10, 1970. Age 65

33—**Hickman, Elizabeth** d. May 28, 1864. Age 64

10—**Hickman, John B** d. March 11, 1859. Age 23

21—**Hickman, Jonathan** Born at sea on the passage from England to Halifax, d. May 18, 1817. Age 100 years and 5 months

32—**Hickman, Kella** Youngest daughter of Jonathan and Susanna Hickman, d. Aug. 12, 1871. Age 10 years

22—**Hickman, Mary Ann** Wife of Henry Hickman, d. March 11, 1857. Age 28

34—**Hickman, Mary Margaret** d. April 28, 1878. Age 14 and **Charles Henry** d. June 25, 1878. Age 10. Children of Henry and Ann Hickman

30—**Hickman, Thomas James** d. Oct. 5, 1870. Age 26

25—**Hickman, Wilson** d. January 12, 1816. Age 52

20—**Rose, John P** No inscription

28—**Tibbo, Susannah** Daughter of George and Esther Tibbo, d. 18? and (J)**Tamsey**, age 4 years

37—**Symes, Jane** Wife of John Symes, d. Jan 6, 1868. Age 61

5—No surname inscription Children **Ann, Eleanor, Eleanor A,** and **Benjamin**

35—No surname inscription d. 1875. Age 56

3—No inscription

19—No inscription

2—Handrigan, Pardy, Miller, Tibbo, Welsh, Downey, Gould, Lake, Blagdon, Osmond, Major Side #1 Bros John T. Handrigan, age 36; Matthew Pardy, age 29; John Tibbo, age 26; Philip Downey, age 22 who were lost at sea on the schooner TUBAL CAIN.

Side #2 Bros William E. Lake, age 30; Saul Major, age 25 who were drowned May 10, 1906.

Side #3 Bros Thomas Miller, age 29; George T. Welsh, age 23; George Gould, age 23; Philip Blagdon, age 26 who were lost at sea on the NELLIE HARRIS

On October 22, 1954, this brief article appeared in the *Daily News*:

FIND TOMBSTONE OF EARLY SETTLER

Grand Bank (special). Workmen excavating under the Frazer Hall here on Tuesday unearthed a tombstone of one of the earliest residents of Grand Bank. The tombstone, although broken in two pieces, clearly bears the inscription "Esther Forsey, died July 19th, 1827 aged 76 years", which indicates the person was born here over 200 years ago. The Frazer Hall was erected 50 years ago, being opened on October 26, 1904.

APPENDIX B

Main Street Methodist Gravestones

𝕿he oldest stone dates 1877; the latest 1937. There are 71 in the 1800s and 55 in the 1900s. Six stones show children died from diphtheria, and for those markers indicating shipping disaster, I have noted the ship.

Marker Number:

102—**Belbin, Elizabeth** Wife of James Belbin, d. July 27, 1908. Age 66

103—**Belbin, James** Husband of Elizabeth Belbin, d. Sept 28, 1906. Age 67

104—**Belbin, Selina Maud** Daughter of James and Elizabeth, d. March 13, 1907. Age 23

26—**Bell, May** d. July 2, 1884, age 7. **Edith Bell** d. June 24, 1884. Children of George and Amelia Bell. Diphtheria

81—**Bradley, Christianna** Wife of Samuel Bradley, d. Feb 4, 1915. Age 74. **Henry Bradley** Son of Samuel and Christianna Bradley; husband of A.J. Bradley. Drowned at sea July 2, 1889. Age 25

83—**Bradley, Claudie** Son of d. Bradley. Born Oct 31, 1902; d. June 2, 1906

82—**Bradley, Samuel** Husband of Christianna Bradley. d. Sept 5, 1883. Age 58

71—**Buffett, Benjamin R.** d. April 9, 1894, age 66. **Dinah P. Buffett**, d. Dec 6, 1898. Age 65. Both of Grand Bank

101—**Buffett, George** d. June 12, 1886. Age 80

37—**Buffett, James Samuel** d. Sept 17, 1878. Age 11. **Margaret Buffett** d. July 24, 1881. Age 6. Children of Thomas and Hannah Buffett

97—**Buffett, Maxie** d. Nov 9, 1899. Age 3

78—**Buffett, Sarah** Wife of Wm Buffett, b. March 30, 1815, d. Jan 3, 1894. **William Buffett** b. Oct 11, 1807, d. Jan 21, 1894

98—**Buffett, Violet** Child of George and Julia Buffett. d. Sept 22, 1892. Age 13

77—**Camp, Amelia** d. March 18, 1887. Age 36

111—**Churchill, Joseph** Who lost his life at Reserve Mines, C.B. Nov 12, 1907. Age 31 **Eleanor Florence Churchill** Age 3, Child of Margaret and Joseph Churchill

117—**Courtney, Dinah Maria** Wife of Henry Courtney. d. Dec 19, 1900, age 31

116—**Courtney, William Geo.** Only child of Henry and late Dinah Courtney d. June 13, 1914. Age 17

67—**Dodman, Charles Henry** Drowned at sea July 24, 1901. Age 19. **Frederick James Dodman** d. Jan 11, 1895. Age 3. Sons of Charles and Esther Dodman

68—**Dodman, Esther** Born Oct 23, 1848; d. Sept 27, 1907

34—**Evans, Christianna B** d. 1885. Age 44

35—**Evans, Thomas Hollett** Son of William and Christianna d. April 20, 1891. Age 20

6—**Foote, George and Clarence** Who were lost at sea in the August Gales of 1892 on the way home from St. John's, NF. Ages 17 and 22 years (Note: This schooner was the *Maggie Foote*.)

23—**Foote, Esther Ann** Wife of George Foote d. Dec 23, 1888. Age 54

5—**Foote, Jane Symes** Daughter of Morgan and Kezia Foote. b. Aug 27, 1867; d. Dec 8, 1927

3—**Foote, Kezia** d. Nov 17, 1910. Age 75

4—**Foote, Morgan** d. April 18, 1888. Age 56

7—**Foote, Morgan** Son of John and Emma Foote d. Oct 2, 1889 Age 2

1—**Foote, Robert** Child of T and B Foote. b. Nov 28, 1889; d. Dec 27, 1889

55—**Forsey, A.** Illegible

85—**Forsey, Ann** d. Aug 15, 1890. Age 67

52—**Forsey, Annie Simms** Daughter of Jacob and Sarah Forsey. d. May 27, 1882. Age 2 months

93—**Forsey, Boyd** Son of Charles P. Forsey. d. Jan 1, 1889 Age 1

58—**Forsey, Christianna** Wife of late George E. Forsey. d. April 5, 1921. Age 78

59—**Forsey, George** Husband of Christianna Forsey. d. Oct 8, 1894. Age 53

92—**Forsey, Georgina** Child of Charles and Mary Ann Forsey. d. July 30, 1882. Age 3

94—**Forsey, Georgina** d. Oct 26, 1883. Age 1

56—**Forsey, J.A.**

53—**Forsey, Jacob Aaron** Son of Jacob and Sarah Jane Forsey. b. May 14, 1883. d. Dec 3, 1883

51—**Forsey, Jacob** b. May 30, 1856 and **Aaron Forsey** b. April 11, 1859 who were lost at sea Dec 13, 1882. Age 26 and 23 (Note: *Ernest J.S. Simms*, owned by Jacob Forsey and captained by Aaron Forsey of Grand Bank, disappeared in the tail end of a hurricane which swept along the South Coast.)

94—**Forsey, Jane** Wife of the late Geo R. Forsey 1845-1927 and **Mary Josephine** 1888-1889

106—**Forsey, John** b. Dec 3 1838, d. July 14, 1929 and **Christianna**. b. Oct 14, 1837, d. Aug 9, 1901

59—**Forsey, Minnie Lucretia** Daughter of George and Christianna Forsey. d. April 15, 1888, age 11

48—**Forsey, Philip N** b. June 30, 1873, drowned at sea Oct 4, 1898 (See Chapter 7, Directory of Banking Schooners, 1898)

125—**Forsey, Robert C** b. April 20, 1834, d. Jan 2, 1907. Age 73 (Note: Robert Forsey was lost on the *Tubal Cain* which disappeared Jan 2-10, 1907, while returning to Grand Bank from Halifax.)

32—**Forsey, Samuel F** b. Sept 2, 1875, d. June 3, 1885

54—**Forsey, Sarah Jane** Wife of Jacob Forsey b. Nov 15, 1859, d. Nov 6, 1937 and **Robert Forward**, father of Sarah Jane Forsey, b. Nov 1829. Lost at Sea 1862 (Note: Schooner *Watchword* was owned by Forward and was lost with crew.)

16—**Forward, Ambrose** d. Dec 28, 1888. Age 61. Also his wife **Olivia**, d. April 2, 1924. Age 79

18—**Forward, Elic** Son of George and Maria Forward d. Oct 10, 1882. Age 3 years

17—**Forward, Elic 2nd** Son of George and Maria Forward who was lost at sea Nov 8, 1903. Age 27

20—**Forward, George** d. March 22, 1930. Age 83

19—**Forward, Maria** Wife of George Forward d. Mar 3, 1927 Age 76

41—**Fowler, Amelia** Wife of Samuel Fowler d. June 29, 1884. Age 28

123—**French, Stephen** Child of John and Julia French, d. April 3, 1907. Age 1 year

?—**Grant, George Thomas** Son of John and Jane Grant, d. Jan 11, 1885. Age 5

75—**Grandy, Esther Ann** Wife of Aaron Grandy d. Dec 16, 1899 Age 66

22—**Green, Spark** Child of George and Agnes Bennett, d. Aug 8, 1906. Age 1 year

9—**Harding, George** d. Feb 8, 1908. Age 77 and his wife **Susanna Collins** d. Nov 27, 1880. Age 39

10—**Harding, Willie Berkley** Child of Isaac and Esther Harding

43—**Harris, Beatrice** Only child of Samuel and Mary Harris. Died of diphtheria, Nov 23, 1877. Age 13 months

47—**H.H.** (No inscription)

45—**Harris, Berkley** Only child of Eli and Catherine Harris. Died of diphtheria June 8, 1883. Age 4 years

2—**Harris, Eleanor** d. Nov. 2, 1889 Age 79

44—**Harris, Harry** child of Eli and Catherine Harris

119—**Hickman, Ann** Wife of Henry John Hickman d. Feb 9, 1924 Age 94

13—**Hickman, Bertha Nina** Daughter of Thomas A. and Maria Hickman. d. April 16, 1887. Age 10

63—**Hickman, Dinah** Wife of Robert A Hickman d. Jly 15, 1882 Age 37

80—**Hickman, Elizabeth** Wife of James W Hickman d. Aug 3,1901 Age 48

122—**Hickman, Elizabeth** Wife of Wilson Hickman d. Apl 17,1907 Age 61

13—**Hickman, Henry John** Husband of Ann Hickman d. Oct 17, 1902

79—**Hickman, James William** d. Nov 16, 1894. Age 50

40—**Hickman, James** d. Sept 27, 1884. Age 95

12—**Hickman, Jonathan** d. May 29, 1882. Age 84

38—**Hickman, Mary** Wife of James Hickman. d. Feb 1, 1884. Age 89

15—**Hickman, Susanna** Wife of Jonathan Hickman d. May 22, 1886 Age 60

14—**Hickman, Thomas A.** Lost at sea Oct 17, 1897. Age 55 (Note: The 57-ton *Mikado* left Grand Bank for Halifax laden with dried cod and disappeared. She was owned and commanded by Thomas Alex Hickman.)

36—**Hickman, Thomas** d. Feb 19, 1884

121—**Hickman, Wilson**Husband of Eliza. Hickman d. June 21, 1906 Age 68

65—**Higgins, Maria** Wife of John Higgins d. Oct 18, 1895

70—**Hiscock, Laura** Daughter of George and Jane Hiscock, who died of diphtheria June 20, 1889. Age 11

120—**Hiscock, Georgie** Child of Josiah and Beatrice Hiscock, b. Oct. 23, 1901; d. May 12, 1904

68—**Hiscock, Josiah** A native of Trinity d. at Grand Bank, Aug 26, 1898. Age 82

29—**Hiscock, Mahala** d. Jan 13, 1894. Age 84

50—**Hiscock, Mary** b. Dec 20, 1835, d. Jan 15, 1908. Age 73

90—**Hudson, Alan** d. Nov 4, 1898. Age 37

91—**A.H.** undecipherable

21—**Hyde, Samuel B** b. Oct 22, 1900, d. Nov 17, 1900 and **Christie P. Hyde** b. Nov 7, 1903 d. June 17, 1906

33—**Kendell, Annie** Daughter of Francis and Emma Kendell. d. March 4, 1887. Age 18

31—**Lawrence, Sarah** b. Jly 22, 1840 d April 26, 1899 Also husband **Benjamin Lawrence** b March 11, 1835 Drowned at sea Sept 4, 1870. (Note: This was the *Elizabeth*, owned by Benjamin Lawrence and lost with 4 crew.)

74—**Lempriere, Alfred T** Son of A&H Lempriere d. Mar 12, 1887 Age 1

11—**Lovell, Helen** Wife of Benjamin Lovell d. April 5, 1888 Age 62 Also **Jennie** d. April 18, 1888. Age 18

115—**Matthews, Henry Garfield** Child of John W and M Matthews d. July 30, 1902. Age 3 months

24—**Mitchell, Jane** Wife of Will M Mitchell d. Mar 12, 1885 Age 26

30—**Newhook, Lavinia** Wife of Albert Newhook d. of diphtheria Nov 9, 1884. Age 23 and son **Benjamin** d. Oct 6, 1884. Age 9 mths

8—**Normore, Robert** of Belle Isle, Conception Bay, a member of the crew of the "Myrtle" drowned in doing his duty at Grand Bank Oct 18, 1897. Age 27 (Note: *Myrtle* was owned by Foote's business, but was not lost with crew. Normore may have been washed overboard.)

76—**Oldford, Thomas** Husband of Frances Mary Oldford d. Sept 9, 1899 Age 47

66—**Pardy, William** d. Sept 5, 1885. Age 75 also his wife **Esther** d. May 29, 1885. Age 67

60—**Parsons, Max** Child of Selby and Louisa Parsons b. Oct 8, 1893, d. March 6, 1896

46—**Patten, Harriet** Child of Charles and Eleanor Hickman d. of diphtheria Nov 16, 1884

107—**Patten, George** Husband of Julia Patten who died at Halifax, N.S. Sept 2, 1902. Age 38

112—**Patten, Lizzie E** Wife of Walter Patten d. at Louisburg, C.B. Aug 4, 1905. Age 31

42—**Peach, Gertie** Child of Harry and Mina Peach d. Jan 28, 1889. Age 11 months

49—**Riggs, Dinah** Wife of William Riggs d. May 13, 1882. Age 24

124—**Riggs, Mary Grace** and **Clarence** Wife and child of John Riggs. d. April 11, 1906. Age 44 and March 24, 1907. Age 3 years

113—**Riggs, May** Child of Walter and Lizzie Patten d. Aug 12, 1900 Age 5 months

64—**Rose, Elizabeth Forsey** Wife of Jonathan Rose. d. April 21, 1910. Age 84

84—**Rose, George** Husband of Ann Rose d. Aug 22, 1885. Age 65

61—**Rose, Jonathan** Husband of Elizabeth Rose d. Aug 8, 1885 Age 69

89—**Simms, George** Stipendiary Magistrate and Sub-collector of H.M. Customs d. May 5, 1893. Age 64

39—**Simms, Jabez** Son of George/Amelia Simms d Feb 2, 1883 Age 5

57—**Tibbo, Eleanor Lemon** Wife of Samuel Tibbo d Jan 22,1894 Age 49

108—**Tibbo, Ewart** Son of George/Letitia Tibbo d Feb 15, 1907 Age 2

88—**Tibbo, George** d. Aug 17, 1881. Age 24

126—**Tibbo, Louisa** Wife of Wilson Tibbo d. Sept 11, 1900. Age 75

62—**Tibbo, James** Child of James/Mary Tibbo d. Dec 22, 1888. Age

109—**Tibbo, Norman** b. Aug 16, 1891 d. Sept 12, 1903 and **Ruby Maud** b. Nov 8, 1897, d. Sept 26, 1898. Children of W H & J E Tibbo

110—**Tibbo, Susie** Daughter of W & J Tibbo b. June 26, 1888, d. Aug 15, 1888

114—**Tibbo, Wilson H** Son of Simeon and Grace Tibbo Who was drowned while bathing in Garnish River Sept 5, 1907. Age 28 and **Simeon Noel Tibbo** d. Dec 29, 1929. Age 83 and **Grace Tibbo** Wife of Simeon d. Dec 12, 1922. Age 75

105—**Wood, Alfred Charles** Son of Andrew and Sophie Wood d. May 5, 1903. Age 7

72—**Wood, Andrew** Of Leith, Scotland d Grand Bank Jan 9, 1900 Age 69

73—**Wood, Andrew Lisk** Son of Wm & Esther Wood d Jan 3, 1893 Age 2

Seven stones with indecipherable surnames.

APPENDIX C

Fortune Road Salvation Army Gravestones

𝕿his, the earliest Salvation Army cemetery in Grand Bank, is located on Fortune Road. It has only fifteen stones — the oldest dates 1904; the most recent, with the exception of one, 1919.

Marker Number:

2—**Ansty, John Ben** Son of Samuel and Elizabeth Ansty d. at Pushthrough Nov 22, 1918. Age 19

14-**Belbin, Ann Elizabeth** wife of George L. Belbin d. Aug 19, 1918. Age 49

15—**Clements, Charles Henry** child of George and Hannah Clements d. Nov 17, 1918. Age 8 years

4—**Hickman, Maria F.** child of Henry and Sarah Hickman b. Feb 23, 1913 d. Nov 20, 1918. Age 5

6—**Hiscock, Hector** child of Adj. & B. Hiscock d. Jan 30, 1909

12—**Morris, Thomas** husband of Susan Morris d. April 10, 1917. Age 57. Also **Samuel Morris** Drowned at Sea Oct 14, 1919. Age 20. Also **William Barnes** Drowned at Sea Oct 14, 1919. Age 26 years

8—**Parsons, Emmaline** wife of John Parsons d. Sept 27, 1910. Age 38 years. **Nellie** child of John and Emmaline Parsons d. June 10, 1909 Age 1 year

1—**Riggs, William** husband of Caroline Riggs d. Jan 21, 1917. Age 81 Also **Caroline Riggs** wife of William Riggs d. April 21, 1917. Age 75

9—**Rose, Susie** wife of Charles Rose d. Aug 30, 1915. Age 29

11—**Scott, Susie** 1885-1973

3—**Thorne, J.** 3149 Private Royal Newfoundland Regt. 10th Dec 1917. Age 19

5—**Thorne, Virginia** daughter of Alice and Thomas Thorne d. Nov 21, 1911. Age 15

13—**Vallis, Willie B** child of Edwin and Maggie Vallis d. Dec 19, 1917. Age 1 year

7—**Warren, Annie** wife of James Warren d. June 12, 1918. Age 45

8—**Way, George** b. at Bonavista Nov 30, 1836. d. at Grand Bank, July 24, 1910. Age 74

APPENDIX D

Grand Bank Built Schooners and their Fate

Several local historians have commented on the extent of shipbuilding in Grand Bank. One of the first to do so was Rev. Lench in the 1912 edition of *Newfoundland Quarterly* saying that "Until recent years Grand Bankers built their own schooners and we can remember seeing a dozen vessels on the stocks in one shipbuilding season. From the early morn until the setting sun the otherwise monotonous winter days were made lively by the ringing of the hammers of the ships' carpenters."

Percival Hickman (1886-1966), a Grand Bank marine insurance businessman, kept his own personal diary, studied the history of the town and, in the early 1960s, used his notes to publish a brief account of the town's rise. Hickman wrote, "And so the eighteen-nineties saw an era of shipbuilding. There are many now living who can recall the shipbuilding boom that followed the start of the Bank fishery. There have been as many as seven schooners on the blocks at one time...ranging in size from forty to eighty tons."

Aaron Buffett, in his short history of Grand Bank, wrote of shipbuilding in Grand Bank and identified the areas where schooners were built and launched:

> One was the site where now stands the stores of J.B. Foote and Sons Ltd.[A] A second and third were the sites now occupied by...Forward and Tibbo.[B,C] Another was where the store of J.B. French and others stand.[D] A fifth paralleled Water Street and occupied the sites of the store of Grand Bank Fisheries.[E] And the (sixth) and the seventh was where Mr. Fred Parsons had his dwelling house.[F,G] Since the nineties a dozen or so vessels have been built, the last one being the *D.J. Thornhill*[H]...

These areas today are:

a. Toward the northeast of the stores of J.B. Foote and Sons Ltd. and the Western Marine Insurance Building.

b,c. On the lower bank below the three buildings of Forward and Tibbo, Sharon's Nook, Strowbridge's Barbershop (Walters Woodworking).

d. On upper bank, today's Water Street, near J.B French's confectionary store which is today Piercey and Co., Clip n' Style, MidTown Fashions. In 1878-79 *Daisy Dean* was built a little north of this store (Harding's Forge was once located behind it). According to local tradition she slipped off her blocks during the night —a bad omen. The next year she was lost with crew.

e. Near the former Buffett's Warehouse (today the Brumac building).

f,g. Between J.B. Patten's Store and the Bridge.

h. Point of Beach where the Grand Bank Seafoods Fish Plant is located.

Several years ago Clarence Griffin, who was keenly inter-

Grand Bank, early 1960s, facing northward. The likely shipbuilding sites of 1890-1935 are indicated.

260

ested in shipbuilding and local history, told me he firmly believed there were hundreds of schooners built in Grand Bank. He had frequently asked older men of the shipbuilding industry — his informants lived and worked prior to 1900.

While "hundreds of schooners" may be an over-estimation, no doubt there were more built than are recorded below. The following, and this compilation is by no means complete or exhaustive, were built in Grand Bank. The information came from two main sources: a list submitted to the *Daily News* in the 1930s by vessel owner William Forsey, and Victor Kendall's *List of Ships on the S.W. Coast of Newfoundland 1861-1889*. The following compilation does not include the several boats built and launched by the Grandy brothers' shipbuilding enterprise of the 1950-60s.

What happened to several of the early locally-built schooners is not known. Only a few (and incomplete) records are available and these records indicate that some vessels, after many long years of good service and heavy work, fell to pieces or rotted near their home; many were sold out of Grand Bank usually to St. Pierre or to Newfoundland's North East coast including such places as Greenspond, Newtown and Musgrave Harbour.

Courtesy Ruth Gosse

Tern schooner *General Ironsides* on her launching in the fall of 1920 in an area northeast of J.B. Foote's store. *General Allenby* and *General Currie* were also built on this site. The tall house in the centre is the Thorndyke.

Schooner	Owner	Fate of Schooner
Beothic	Wm & Simeon Tibbo	No oral/written record
Kitty Clyde	Benj & Geo Buffett	Sold NE coast, beached 1940s
Steadfast	W Buffett & G Penny	No oral/written record
Mary Alice	W Buffett & G Penny	No oral/written record
Nellie Gray	George R. Forsey	No oral/written record
A.B. Coen	Geo & Ths Hickman	No oral/written record
Esther	Daniel & Philip Cox	No oral/written record
Sarah Jane	Wm Evans	Lost with 10 crew, Aug. 1886
Royal Albert	Henry Evans	Beached at Grand Bank, 1887
Frances	Joseph Evans	No oral/written record
Theresa	Joseph(or John)Evans	Sold on Western Shore
Antelope	Jonathan Rose	Prob. sold in Burin, lost 1893
Johnnie Rose	Charles Rose	Sold to foreign country
Lizzie Bell	Charles Rose	Sold to St. Pierre, 1899
John B. Foote	Morgan Foote	No oral/written record
Jennie B. Foote	Morgan Foote	No oral/written record
Smuggler	Morgan Foote	Wrecked NE Coast, Dec. 1921
Samuel J. Foote	Thomas Foote	Sold St. Pierre, April 1900
Daisy Dean	Robert Courtney	Lost with 4 crew, Nov. 1880
Pointer	"Pointer" John Forsey	No oral/written record
Grand Master	"Pointer" J. Forsey	Wrecked at St. Pierre Hr. 1885
George R. Hyde	Ambrose Hyde	No oral/written record
Dauntless	Thomas Harris	Abandoned at sea, 1863
George C. Harris	Samuel Harris	renamed Kitchener Aban'ed Atlantic
Emily Harris	Samuel Harris	Sold & broken up Burin, 1919
Mary F. Harris	Samuel Harris	Wrecked Labrador Nov 6, 1919
Nellie Harris	Samuel Harris	Lost with 6 crew, Nov. 4, 1906
Wallie G	Spencer(Fortune)	Lost Nova Scotia, 1933
Castle Carey	Samuel Harris	Abandoned at sea Feb. 23, 1922
Ruby	Samuel Harris	Wrecked Louisbourg, N.S. May 5, 1910
Bessie Mcdonald	Samuel Harris	Wrecked Old Perlican Nov. 9, 1932
Blanche Forsey	Samuel Harris	Wrecked Blanc Sablon July 26,'29
General Allenby (tern)	Harris Export Co Ltd	Wrecked Oporto, Jan. 1922
General Currie (tern)	Harris Exp. Co Ltd	Wrecked St. Pierre, 1922
General Ironsides (tern)	Harris Exp. Co Ltd	Wrecked & sold to Portugal, 1923

Roberta Ray (tern)	Harris Exp. Co Ltd	Abandoned at sea March 19, 1921
Idol or (Idler)	William Buffett	Lost with 4 crew Oct. 16, 1876
Julia Forsey	Geo A. Buffett	Wrecked at N.S., May 31, 1918
Sunbeam	Geo A. Buffett	Burned Pugwash Harbour ?
Occident	Geo A. Buffett	Sold & wrecked West Coast, Dec. 4, 1927
Orion	Geo A. Buffett	Lost 17 crew St. of Belle Isle, Oct 5, 1907
Pleadias	Geo A. Buffett	Wrecked West C. Nov 16, 1925
Rosanna Hickman	Samuel Hickman	Sold to foreigners, 1887
R.J. Pincent	Simeon Tibbo	Wrecked Dantzig Cove May 2, 1891
George E. Tibbo	Simeon Tibbo	Wrecked Labrador Sept. 26, 1927
Mary Florence	Samuel Tibbo	Wrecked Rose Blanche
Winnie Pierce	Samuel Tibbo	Wrecked 1927
W.H. Tibbo	George Tibbo	No oral/written record
Princess Royal	George Tibbo	Sunk in collision, 1872
Mary	John Hiscock	No oral/written record
Annie Rose	Rose & Riggs	Sold to a foreign country, prob. Canada
John and Helen	Thomas Riggs	Broken up in G.B. Harbour, 1877
Carrie E	Aaron Grandy	No oral/written record
Lizzie Bennett	Benj. Bennett	Wrecked on the Labrador, 1908
George Foote	Foote Bros	Lost with 17 crew on Banks, Aug 1892
Maggie Foote	Foote Bros	Lost with 5 crew off Cape Race, Aug 22, 1892
Clarence Foote	Bowering Bros/Foote	Lost with 5 crew Aug. 16, 1893
Grand Banker	Geo. & Chas. Forsey	Sold to St. Pierre, fate obscure
Emma Martell	George Forward	Broken up at Rose Blanche, 1906
Prince of Wales	Geo&Thomas Simms	Lost with 4 crew, Dec. 1875
Pointer (II)	Chs & Benj Pardy	No oral/written record
George Kendall	Jonathan Evans	Abandoned in the Atlantic
Selena Forsey	Joshua & John Forsey	Wrecked Oct. 19, 1901
Lucretia Camp	John Camp	Wrecked between 1880-1885
Artolan	George Bell	No oral/written record
Pilot	Charles Forsey	No oral/written record
Mary Bell	Geo & Samuel Bell	No oral/written record
Ernest J.S. Simms	Thomas A. Hickman	Lost with 5 crew in Gulf, Dec. 13, 1882
Bertha Hickman	Thomas A. Hickman	No oral/written record
Village Belle	James Hickman	Sold north, No record
W.M. Mitchell	James Hickman	Broken up at Grand Bank, 1904

Myrtle	John B. Foote	Wrecked Sydney, May 22, 1938
Cora	John B. Foote	Wrecked Sydney, Nov 10, 1910
Esther Tibbo	Jonathan Tibbo	Sold to St. Pierre 1890-93, broken up
Sisters	Aaron Forsey	No oral/written record
Three Sisters	Jonathan Hickman	No oral/written record
Grace Tibbo	Simeon Tibbo&Sons	Wrecked Rose Blanche, Mar. 26, 1912
Prospector	Simeon Tibbo&Sons	Wrecked at St. Pierre
Tubal Cain	Simeon Tibbo&Sons	Lost 7 crew in Gulf, Jan. 2-10, 1907
Linda Tibbo	Simeon Tibbo&Sons	Sold N E Coast, obscure
Carl Tibbo (tern)	Simeon Tibbo&Sons	Wrecked Seldom, Nov. 20, 1919
George Rose	C. Forward/R. Rose	Wrecked Labrador Sept 26, 1927
Sentinel	Thomas Foote	Wrecked Rose Blanche, Feb. 1930
Maude Foote	Thomas Foote	Sold Fortune Bay, obscure
Passport	Thomas Foote	Sold, lost with crew NE Coast Dec. 5, 1921
Lucy Howse	J. Smith (Hr. Breton)	Sunk by German sub Mar. 13, 1917
D.J. Thornhill	John Thornhill	Abandoned in Gulf, January 1943

APPENDIX E

Directories of 1816, 1864, 1870, 1892 and 1936 Knight's List of Subscribers

Rev. Richard Knight, who brought the Wesleyan denomination to Grand Bank in 1816, fortunately kept a list of his subscribers for the new Grand Bank church he proposed to build. Merchant Edward Evans collected the church fees at his shop on Water Street.

The following is Knight's first list shows only men. (It may not show all homeowners of the town.) Most likely the list was first handwritten and transcribed by a person unfamiliar with local surnames and several names may be misspelled, e.g., Lambord (Lambert), Landrigan (Handrigan), Philben (Belbin) and Mouster (Monster).

Bask, John	Francis, John	Montory, John
Brice, Henry	Gale, John	Mouster, James
Buffett, Reuben	Grandy, Philip jr	Osmond, Benjamin
Chilcott, Robert	Hamlyn, William	Parsons, Benjamin
Collier, Jasper	Hickman, Jonathan	Parsons, Thomas
Cox, Thomas	Hickman, James	Patten, Charles
Croker, Thomas	Higgins, Thomas	Patten, Edward
Davis, George	Keef, John	Peckford, Samuel
Dinman, Francis	Lambord, James	Philben, Robert
Durrant, James	Landrigan, Thomas	Pitt, Joseph
Evans, William	Lewis, John	Rose, Robert
Foote, John sr	Lovell, Benjamin	Russel, Thomas
Forsey, George	Mackay, James	Tibbo, John
Forward, Ambrose	Makeley, John	

Hutchinson's Directory for 1864-65
Grand Bank Entry

Note: Hutchinson's list of occupations in Newfoundland enumerates people in various government positions and specific trades. The majority of employed people (labourers and fishermen) in Grand Bank were connected with the fishery and their names are not listed.

Thomas Bird	watchmaker
Josiah Blackburn	stipendiary magistrate
Edward Evans	J.P., M.H.A., merchant
William Evans	letter carrier
Jonathan Hickman	post master
Rev. J.S. Phinney	(clergy)
Cyrus Wood	school teacher

McAlpine's Maritime Provinces Directory, 1870
Grand Bank

Note: Often these directories listed only men, and then only those over a certain age; for example, twenty-five. Possibly some of these people, like Weymouth, lived in Molliers, a small town a few miles east of Grand Bank.

Bennett, Robert fisherman	Hawkins, Jonathan fisherman
Buffett, William sr fisherman	Hickman, Charles planter
Courtney, Robert planter	Hickman, George fisherman
Cox, Philip fisherman	Hickman, Robert fisherman
D'Eugene, Auguste cooper	Hickman, Thomas fisherman
Evans, Edward merchant	McGregor, Edwin physician
Evans, Henry fisherman	Nicolle, Edward fisherman
Evans, Joseph fisherman	Nicolle, Philip fisherman
Evans, William G. planter	Power, Mark fisherman
Forsey, John fisherman	Rose, Jonathan planter
Forsey, George G. trader	Scott, John trader
Forsey, Aaron planter	Stoodley, George fisherman
Harding, George blacksmith	Weymouth, William fisherman

McAlpine's Newfoundland Directory, 1898
Grand Bank

Note: These Grand Bank surnames are reproduced as they appear in the Directory; alphabetical order is not accurate and there are various spellings (or mis-spellings) of names. In this directory the only women listed are widows. Housewives, store clerks and women who worked on beaches are not given.

To distinguish between those who have the same name, the father's name is in brackets.

Ayre Hester	widow of John
Anstey Samuel	fisherman
Anstey Wm	fisherman
Abbott Thos	fisherman
Ahier Elias	fisherman
Butt John T	carpenter
Bethune Alex	carpenter
Bethune Ken	carpenter
Banfield Dav	carpenter
Brown Michael	fisherman
Brewer Mrs.	widow of Benj
Bell Geo	preventive officer
Buffett G A,(j.p.)	general merchant
Buffett Aaron	gentleman
Buffett Dinah	widow of Benjamin
Butt Geo	fisherman
Butt Thos	fisherman
Butt Richard	fisherman
Butt Wm	fisherman
Belben Jas, sr	fisherman
Belben Jas, jr	fisherman
Bradley Christianna	widow of Samuel
Bradley Samson	fisherman
Bradley Nancy	widow of Henry
Bradley Emma	widow of William
Brown John	fisherman
Butler Wm	fisherman
Belbin Wm	fisherman
Bearns Jane	widow of George

Bambury Wm	fisherman
Bevis Mary	widow of John
Banfield Henry	fisherman
Bennett Philip	fisherman
Camp John	custom's officer
Courtney William G	master mariner
Courtney Henry H	fisherman
Cross Edw	fisherman
Cox Philip	ships' carpenter
Cox Esther	widow of Daniel
Chancey Robert	shop keeper
Camp Geo	fisherman
Clements Wm	labourer
Clements Saml	fisherman
Clements Geo	fisherman
Clements Charles	fisherman
Courtney Lydia	widow of Robert
Dunford Geo	shop keeper
Dunford Robert	fisherman
Dunford Ann	widow of Samuel
Dodman Charles	fisherman
Dodman Alford	mariner
Downey Levi	fisherman
Dodge Ann	widow of Edward
Douglas Geo	fisherman
Dear Samuel	fisherman
Diamond Benjamin	fisherman
Dicks William	fisherman
Evans William P	mariner
Evans, Elizabeth	widow of William
Evans Jos sr	master mariner
Evans Esau	sailor
Evans Charlotte	widow of Thomas
Evans Jonathan	master mariner
Evans Ambrose	seaman
Emberly Samuel	fisherman
Evans John	seaman
Forsey William	clerk
Forward Charles	clerk
Forsey Robert F	master mariner
Forsey Joshua	master mariner
Forsey John L(of John)	carpenter

Forward Geo	fisherman
Forward Sarah	widow of Ambrose
Forward Edward	fisherman
Forward Lavinia (Olivia?)	widow of Ambrose
Forsey John Lovell	fisherman
Forsey Stephen	fisher
Forsey Samuel B	master mariner
Forsey Aaron sr Geo	fisherman
Forsey John Ambrose	fisherman
Forsey Robert (Aaron)	fisherman
French Morgan	lobster packer
Forsey John (Geo)	farmer
Forsey John (John)	farmer
Forsey Frederick	lobster packer
Francis Benjamin	fisherman
Francis Jane	widow of John
Francis Jos(son of Benj)	fisherman
Francis Solomon	fisherman
Francis Elizabeth	widow of Joseph
Francis Thomas (Benj)	fisherman
Francis John (Benj)	fisherman
Forsey Robert Chilcot	farmer
Forsey Philip	lobster packer
Forsey Frances	widow of George
Forsey Christianna	widow of George
Forsey Sarah Jane	widow of Jacob
French John B	lobster packer
French William	fisherman
Fowler Samuel	fisherman
Forward Jonathan T	mariner
Francis Jos sr	fisherman
Fox William	lobster packer
Francis Thomas (Jos)	fisherman
Foote Thomas	merchant
Foote Kezia	widow of Morgan
Foote John B	merchant
Foote Amelia	widow of George
Forsey John sr	farmer
Forsey Aaron sr(John)	carpenter
Grandy Aaron	master mariner
Grandy George	mariner

Grandy Jane	widow of Thomas
Grandy Charles	seaman
Grant John jr	fisherman
Grant John sr	farmer
Grant Caleb	farmer
Grant Edwin	mariner
Green Mary	widow of George
Gillard Philip	lobster packer
Gregory Albert	fisherman
Harris Eli	master carpenter
Harris Samuel	merchant
Hartling Mary	widow of William
Hause Elias	fisherman
Hiscock Josiah jr	fisherman
Hickman William	fisherman
Hines George	fisherman
Hines Elizabeth	widow of William
Hickman John Henry	fisherman
Hickman Henry sr	shop keeper
Hickman Joshua	mariner
Hickman Sarah	widow of Jabez
Hickman Jane	widow of Thomas
Hickman Mary	widow of George A
Hickman Priscilla	widow of Samuel
Hickman Maria	widow of Thomas A
Hickman Ellen	widow of George
Hickman Albert	clerk
Hiscock Joseph	master mariner
Hickman George T	telegraph operator
Hickman Morgan	fisherman
Hickman Henry(Morgan)	fisherman
Hiscock John	farmer
Hanlon Robert	fisherman
Hickman George Ed.	master mariner
Hickman Charles	ship carpenter
Hickman Jonath'n (Jon)	fisherman
Hickman Jonathan sr	farmer
Hickman Jas W	master mariner
Hiscock Francis	master mariner
Hickman John R	fisherman
Handrigan Michael	fisherman
Handrigan John T	fisherman

Handrigan William	fisherman
Handrigan Morgan	fisherman
Hyde George F	master mariner
Hyde Mary	widow of Ambrose
Hickman George W	farmer
Harding George sr	blacksmith
Harding George jr	iron worker
Harding Isaac	lobster packer
Harding Herbert	canmaker
Heffernan Elihu	shop keeper
Hudson Jas	fisherman
Hiscock Josiah sr	light keeper
Hiscock Mary	widow of Josiah
Hickman Robert A	fisherman
Hollett Benjamim	fisherman
Hiscock George	master mariner
Higgins John	master mariner
Hickman Jonathan (Geo)	carpenter
Hickman Wilson	fisherman
Hollett James	fisherman
Innes James	fisherman
Kelly James	fisherman
Keating Richard	fisherman
Keating John	fisherman
Keating Philip	fisherman
Keating David	fisherman
Keating Luke	fisherman
Keeping Snook	fisherman
Lee Joseph	fisherman
Laurence Charles	fisherman
Lovell George	fisherman
Lovell Jane	widow of Wilson
Lovell Stephen	fisherman
Lucas Josiah	gentleman
Lucas Henry	fisherman
Lambert Samuel	fisherman
Lambert John	fisherman
Lee Robert	labourer
Lee George	fisherman
Lee Henry	fisherman
Matthews Henry	fisherman
Matthews John W (Chas)	master mar'er

Matthews Mary	widow of Charles
Matthews George	fisherman
Matthews Benjamin	fisherman
Matthews Morgan	fisherman
Matthews William sr	fisherman
Matthews John (Wm)	fisherman
Matthews Wilson (Wm)	fisherman
Matthews Thos Fox	fisherman
Matthews Joseph	fisherman
Matthews John Rd	fisherman
Matthews Wilson (Jos)	fisherman
Matthews William Poole	fisherman
Matthews William T	fisherman
Matthews John (Wm)	fisherman
Moores Elizabeth	widow of James
McDonald Allan	physician
Millington James	shoreman
Munden George	fisherman
Morris Thomas	fisherman
Murphy William	fisherman
Nicolle Edward	fisherman
Nicolle Philip jr	fisherman
Nicolle Philip sr	fisherman
Nicolle Henry	fisherman
Nicolle Joshua	fisherman
Noseworthy Richard	fisherman
Noseworthy Wilson	fisherman
Noseworthy John	fisherman
Nurse Rev James	methodist minister
Nurse Susan	widow of James
Osmond John	fisherman
Oldford Thomas	constable
Osmond George	farmer
Osmond William	fisherman
Patten John B	master mariner
Patten George	master mariner
Penwell William	fisherman
Penwell John	fisherman
Penwell Thomas	fisherman
Pike Thomas	fisherman
Patten John	farmer
Patten Albert	shoemaker

Patten Simeon	fisherman
Patten Aaron	fisherman
Patten Philip (Simeon)	fisherman
Patten John T	fisherman
Patten Sarah Ann	widow of Edward
Parsons John R	fisherman
Parsons Morgan	fisherman
Parsons Dinah	widow of John
Pardy Benjamin	seaman
Patten Charles	carpenter
Patten Philip sr	carpenter
Patten Cyrus R	fisherman
Piercy Samuel	master mariner
Parsons Selby	sail maker
Pardy Charles (Wm)	master mariner
Pardy Samuel	mariner
Pardy Frederick	fisherman
Pardy Reuben	fisherman
Pardy Charles (John)	fisherman
Pardy Jos	fisherman
Poole Mary	widow of Reuben
Rendell George	fisherman
Ro(a)lph Samuel	fisherman
Ro(a)lph Robert	fisherman
Rose Robert sr(Samuel)	farmer
Rose Wilson (Robert)	fisherman
Rose Thomas J	fisherman
Rose Jas (Jonathan)	lobster packer
Rose John (Jas)	seaman
Rose John sr	seaman
Rogers Joshua	fisherman
Rogers Benjamin	fisherman
Rose Charles sr	master mariner
Rose Robert C	mariner
Riggs Richard	fisherman
Riggs John (Richard)	fisherman
Riggs Henry	fisherman
Riggs Thomas	fisherman
Riggs George Benj	fisherman
Riggs John (Thomas)	fisherman
Riggs Robert	fisherman
Rose George	seaman

Rogers William	fisherman
Rogers Robert	fisherman
Riggs Mary	widow of Henry
Riall Jas W	fisherman
Rose Wilson (George)	fisherman
Rose Samuel (George)	fisherman
Rose Abner	fisherman
Rose Susan	widow of Samuel
Rose Robert (George)	fisherman
Rose Archibald	fisherman
Rose Ann	widow of George
Rose Charles (George)	fisherman
Rose Susan	widow of Wilson
Riggs William sr	fisherman
Riggs Amelia	widow of Morgan
Riggs William jr	master mariner
Riggs Harriet	widow of George
Rose Samuel James	mariner
Stoodley Samuel	fisherman
Simms Elizabeth	widow of Thomas
Stoodley John	fisherman
Stoodley Susan	widow of Frank
Simms Aaron	fisherman
Simms Amelia	widow of George
Stoodley Thomas	tinsmith
Stone Christopher	bricklayer
Stoodley Robert	fisherman
Stoodley Henry	fisherman
Stoodley George	fisherman
Thornhill John	fisherman
Thornhill George	fisherman
Tibbo George sr	mariner
Tibbo Jonathan jr	mariner
Tibbo Wilson H	master mariner
Tibbo Jonathan sr	master mariner
Tibbo John F	mariner
Tibbo George (Jon'an)	mariner
Tibbo Robert (Jon'an)	mariner
Tibbo Samuel sr	master mariner
Tibbo Simeon Noel	general dealer
Tibbo Samuel jr	fisherman
Tibbo Wilson (Thomas)	fisherman

Trim(m) John	fisherman
Thornhill James	fisherman
Thornhill Luke	fisherman
Thornhill Christiana	widow of William
Trim George	fisherman
Trim Henry	fisherman
Trim William	fisherman
Trim Jane	widow of Henry
Thorn Thomas	fisherman
Vincent Thomas	fisherman
Weeks Eli	fisherman
Welsh Edwin	fisherman
Way Josiah	mill wright
Wooden Thomas	fisherman
Williams John sr	fisherman
Wines Henry	fisherman
Welsh Joshua	fisherman
Welsh John (John)	ships' carpenter
Welsh John sr	fisherman
Wines Isaac	fisherman
Way George	shoe maker
Warren Aaron	fisherman
Warren James	fisherman
Warren Albert	fisherman
Warren William	fisherman
Woundy James	mariner
Wooden Benjamin	fisherman
Weymouth Jacob	fisherman
Walsh Thomas sr	fisherman
Walsh Thomas (Thomas)	fisherman
Woods William	blacksmith
Woods Andrew S	tinsmith
Way W P	teacher
Williams Henry	fisherman
Williams Charles sr	farmer
Williams John	fisherman
Williams Charles jr	fisherman
Whittle Benjamin	fisherman

Newfoundland Directory, 1936
Grand Bank Section

Note: These Grand Bank surnames are reproduced as they appear in the 1936 Directory; abbreviations of occupations; various spellings (or mis-spellings) of names; and, although a few working women are included, housewives and women who worked on the beaches drying fish were not listed in the directory.

Ahier Miss Esther hsekpr

Ahier Joshua fshrmn

Almeda Augustina hsekpr

Anderson John clk Bank of Nova Scotia

Anstey Miss Annie hsekpr

Anstey Miss Laura hsekpr

Anstey Miss Lizzie clk P. Dunford

Anstey Henry lab

Anstey Saml Sr fshrman

Anstey Saml Jr fshrman

Anstey Wm fshrmn

Ashcroft Miss Jane hsekpr

Baker Arthur fshrmn

Baker Miss Bessie hsekpr

Baker Felix fshrmn

Baker Frederick fshrmn

Baker John fshrmn

Baker Walter fshrmn

Bambury Wm fshrmn

Bearnes Jacob lab

Bearns Samuel fshrmn

Belbin Absalom lab

Belbin George fshrmn

Belbin James fshrmn

Bennett Cecil fshrmn

Bradley Henry clk G & A Buffett

Breon Berkely fshrmn

Bolt Thomas fshrmn

Brown Angus fshrmn

Brown George fshrmn

Brown John fshrmn

Brown Robert fshrmn

Buffett Aaron mer G & A Buffett

Buffett, G & A Ltd. **vessel owners, general merchant, ex & importers**

Buffett Miss Jean clk G & A Buffett

Buffett Thomas fshrmn

Buffett Miss Violet clk G & A Buffett

Buffett Wilfred clk

Bullen John fshrmn

Burke J B MD

Burke Stanley fshrmn

Butler Charles fshrmn

Butler John fshrmn

Butler Miss Mary hsekpr

Butt Richard fshrmn

Butt Thomas fshrmn

Butt William fshrmn

Camp Henry lab

Camp John lab

Carberry William fshrmn

Carr P L mgr Grand Bank Fisheries

Clements Charles fshrmn

Clements George fshrmn

Clements Henry fshrmn

Clements Miss Minnie hsekpr

Clements Samuel fshrmn

Comben Geo fshrmn

Comben Robert fshrmn

Coombs Charles fshrmn

Cornish Thomas fshrmn

Courtney William lab
Crews William fshrmn
Crowley Hubert fshrmn
Crocker W fshrmn
Crowley Mrs Christina
  hskpr Crowley James
  lab
Diamond George
  fshrmn
Dicks William fshrmn
Dodman Les
  clk William Forsey
Dodman Les lab
Dollimount Abraham
  fshrmn
Douglas George fshrmn
Downey Theodore
  fshrmn
Drake Arthur fshrmn
Drake Denis fshrmn
Drake John fshrmn
Dunford George
  mgr Grand Bank
  Fisheries
Dunford Maxwell
  clk Grand Bank
  Fisheries
Elms Robert lab
Elms Reuben fshrmn
Emberley Fred fshrmn
Emberley William carp
Evans Miss Bessie
  clk William P. Evans
Evans Miss Eleanor
  hsekpr
Evans William mer
Eveleigh Ches fshrmn
Eveleigh Miss M

clk R. Dunford
Fizzard John fshrmn
Fizzard William fshrmn
Follett Benjamin lab
Follett Edward fshrmn
Follett George capt
Follett Miss Mary
  hsekpr
Follett Stanley fshrmn
Foote Ambrose mer
Foote Miss Cora
  clk Bank of
  Nova Scotia
Foote George mer
Foote J B & Sons Ltd
  gen dealers
  imports & ex
Foote Miss Kezia
  clk J B Foote &
  Sons Ltd
Foote Robert
  clk Forward & Tibbo
Foote Thomas lab
Forsey Aaron lab
Forsey Aaron fshrmn
Forsey Miss Annie
  clk Grand Bank
  Fisheries
Forsey Mrs. A hsekpr
Forsey Ches
  clk William Forsey
Forsey Curtis
  Mgr William Forsey
Forsey Hedley fshrmn
Forsey John lab
Forsey Leonard fshrmn
Forsey Leonard lab
Forsey Miss Mabel opr

Forsey Miss Meta
  clk S. Piercy
Forsey Reuben
  clk Grand Bank
  Fisheries
Forsey Robert lab
Forsey Samuel
  agt Canada Packers Ltd.
Forsey Stephen capt
Forsey WM
  vessel ownr,
  mer, ex & im
Forward & Tibbo
  vessel ownrs,
  mer, ex & im
Forward Charles mer
Forward Miss Sarah
  clk Forward & Tibbo
Fowler Samuel fshrmn
Fox Lawson
  cook Customs Boat
Fox Samuel fshrmn
Fox William Jr lab
Fox William Sr lab
Francis Eli fshrmn
Francis John fshrmn
Francis Jos fshrmn
Francis Solomon fshrmn
Francis Solomon lab
French George line
  repairer
French John mer
French Ray
  clk J French
French William lab
Garland Mrs Thomas
  hsekpr
Gillard Miss Bella

clk G & A Buffett
Gillard Robert fshrmn
Grand Bank
Fisheries
  vessel ownr,
  mer, ex & im
Grand Bank Phar-
macy
  chemist, druggist
Grandy George fshrmn
Grandy Harry fshrmn
Grandy Hugh fshrmn
Grandy Mrs John hsekpr
Grandy Stephen fshrmn
Grant Edwin fshrmn
Grant William lab
Green Benjamin lab
Green Frederick fshrmn
Green John fshrmn
Gregory Dan fshrmn
Griffin Henry fshrmn
Guy Hubert teacher
Haines George fshrmn
Handrigan George
  fshrmn
Handrigan John fshrmn
Handrigan Miss Minnie
  clk J B Foote & Son
Handrigan Morgan
  barbr
Handrigan Morley
  fshrmn
Handrigan Robert
  fshrmn
Handrigan Stanley
  fshrmn
Hanlon John fshrmn
Harding Miss Bessie

clk G & A Buffett
Harding George
  blksmith
Harding Herbert lab
Harding John
  clk Grand Bank
  Fisheries
Harding William lab
Harding William
  clk G & A Buffett
Harris Miss Christie
  clk Grand Bank
  Fisheries
Harris Eli lab
Harris George lab
Harris John R fshrmn
Harris Sydney capt
Harris Thomas capt
Hatcher Mrs W hsekpr
Haskell Robert fshrmn
Hawkins Edward
  fshrmn
Hawkins Elias fshrmn
Hawkins Jonathan
  fshrmn
Hayward Wallace
  fshrmn
Hayward William lab
Hickman Miss Alice clk
Hickman Chester
  fshrmn
Hickman Clarence
  fshrmn
Hickman Mrs George
  hsekpr
Hickman George lab
Hickman George
  fshrmn

Hickman Henry fshrmn
Hickman Henry lab
Hickman James fshrmn
Hickman James lab
Hickman James fshrmn
Hickman John J fshrmn
Hickman Jonathan lab
Hickman Jos fshrmn
Hickman Morgan
  fshrmn
Hickman Percival lab
Hickman Robert lab
Hickman Ronald fshrmn
Hickman Samuel lab
Hickman Thomas
  fshrmn
Hickman William
  fshrmn
Hickman Wilson fshrmn
Hiscock George lab
Hiscock Josiah capt
Hiscock Miss Mary clk
Hiscock Miss Tilly tchr
Hollett Edward lab
Hollett James fshrmn
Hyde George lab
Hyde John
  sub collector
  HM Customs
Hyde Norman lab
Keating David lab
Keating Miss Elsie clk
Keating John fshrmn
Keating Luke fshrmn
Keating William lab
Keeping Heber fshrmn
King George fshrmn
Laing Gerald K

Mrg Bank of
  Nova Scotia
Lambert Ambrose lab
Lawrence Jos lab
Lee Benjamin fshrmn
Lee Foot laundry
Lee George fshrmn
Lee Henry fshrmn
Lee Henry lab
Lee Morgan lab
Legge Henry fshrmn
Loveys John lab
Lucas Boyd lab
Lucas Miss Caroline
  clk Forward & Tibbo
Lucas Henry fshrmn
Martin Alfred fshrmn
Matthews Arthur
  fshrmn
Matthews Charles
  fshrmn
Matthews Cross fshrmn
Matthews George
  fshrmn
Matthews Jacob fshrmn
Matthews James fshrmn
Matthews John fshrmn
Matthews John H
  fshrmn
Matthews Leonard
  fshrmn
Matthews Robert
  fshrmn
Matthews Mrs R hsekpr
Matthews William
  fshrmn
Matthews William barbr
Matthews William lab

Miller Edward fshrmn
Miller Frederick lab
Miller George fshrmn
Miller John fshrmn
Moore James fshrmn
Moore John fshrmn
Moulton George fshrmn
Moulton James fshrmn
Mullins John fshrmn
Murphy Ambrose
  fshrmn
Murphy Edward seamn
Murphy Thomas fshrmn
Nicholle John fshrmn
Noseworthy James
  fshrmn
Noseworthy John
  fshrmn
Noseworthy Wilson
  fshrmn
Nurse George lab
Osbourne John lab
Osbourne Wilson
  blksmth
Osmond Clyde fshrmn
Osmond Garfield
  fshrmn
Osmond George fshrmn
Osmond William
  fshrmn
Pardy Ben fshrmn
Pardy Benjamin fshrmn
Pardy Charles fshrmn
Pardy Elias fshrmn
Pardy Samuel fshrmn
Pardy William Jr lab
Pardy William fshrmn
Parsons Frederick capt

Parsons John R fshrmn
Patten Cecil tsmn
Patten Cyrus lab
Patten George machnic
Patten Gerald
  clk J B Patten & Sons
Patten Gus
  clk J B Patten & Sons
Patten J B & Sons Ltd
  gen ex & im dried fish
Patten Louis lab
Patten Miss Margaret
  clk J B Patten & Sons
Patten Samuel
  mgr J B Patten & Sons
Penwell Jacob fshrmn
Penwell John opr
Penwell William lab
Piercy Alec
  clk S Piercy
Piercy Henry garage
Piercy Miss Myrtle
  clk S Piercy
Piercy S
  dealer dry goods,
  prov, vess
Pike Joseph fshrmn
Pike Thomas lab
Poole Charles lab
Price John fshrmn
Price Thomas Jr fshrmn
Price Thomas Sr
  fishrmn
Prior Albert fshrmn
Prior Charles fshrmn
Pynn James lab
Ralph John fshrmn
Ralph Steve fshrmn

279

Riggs Bert lab
Riggs Clyde lab
Riggs Edward fshrmn
Riggs Ernest
 clk John R Riggs
Riggs George fshrmn
Riggs Harry fshrmn
Riggs Robert fshrmn
Riggs William fshrmn
Rodgers Benjamin
 fshrmn
Rodgers Edward fshrmn
Rodgers Garfield
 (fshrmn)
Rodgers George Jr
 fshrmn
Rodgers George Sr
 fshrmn
Rodgers Harry fshrmn
Rodgers James R
 fshrmn
Rodgers James Jr lab
Rodgers James Sr
 fshrmn
Rodgers John fshrmn
Rodgers Joseph lab
Rodgers Louis fshrmn
Rodgers Luke lab
Rodgers William lab
Rose Abner fshrmn
Rose Arch fshrmn
Rose Charles lab
Rose Charles fshrmn
Rose Charles capt
Rose Mrs George hsekpr
Rose George fshrmn
Rose Miss Grace
 clk J B Patten & Sons

Rose James lab
Rose John lab
Rose Mrs Martha wid
Rose Miss Nellie
 clk Grand Bank
 Fisheries
Rose Robert lab
Rose Samuel fshrmn
Rose Miss Susan
 clk Grand Bank
 Fisheries
Rose Thomas tchr
Rose Wilson lab
Ruelokke Charles lab
Ryall Charles lab
Saunders Ambrose
 fshrmn
Shute Miss Annie
 J R Riggs
Shute John fshrmn
Skinner Abraham
 fshrmn
Skinner Arthur fshrmn
Skinner Miss Edith
 clk W Forsey
Smith Alec capt
Smith John capt
Smith Joseph fshrmn
Smith Leo fshrmn
Smith Leslie fshrmn
Smith Renold fshrmn
Smith Robert fshrmn
Smith William J fshrmn
Snook Benjamin fshrmn
Snook Levi fshrmn
Snook Thomas fshrmn
Squires Cyril capt
Stoodley Alan

 clk Bank of
 Nova Scotia
Stoodley Alex lab
Stoodley George fshrmn
Stoodley Henry fshrmn
Stoodley John barbr
Stoodley John lab
Stoodley Raymond
 fshrmn
Stoodley Robert electrcn
Stoodley Robert lab
Stoodley Samuel
 tnsmith
 Thomas Stoodley
Stoodley Thomas
 tnsmith
Strowbridge Charles
 fshrmn
Thomas Charles fshrmn
Thomasen Henry capt
Thorndyke Hotel
 Mrs J Thornhill,
 propr'ss
Thorne George fshrmn
Thorne James fshrmn
Thorne Joseph fshrmn
Thorne William fshrmn
Thornhill Arch fshrmn
Thornhill Frank capt
Thornhill Isaac fshrmn
Thornhill Jacob fshrmn
Thornhill James fshrmn
Thornhill Miss Jane
 clk Forward & Tibbo
Thornhill John capt
Thornhill John F fshrmn
Thornhill Nelson
 fshrmn

Thornhill Reuben capt
Thornhill Thomas
  fshrmn
Thornhill Wallace
  fshrmn
Thornhill William
  fshrmn
Thornhill William capt
Tibbo Aaron lab
Tibbo Mrs C hsekpr
Tibbo Felix mer
Tibbo George lab
Tibbo George Sr lab
Tibbo Merril
  relieving off
Tibbo Samuel fshrmn
Tibbo Willis
  clk G & A Buffett
Tibbo Wilson fshrmn
Tizzard William fshrmn
Trim Miss Byatt hsekpr
Trim Morgan fshrmn
Trim William fshrmn
Vallis Edward fshrmn

Vallis William shoe
  shiner
Vincent Gabriel fshrmn
Walsh Howard lab
Walsh James fshrmn
Walsh James lab
Walsh John barbr
Walsh John fshrmn
Walsh Thomas tcher
Warren Albert tmstr
Warren Albert storekpr
Warren Frederick
  fshrmn
Warren George seamn
Warren George fshrmn
Warren James fshrmn
Warren Levi tmstr
Walters Charles fshrmn
Walters Edwin lab
Walters William fshrmn
Watts William lab
Weatherall Jas fshrmn
Weymouth Hector
  fshrmn

Weymouth Jacob
  fshrmn
Weymouth Sydney
  fshrmn
White Corbett fshrmn
White George fshrmn
White Gilbert lab
White William fshrmn
Whiteway Douglas
  fshrmn
Whittle William lab
Williams Charles
  fshrmn
Williams Clarence capt
Williams Mrs Hannah
  wid
Williams William Jr
  fshrmn
Williams William
  fshrmn
Wood William
  blcksmith
Woolfrey Rev W J
  methodist minister

APPENDIX F

Past Masters of Fidelity Lodge

George Robert Forsey 1877, 1878, 1879, 1880, 1882, 1885, 1888, 1902, 1903, 1907, 1915
Thomas Alex Hickman 1881
George Abraham Buffett 1883, 1887, 1889, 1893, 1894, 1905
Samuel Tibbo 1884, 1886, 1896, 1901, 1904
Allan MacDonald, M.D. 1890, 1897, 1900, 1911, 1912
Alfred Lempriere 1891
Samuel Harris 1892
Thomas Foote 1895
Selby Parsons 1898
William Forsey 1899, 1908
Elihu Hefferman 1906
George Dunford 1909, 1913, 1914, 1917, 1918, 1922, 1923, 1925, 1943, 1945
Aaron F. Buffett 1910, 1919, 1924, 1931
Henry Camp 1916, 1920
George Harding 1921
Henry Evans 1926
John F. Hyde 1927
George Foote 1929
Gerald K. Laing 1934, 1935
Harold Patten 1936, 1952, 1953
Donald W. Tibbo 1937, 1942
James M. Dunford 1938, 1939, 1944

Clayton Camp 1940
Reuben P. Forsey 1941, 1946, 1947, 1950, 1951
Wilfred M. Buffett 1948, 1949
George A. Welsh 1954, 1955
Clarence W. Handrigan 1956, 1957, 1971
Harry Piercy 1958, 1959, 1964, 1969, 1970
G. Buffett Tibbo 1960, 1961
Frank S. Riggs 1962, 1963
Reuben Ralph 1965, 1966
Walter P. Forsey 1967, 1968, 1972
William J. Welsh 1973, 1974, 1988, 1989
Lance G. Ralph 1975, 1976
Caleb W. Green 1977
Eric C. Grandy 1978, 1979
Clayton Lloyd Trimm 1980, 1984
Bennett A. Wiseman 1981
Eli J. Matthews 1982
Kelvin Matthews 1983
Thomas Harvey Brenton 1985, 1986
John W. Clarke 1987
Robert C. Parsons 1990, 1991
Norman B. Denty 1992
James E. Cluett 1993
Keith Hillier 1994
Kevin Kelly 1995, 1996

APPENDIX G

Young Women from Grand Bank Who Attended Mainland Colleges

In the fall of 1994 I located a list (compiled by Grace (Patten) Sparkes) of Grand Bank girls who had attended institutes of higher education in Canada. The majority of these girls competed their local schooling in the Methodist Academy and enroled in Mount Allison University. For the purpose of this appendix, I arbitrarily selected attendance up to the 1930s.

Name	Institute of Higher Learning	Year
Elizabeth Hickman	Halifax	1879-84
Ethel Hickman	Mount Allison	Prior to 1900
Emily Harris	Mount Allison	Around 1900
	(Mistress of Liberal Arts)	
Georgina Buffett	Mount Allison (M.L.A.)	1904
Jane Hickman Patten	Mount Allison (M.L.A.)	1904
Mary Harris	Mount Allison ?	
	(Degree in Domestic Science)	
	Simmons College in Boston	
Maria Buffett	Mount Allison 1911 or 1912	
	(Bachelor of Arts)	
Eleanor Harris	Mount Allison (B.A.)	1913
Elizabeth Patten	Mount Allison	1913
	Ladies' College	
	Toronto General	
Cora Foote	Mount Allison	1918
Christie Forsey	Mount Allison (M.L.A.)	1922
Eleanor Forsey	Graduate Nurse Mass. Gen. Hosp.1919	
	Mount Allison	
	Simmons College Boston	
	School of Public Health (R.N.) 1930	
Barbara Dunford	Mount Allison	1925-27
Grace M. Patten	Mount Allison (B.A.)	1928
Violet Buffett	Mount Allison (B.H. Science) 1930	

APPENDIX H

Place Names near Grand Bank

Many of these brooks, ponds, beaches, cliffs, berrypicking grounds and woodcutting areas have long been forgotten by many of our younger generations. Due to modern housing or industrial buildings, several places have disappeared. Grand Bank Seafoods Plant is built over Point of Beach and Nigger Ralph's Pond has disappeared in the housing development on the northwest side of Main Street, or Fortune Road as it was once known. The Grand Bank water supply dam covers First Western Falls.

Many familiar areas are not listed. The geographical range of this list lies roughly a half mile from Grand Bank's centre. Many locations and the origin of the names were supplied through interviews with local people; unfortunately, most could not identify how (or for whom) the location was named.

Admiral's Cove
Admiral's Cove Pond
The Bank
Beggar's Hill
Bennett's Hill
Bernell's Brook
Bill's Hole
Black Duck Pond
Boy's Place
Bragg's Path
Break Heart
Bull Path
Capelin Cove
Clarke's Garden
The Commons
Country Pond
Cow Nap
Devil's Cave/Drums

Duchene's Well
Dunford's Rock
Eternity Rock
Evan's Head
Farmer's Hill
First and 2nd Western
George's Brook
Green Knob
*Greenwood Farm
Grigger's Garden
Gumbo Runs
Harry's Long Pond
Hill of Green
Jane's Pond
Jim Albert's Drong
Kelly's Cove
L'Anse au Paul
Lobster Pond

Louis Hill
Martha's Mish
Nigger Ralph's Pond
Old Road
Point Bouilli
Point of Beach
Pond Gut
Sally's Rock

Sam's Knob
Simm's Ridge
Spruce Road
Squire's Hill
Taylor's Knob
Trimm's Beach
Uncle Bob's Garden

*Ben Matthews and his wife Kate composed the song "The Greenwood Farm" after they sold it to George C. Harris in the 1930s. Located in the general area of today's Greenwood Avenue, it was a pasture for Harris' seven or eight milk cows. In the early 1950s, Harris sold the Greenwood Farm to Robert Stoodley (mechanic). Ben and Kate Matthews are the grandparents of the late Almeda Eveleigh.

Byatt Cumben and Georgie (Rose) Jones remembered the verses:

> The Greenwood Farm is the pride of my heart,
> I love it so and so does Kate
> With a smile on her brow
> I seem to see her now
> Tying up the old stave gate.
>
> (Chorus)The Greenwood Farm is going to be sold,
> It would make you blood run warm
> To see eight hundred dollars paid down,
> Paid down for the Greenwood Farm.
>
> If someone happen to bring along my dinner
> I would sit down and eat it in the warm
> And I heard a voice saying
> What's ya doing over there
> I'm working in the Greenwood Farm
>
> Over in the farm there's a big flat rock
> And on it the sun shines warm
> It would do your heart good
> If you'd only look around
> When you're over in the Greenwood Farm

APPENDIX I

Student Interview with Curtis Forsey in 1972
Forsey's Brief History of Grand Bank

The first settlers in Grand Bank were here in the early seventeen hundreds. They could have been French people. It has never been recorded in history who they were, but apparently they were French. In those days, St. Pierre was populated; and some Frenchmen often left St. Pierre and came to the Mainland of Newfoundland and settled.

We have some of our descendants today in Lamaline and on the West Coast — the Tibbos for instance who may be descendants of French people. The name Buffett is French. They came from the Western Shore. In 1720 there were twenty-six people living in Grand Bank. Everyone living in Grand Bank came out to Harbour Breton, Hermitage, and Burin where the English firm, Newman & Co. had businesses established, and they came out with young men. My ancestors, my great, great, great, great, great grandfather came out from England as a young man, as did yours no doubt, and everybody elses, and then they got mixed up with the French.

Back in the early days the people of Grand Bank fished for Harbour Breton when Newman & Co. was established, and of course they fished for St. Pierre because in the late 1880s and 1890s there was considerable business done in the bait business. There were people here and all around Fortune Bay with their little schooners and seines. They used to carry bait to St. Pierre and sell it, and supply the French bankers.

The Newfoundland Government brought in the Bait Act during the latter part of the 19th century which forbid Newfoundlanders to sell bait to the French, and it is supposed that this was one of the things that brought on the French trawler — the steam trawler. Newfoundlanders were deprived of the bait and the reason for that was they were selling the Frenchmen bait to catch fish. They were putting it in our markets in competition with us. The Newfoundland government was persuaded to forbid all foreign vessels in taking bait from Newfoundland waters. That created quite a problem because they then started smuggling the bait to the French. Therefore "revenue cutters" were introduced to help enforce the Bait Act.

Newman & Co. were the pioneers of the salt cod fish business in Fortune Bay and other parts of this coast. They supplied the fishermen and they took their fish as payment for goods that were supplied to them. It not only applied to Fortune Bay but Placentia Bay as well. You have the same situation in Burin. Newman's collected the fish and exported it to various European countries where they had markets — Spain and Portugal chiefly.

Around the turn of the century all of the people got into the fish business. Around the 1880s and 1890s, this part of the coast discontinued their connections with Harbour Breton and more or less went into the business themselves. They collected their own fish and supplied the fishermen (collected the fish and sold it themselves). In some cases they marketed it to a foreign country. And about the early 1900s, the exporters of Grand Bank went on their own. They supplied their own fish, collected it, made it, processed it and

Blackburn Road facing eastward. William Forsey's home (father of Curtis Forsey) is far left, and centre is the home in the Queen Anne style built by Garfield Harris (later Dr. John Burke, and later Grand Bank Dental Clinic). The water tower was built in 1958-59 on the highest point of land within the town, but by 1970 it had deteriorated and was taken down.

shipped it to such countries.

The early pioneers in Grand Bank in that business were Samuel Harris and George A. Buffett. They were the first two who went on their own as exporters. Previous to that, most of our fish went to St. John's and the St. John's merchants exported.

Around the beginning of the century, the people around here decided they were going to handle their own fish and export it under their own name, which they did and that continued as long as the salt cod fish business lasted.

Appendix J

𝕴n April 1936, the Grand Bank schooner *Partanna* disappeared off the Southern Avalon. Her story has been written in several Newfoundland books which identify her twenty-five crew. From Grand Bank were: Edwin Walters, Clyde Riggs, Robert Rose, Felix Baker, James Moore, William Dunford, Willoughby Mullins, Clayton Welsh, Morgan Hickman, Wilson Hickman, Norman Burt, and Stanley Burt. Chesley, the youngest son of Stanley Burt, composed and sang this song which helped him overcome the grief of the disappearance and loss of a father.

Mystery of the *Partanna*

I'll tell you a story if you'll listen to me,
A story of heartaches, sorrow and grief
About the schooner *Partanna*, it's a mystery I'm
sure
How she sailed to the Grand Banks
    to return no more.

It was on a Monday, and the fog was so thick
As she sailed for the harbour with her
    whole crew on deck.
All their wives and children watched her that day,
With her sails full of wind, she sailed out the bay.

It was Easter they said she'd return,
We were watching and waiting,
    for all were concerned.
We watched from the cape, and we
    watched from the shore,
But the schooner *Partanna* would return no more.

We waited three long weeks for our
    loved ones and friends,
Just hoping and praying they'd return again.
But soon the bad news was brought to our door
The schooner *Partanna* would return no more.

Some say she was sunk by a ship made of iron,
Or maybe she ran on the Keys in a storm.
But still it's a mystery how she sank I'm sure,
But the schooner *Partanna* will return no more.

Lost were twelve men from Grand Bank,
    Garnish lost ten,
One from Little Bay East, Bay L'Argent and Burin.
There were husbands, brothers and fathers to be,
All, like the *Partanna*, they were lost to the sea.

We have searched for clues for many a year,
But all we have found are heartaches and tears,
But still it's a mystery how she sank I am sure,
But the schooner *Partanna* will return no more.

Appendix K

Crew List of Three Banking Vessels, 1935

Owned by G.& A. Buffett, these salt cod banking schooners drew the majority of their crews from Fortune Bay.

Pauline C. Winters	Nina W. Corkum	Freda M
Capt. Sidney Harris	Capt. John Smith	Capt. George Follett
Eugene Ridgley	Sam Fox	Geo King
Tom Grandy	Philip Grandy	Frank Banfield
Hubert Grandy	Robert Smith	Charles Anstey
Horatio Brown	George S. Warren	George Bungay
Thomas R. Grandy	George Brown	Henry Skinner
Aaron White	Sam Pardy	Sam Bungay
Ernest Grandy	Alec Bond	W. E. Anstey
Richard Rose	Ambrose Tapper	Ches Thornhill
Curtis Forsey	John J. Skinner	Tom Thornhill
Simeon J. Skinner	Chas Skinner	John Bird
William Skinner	R. J. Skinner	Olaf West
Garfield Vallis	James Snook	Percy Miles
George Keeping	Onslow Drake	Wilbert Grandy
Edgar Hillier	James Penwell	Garfield Anstey
John P. Miller	Reg Pardy	W. J. Moulton
Matt Cross	Reg Barnes	Dan Skinner
Charles Royle	John Labour	Arch Scott
George Pope	Charles Barnes	James Keeping
Isaac Wells	Edward Pope	George Miller, Jr.
Jonas Pardy	Caleb Bungay	Thomas Bond
Ken Pike	Edward West	Fred Buffett
Sam Pynn	Albert Elms	George T. Cluett
George Douglas	Arthur Trimm	Horatio Cluett
Jacob Penwell	Augusta Almeda	

Season's Catch	*Season's Catch*	*Season's Catch*
3064 quintals	3021 quintals	4613 1/2 quintals

Crew List of Four Banking Schooners, 1937

All four bankers relied on men from Fortune Bay to compliment their crews. Note: To place the list side by side for comparison, some names have been abbreviated. The place of residence is given for the crew of *D.J. Thornhill*.

Pauline C. Winters	Freda M	L.A. Dunton	D.J. Thornhill
Capt. Sidney Harris	Capt. Geo Follett	Capt. Clar Williams	Capt. John Thornhill, Grand Bank
Richard Rose	George White	Thomas Anstey	Charles Parsons, Grand Bank
Hubert Grandy	Stan Lawrence	George Anstey	Matt Cluett, Frenchman's Cove
J. S. Miller	Felix Johnson	George Keeping	George Hickey, English Harbour E.
William Baker	Elias Pardy	J. Hackett	William Fudge, Belleoram
George Nurse	John Skinner	James Keeping	Ambrose Thornhill
John Barnes	George Bungay	T. Kearly	Alex Price, Grand Bank
George Miller	Harry Skinner	George Good	Albert Elms, Grand Bank
Tom Hatch	Sam Bungay	William Thornhill	Alex Bond, Grand Bank
George T. Hatch	Caleb Bungay	Tom Herridge	Frank Hoben, Frenchman's Cove
James Myles	Hugh Scott	William Pardy	George Barnes, Grand Bank
Rudolph Banfield	Tom Bond	Ches Rose	Frank Bond, Frenchman's Cove
Tom Harris	Garfield Osmond	Philip Vallis	Reuben Pardy, Bay L'Argent
Robert Harris	Tom Thornhill	Aaron Myles	John Pike, Bay L'Argent
Allen Hatch	W.J. Moulton	Freeman Clarke	Wilson Dodge, Lally Cove
Jonathan Hiscock	William Grandy	Edgar Rideout	Steven Cluett, Frenchman's Cove
Joe Grandy	Olaf West	Joseph West	Albert Grandy, Garnish
George R. Barnes	George Wells	Man Herridge	John Cluett, English Harbour E.
Walter Barnes	William James Price	Herbert Myles	Pat Hynes, English Harbour E.
Jonas Pardy	Philip Price	Jonthan Keeping	Joe Hackett, English Harbour E.
Max Follett	Rex Miles	Manuel Cox	George Saunders, English Harbour E.
Sam Ridgley	Fred Buffett	Alfred Martin	George Cluett, Garnish
William Ridgley	Alex Banfield	Reg Buffett, Fortune	
Jonathan Baker	George F. Tibbo		
	Philip Green		
Season's Catch	*Season's Catch*	*Season's Catch*	*Season's Catch*
4026 7/8 quintals	4542 1/16 quintals	3358 7/8 quintals	4020 1/2 quintals

Appendix L

Grand Bank Councillors up to 1995

1. Alcock, Ruby
2. Baker, Allen
3. Bartlett, Newman
4. Buffett, Wilfred
5. Buffett, Bruce
6. Burfitt, William
7. Cooper, George
8. Cumben, John
9. Dunford, Max
10. Emberley, Roger
11. Emberley, Randolph
12. Fizzard, Stanley
13. Foote, John
14. Foote, George
15. **Forsey, Curtis
16. Gillard, Philip
17. Grandy, Max
18. Grandy, Harry
19. Grandy, Hubert
20. Green, Caleb
21. Harding, George
22. Harris, Earl
23. Hickman, George Edward
24. Hickman, Percival
25. Hillier, Onslow
26. Hiscock, Winfield
27. *Large, Ann
28. Matthews, Thomas
29. Matthews, Ambrose
30. Matthews, Norman
31. **Matthews, Rex
32. May, Alpheus
33. Melendy, John
34. Patten, George
35. Patten, Howard
36. Patten, Cecil
37. Rideout, Wayne
37. Riggs, Philip
38. Rogers, June
39. Rogers, Clarence
40. Rose, George
41. Rose, Bruce
42. Russell, Harold
43. Smith, Florence
44. **Snook, T. Maxwell
47. Stoodley, Robert
48. Stoodley, Philip
49. **Stoodley, Samuel
50. **Tessier, Frederick
51. Thorne, George
52. Tibbo, William
53. Tibbo, George E.
54. Trimm, Arthur
55. Warren, Harold
56. Warren, Bruce
57. **Welsh, Clayton
58. Welsh, George
59. Welsh, William

*The first woman elected to council
**Grand Bank Mayors

Sources

Books:

Andrieux, J.P. *Marine Disasters of Newfoundland and Labrador*. O.T.C. Press, 1986.

Andrieux, J.P. *Shipwreck at St. Pierre*. Ontario: W. F. Rannie, 1982.

Barbour, Job. *Forty-Eight Days Adrift*. St. John's: Breakwater, 1983.

Bebb, Trevor. *Quest for the Phantom Fleet*. Lockeport, N.S., 1992.

Dictionary of Newfoundland and Labrador Biography. St. John's: Harry Cuff Publications, 1990.

Encyclopedia of Newfoundland and Labrador Vols 1 - 5. St. John's: Newfoundland Book Publishers, 1984.

Fidelity Lodge Centenary Book 1876-1976. Grand Bank, 1976.

Fizzard, Garfield. *Master of his Craft*. Grand Bank: Grand Bank Heritage Society, 1988.

Fizzard, Garfield. *Unto the Sea*. Grand Bank: Grand Bank Heritage Society, 1987.

Forsey, Eugene. *A Life on the Fringe*. Toronto: Oxford University Press, 1990.

Horwood, Andrew. *Captain Harry Thomasen — Forty Years at Sea*. Ireland: W. & G. Baird, 1973.

Horwood, Andrew. *Newfoundland Ships and Men*. St. John's: Marine Researchers, 1971.

Taylor, E.; Jackman, D; Hollett, J; et al. *A Changing Fishing Technology in the Community of Grand Bank*. Canada Studies Foundation, April 1977.

Kelland, Otto. *Dories and Dorymen*. St. John's: Robinson Blackmore, 1984.

Lehr, G. and Anita Best. *Come and I Will Sing You*. St. John's: Breakwater, 1985.

Lench, Rev. Chas. *An Account of the Rise and Progress of Methodism on the Grand Bank and Fortune Circuits (Rev. Ed)*. St. John's: Creative Publishers, 1986.

MacDermott, Hugh. *MacDermott of Fortune Bay*. London: Hodder and Stoughton, 1938.

Marsh (Smith), Viola Alfreda. *A Small Town Nurse*. Owen Sound, Ont.: Stan Brown Printers, 1986.

Mosdell, H.M. *When Was That?* St. John's: Trade Printers, 1923.

Newfoundland Historic Trust. *Ten Historic Towns*. St. John's, 1978.

Newfoundland Who's Who 1952. (and other editions of Who's Who) St. John's, 1952.

Parker, John P. *Sails of the Maritimes*. North Sydney, Nova Scotia, 1959.

Parsons, Robert C. *Lost At Sea Volume One*. St. John's: Creative Publishers, 1991.

Parsons, Robert C. *Lost At Sea Volume Two*. St. John's: Creative Publishers, 1992.

Parsons, Robert C. *Toll of the Sea*. St. John's: Creative Publishers, 1995.

Parsons, Robert C. *Wake of the Schooners*. St. John's: Creative Publishers, 1993.

Peach, John. *Diary, 1840-1844*. Archives of the Centre for Newfoundland Studies, Memorial University.

Peacock, Kenneth. *Songs of Newfoundland's Outports*. Ottawa: National Museum of Canada, 1965.

Pitt, David G. *E.J. Pratt The Truant Years 1882-1927*. St. John's: Jesperson Press, 1984.

Sherburne, Andrew. *Memoirs of Andrew Sherburne*. Freeport, N.Y. Books for Libraries Press, 1970. (Reprint)

Smith, Harry J. *Newfoundland Holiday*. Toronto, 1952, pages 234-253.

Thomas, Gordon W. *Fast and Able — Life Stories of Great Gloucester Fishing Vessels*. Gloucester, Mass: Gloucester 350th Anniversary Celebrations, Inc., 1973.

Tocque, Rev. Philip. *Newfoundland As It Was And As It Is In 1877*. Toronto: John B. Magurn, 1878.

Newspapers and magazines:

"Atlantic Guardian Visits Grand Bank." In *Atlantic Guardian*. January, 1948.

Buffett, Aaron. "Grand Bank." In *Daily News*, June 1941.

"Captn. Taverner's Second Survey." In *Newfoundland Quarterly*. Vol. LXXXIX, No. 3, Spring/Summer 1995.

Coish, Calvin. "Grand Bank — Child of the Sea." In *Atlantic Advocate*. January, 1984.

"Couple Reminisce About Early Days in Grand Bank." In *Evening Telegram*. April 11, 1981, p. 21.

Day, David "Lives in the Law: Informal Legal and Social Sketches of the Chief Justices of Newfoundland, 1874 to 1996. *Newfoundland Quarterly* Spring 1996, p. 9.

"Disappearance of Our Sailing Fleet of Foreign Going Vessels." In *Fishermen's Advocate*, December 7, 1932.

Fairbairn, R.E. "Snapshots at the Newfoundland Conference." In *The Christian Guardian*. August 16, 1922.

"Governor of St. Pierre Visits Grand Bank." In undated, unnamed newspaper article located in Seamen's Museum, Grand Bank.

"Grand Bank Owned Vessels Which Were Lost Since 1862." In *Daily News* July 28, 1936, p. 3. (List submitted to paper by Felix Tibbo)

Harrington, Michael. "Offbeat History." In *Evening Telegram*, St. John's. Various editions.

Hickman, Percival. "A Brief History of Grand Bank." In *Newfoundland Quarterly*. Spring 1979.

Lench, Rev. Charles. "Grand Bank: An Interesting Outport." In *Newfoundland Quarterly*. Vol. XII, No. 3, 1912.

Methodist Monthly Greeting Number 13, 1897.

"150th Anniversary for Grand Bank United Church." In *Evening Telegram*. April 26, 1966.

Parsons, Robert. "The Dory on the Coin." In *Newfoundland Quarterly*. Volume XC, No. 2, Spring 1996.

Parsons, Robert. "The Grand Bank Heritage Walk." In *Newfoundland Lifestyle*. Volume 8, No. 3, 1990.

Parsons, Robert. "Three Short Sentences." In *Newfoundland Quarterly*. Volume LXXXVI, No.4, Summer 1991.

"People Who Helped Shape Newfoundland and Labrador." In *Newfoundland Lifestyle* Volume 10, No. 3, 1992.

Perlin, A.B. "The National War Memorial." In *What's Happening*. Vol. 18, No. 1, 1993.

Porter, Marilyn. "Mothers and Daughters: Linking Women's Life Histories in Grand Bank." In *Women's Studies Int. Forum*. Vol II, No. 6 (date unavailable).

"Profile Louise Belbin of Grand Bank." In *Newfoundland Herald* May 3, 1978.

Rughooking: Booklet to accompany mat exhibit *The Fabric of their Lives* (including Louise Belbin's rugs). Date and place of publication unavailable.

Southern Gazette May 20, 1987 and other various editions.

Stoodley, Les. "Remembering." In *Atlantic Advocate*. date unavailable

Taylor, Ernest. "Grand Bank Firm Closes After 75 Years of Service." In *RB Weekender*. February 16-22, 1985.

"Trailblazer (Grace Sparkes)." In *Evening Telegram* March 3, 1996.

Woodland, Bruce. "Newfoundland Schooners Made History." Reprinted from *Trade News*, Department of Fisheries, January, 1959.

Booklets and Pamphlets

Fizzard, Garfield. *History of the Thorndyke.* Brochure.

Grand Bank Fire Department 40th Anniversary Commemorative yearbook. Grand Bank, 1987.

Grand Bank Heritage Walk. Town Council Promotional Brochure, 1987 (reprinted 1992, 1995).

Grand Bank Main Street Newsletter. Grand Bank Main Street Promotional Committee, various editions 1994-1996

Grand Lion 25 Years of Lionism in Grand Bank. Commemorative Yearbook. Grand Bank, 1976.

Memoirs: Reunion Salvation Army School July 5-7, 1991. Commemorative Yearbook. 1991.

Orangism Grand Bank Nfld. 1873-1987 114 Years. Commemorative Pamphlet. Grand Bank, 1987.

Pittman, Lori. "Biography of my Great-Grandfather George R. Diamond Deep Sea Diver." Partanna Academy school paper, 1992.

Shining Through the Century The Salvation Army. Commemorative Yearbook. Grand Bank, 1987.

U. C. School Record. Robert Carr, ed., Grand Bank, 1941.

Unpublished University Papers, Theses and Dissertations:

Carberry, Fred. *A History of Football in St. John's.* St. John's: Maritime History Group, Memorial University of Newfoundland, 1973.

Hillier, Charles Edward. *The Problems of Newfoundland from Discovery to the Legislative Sessions of 1847.* Acadia University, Nova Scotia: August 1963.

Kendall, Victor. *List of Ships on the S.W. Coast of Newfoundland 1861-1889.* St. John's: Memorial University of Newfoundland.

Moulton, Bruce. *A Short History of Grand Bank.* St. John's: Memorial University of Newfoundland, 1969.

Noseworthy, Ronald. *A Dialect Study of Grand Bank.* St. John's: Memorial University of Newfoundland, 1971.

Snook, T. Maxwell. *A History of Grand Bank.* St. John's: Memorial University of Newfoundland.

Public Documents and other Sources:

Grand Bank File in:
  Grand Bank Memorial Library;
  Newfoundland Provincial Reference Library;
  Seamen's Museum;
  Provincial Archives of Newfoundland and Labrador.
  Gravestone markings in various cemeteries, Grand Bank.
Registry of Newfoundland Shipping, Marine Archives, Elizabeth Avenue, St. John's. Many references to schooner statistics were obtained at this source.
Stoodley, Les. Text of speech "What is Grand Bank?" given August 11, 1987, at the State Dinner during the 300th Anniversary Celebrations at Grand Bank.
Student interviews with Curt Forsey, 1972.
Correspondence, interviews (often edited for clarity), and/or personal conversations gathered between 1988-1996: Aunt Susie Baker, Blanche and Harvey Banfield, Newman Bartlett, David Benson, Christie Bradley, Chesley Burt, George Carr, James Carr, Byatt Cumben, Philip Downey, Doris Evans, Chesley Eveleigh, Frank Fizzard, Garfield Fizzard, Alice and Joshua Forsey, Curtis Forsey, Earl Francis, Myrtle Francis, Ruth Gosse, Max Grandy, Ron Grandy, Shirley (Parsons) Grandy, Clarence Griffin, Fred Hancock, George Hickman (Marine Drive), Georgie Jones, Max Keeping, Otto Kelland, Henry Lee, Neil Locke, Alfreda Marsh, Helen Milley and her daughter Hazel, Margaret Mullins, Christie Oakley, George Pardy, Hedley Parsons, Frank Riggs, Clayton Rogers, Fred Rogers, John Smith, Grace Sparkes, Ursula Squires, Clara and Elic Stoodley, Les Stoodley, Fred Tessier, Eric Tibbo, William Tibbo, Charlotte Welsh, Lucy Welsh, Alf White. To each a special thank you. Although the names are one of the last items in this collection, the information they gave remains first rate.

Bert Riggs, Ernest Taylor, Chief Justice T. Alex Hickman, T. Maxwell Snook and Garfield Fizzard were of tremendous assistance, not only for editorial help, but also for their historical expertise and I thank them for their help.

The 70 pictures or illustrations used in this work (other

than those taken by or are the property of the author) are acknowledged next to each picture in the text. If any errors occur in photo credits and/or information, advise the author and efforts will be made to correct it in future editions.

Index of Events and Places

302

Schooner and Vessel Index